SUPERVELOCE

SUPERVELOCE

How Italian Cars Conquered the World

PETER GRIMSDALE

**SIMON &
SCHUSTER**

London · New York · Amsterdam/Antwerp · Sydney/Melbourne · Toronto · New Delhi

First published in Great Britain by Simon & Schuster UK Ltd, 2025
Copyright © Peter Grimsdale, 2025

The right of Peter Grimsdale to be identified as the author
of this work has been asserted in accordance with
the Copyright, Designs and Patents Act, 1988.

1 3 5 7 9 10 8 6 4 2

Simon & Schuster UK Ltd, 1st Floor
222 Gray's Inn Road, London WC1X 8HB

www.simonandschuster.co.uk
www.simonandschuster.com.au
www.simonandschuster.co.in

Simon & Schuster Australia, Sydney
Simon & Schuster India, New Delhi

The authorised representative in the EEA is Simon & Schuster Netherlands BV,
Herculesplein 96, 3584 AA Utrecht, Netherlands. info@simonandschuster.nl

The author and publishers have made all reasonable efforts to contact
copyright-holders for permission, and apologise for any omissions or errors in
the form of credits given. Corrections may be made to future printings.

Simon & Schuster strongly believes in freedom of expression and stands against
censorship in all its forms. For more information, visit BooksBelong.com.

A CIP catalogue record for this book is available from the British Library

Front endpaper image © Chronicle / Alamy Stock Photo
Back endpaper image © Bernard Cahier / Getty Images

Hardback ISBN: 978-1-3985-1303-7
eBook ISBN: 978-1-3985-1304-4

Typeset in Sabon by M Rules
Printed and Bound in the UK using 100% Renewable Electricity
at CPI Group (UK) Ltd

For Beppe Severgnini

CONTENTS

'We declare that the splendour of the world has been enriched by a new beauty: the beauty of speed. A racing automobile with its bonnet adorned with great tubes like serpents with explosive breath … a roaring motor car which seems to run on machine-gun fire, is more beautiful than the Victory of Samothrace.'

Filippo Tommaso Marinetti, *The Futurist Manifesto*

'If you want to be somebody you buy a Ferrari, if you already are somebody, you own a Lamborghini.'

Frank Sinatra

Sprezzatura

On a sunny May Saturday in 1950, Britain prepares to host the opening round of the first ever Formula One world championship. A hundred and fifty thousand people have converged on a recently decommissioned bomber base, RAF Silverstone, for what the organisers are calling 'the greatest occasion in the history of motor racing in this country'. For the vast majority it will be the first time they have ever witnessed such an event.

The circuit following the former airbase's perimeter road is lined with hay bales and ropes to keep spectators – ten deep in places – from crowding onto the track. A hundred and twenty loudspeakers connected by 7 miles of cable will tell them the drivers' positions. *The Times* motoring racing correspondent pays tribute to 'the many people who have helped to raise motor racing in this country to the status of a national sport'.

In 1950, Britain's motor industry is on a roll. Its output is second only to America's and it is the world's biggest exporter of cars. But not since 1922 has a British car won a Grand Prix. Now, inspired by the engineering feats that helped deliver victory over Hitler, hopes are high for success on the track.

Ticket prices are seven shillings, with an extra shilling for the programme. On the cover is a full colour rendering of the much-anticipated BRM Grand Prix machine speeding away from the pits beneath a fluttering Union Jack. But the car is not yet ready to race. Instead, the public are treated to a couple of demonstration laps and hear the hysterical scream of its sophisticated V16 engine, fed by the same Rolls-Royce superchargers that powered Spitfires and Hurricanes to victory in the Battle of Britain. Inside the programme, the wartime spirit is invoked in a call to action exhorting the public to 'get behind the brave new machine. It is YOUR car and YOUR support is needed to complete the job of providing the funds.'

Even more exciting for the crowd is the appearance of the royal family. For many it will be their first sight of the King and Queen and the first time British monarchs have attended a motor race. Joined by Princess Margaret and the Earl and Countess Mountbatten, they make a lap of honour in a regal Daimler landaulette, serenaded by the band of the Grenadier Guards. Before taking their positions on a specially constructed platform opposite the pits, they shake hands with the drivers from ten nations lined up beneath the flags of each participating country.

These men are not newcomers to the sport. Their average age is thirty-nine and three are over fifty, all of them making up for time lost fighting each other. Among them is Tony Rolt, a seven-time escapee from German POW camps and one planned attempt from Colditz, by glider. There is a collective sigh of relief at the absence of the German teams who dominated Grands Prix before the war, though a certain unease is aroused by the four red cars occupying the front row of the starting grid.

The public have little reason to fear their former foes. According to a popular joke among British troops who fought the Italians in North Africa, their tanks have only one forward gear and four reverse. But no one's laughing today, when out of a field of twenty-four almost half the entrants are Italian. As a gesture of magnanimity Alfa Romeo have invited leading British racer Reg Parnell to join them for this event. British hopes rest on the ERAs from English Racing Automobiles further down the grid.

At three o'clock, the royal family take their places and the national anthem is played. When the flag drops the grid in front of the grandstands is engulfed in a haze of exhaust. The shattering cacophony briefly disrupts the royals' smiles as the machines blast down the Farm Straight towards Woodcote Corner. Any hope of a real battle is dashed minutes into the race when Rolt's ERA pulls into the pits and his teammate Leslie Johnson leaves the track, leaping from the cockpit as flames engulf his machine. Rolt manages a few laps more before retiring with a shattered gearbox. There is a weary resignation in the tone of the *Motor Sport* reporter's assessment: 'Thus early the race is robbed of all real interest and we settle down to see a demonstration of Italian supremacy that is to cost £1,000 in prize money.' *The Times* notes that the Alfa Romeos are simply 'far faster than any of their competitors'. They take the first three places; Parnell comes third and the highest-placed British car comes sixth.

The spectators are left to wonder how this can have happened. How is it that Italy, so recently pummelled into submission, its factories flattened by Allied bombs, has emerged from the ruins to set new standards of speed and style, leaving the spectators in disbelief? Equally dismaying is how effortlessly their victory was delivered. Giuseppe 'Nino' Farina, winner of the Grand Prix and soon to be crowned the first Formula One world champion, awes his audience with a masterclass in driving style that leaves a deep impression on the as yet unknown Stirling Moss. 'I saw a man motor racing as though he was reclining comfortably in an armchair, almost nonchalantly. Nothing tense, just a picture of relaxation and ease. Here was a style I had never seen before.' What Moss observes is a peculiarly Italian phenomenon for which there is no word in English: *sprezzatura* – the art of making something difficult look easy, with an effortless grace.

And it's not only in post-war Britain that Italy's former enemies are being given lessons in style. Nino's uncle, Battista 'Pinin' Farina and cousin Sergio are celebrated *carrozzieri*, designers of stylish car bodies. Italians are banned from the 1946 Paris Salon d'Auto, but that doesn't deter the Farinas. With some family friends along for the ride, father and son drive two of their latest creations from their workshop in Turin, over the Alps and up to Paris. They find space just outside the doors of the Grand Palais on the Champs-Élysées and park in full view of the thousands queuing for the Salon. Word gets round and soon their French rivals are compelled to step outside and have a look. '*Ce diable de Farina*,' one exclaims, '*a ouvert son salon personnel*.' ('This devil Farina has opened his own show.') The press pick up on the buzz. '*Antisalon du carrossier Turinois Pininfarina*' goes one headline. Photoshoots are staged featuring the cars gracing various iconic Paris landmarks. Few can disagree that Pininfarina has stolen the Salon.

Dismaying as it is for the Silverstone spectators and the crowd on the Champs-Élysées, automotive aficionados know that there is nothing new about this ability of the Italians to outflank their more powerful and better-equipped neighbours. In 1900, while France made nearly 5,000 cars, Italy's output was too small to be recorded. But by 1907, all of the three main races in the nascent Grand Prix season were won by Italian cars and drivers.

Unlike France, Germany and Britain, nineteenth-century Italy had had no industrial revolution. Wealth was controlled by the nobility, their lands toiled by illiterate sharecroppers. Half the population was illiterate. So how did the Italians do it – and with such *sprezzatura*? It's a question that will be asked again and again in the decades that follow. This is the story of how it was done.

A Car Is Not a Poem

Appropriately, the story of the Italian motor industry begins with a painting. Lorenzo Delliani was noted for his *plein-air* oils capturing his native Piedmont, of which no fewer than forty examples would be on show at the 1905 Venice Biennale. But he was not above accepting more lucrative commissions for portraits, one of which came in July 1899 from a member of the Torinese nobility. Count Emanuele Cacherano di Bricherasio wished to have recorded for posterity a gathering in the library of his family's 300-year-old palazzo in the centre of Turin.

In the painting nine men are seated or stand around a table. Eight are dressed in sombre suits, but in the centre is Bricherasio, sporting a white smoking jacket. In his hand is a pen, poised over a document. Tall, slim and pale, with a 'Kaiser'-style moustache upturned at the ends, he has a stiff Prussian bearing that was not untypical of nineteenth-century northern Italian nobles. However, the book on the table hints at a rather different Germanic influence. The title is obscured in the painting, but the noble count was famous for scandalously displaying a copy of Karl Marx's *Das Kapital* on his desk, which earned him the sobriquet *Il conte rosso*. Given the strict social stratifications of the time, it could be assumed that the rest of the gathering were similarly aristocratic gentlemen of Turin. But the group includes several commoners – a lawyer, a former soldier and the son of a watchmaker. What bound them together was a shared passion: the motor car. The son of one of those attending,

Carlo Biscaretti di Ruffia, described them all as 'gripped by a sort of automotive euphoria'.

Commissioning the painting might have been seen as an act of hubris on the part of Bricherasio, but the moment Delliani captured was truly historic. The document the gathering were about to sign would fundamentally transform not just the fortunes of the city of Turin but the whole of the recently united nation of Italy as it prepared to enter the twentieth century. It would bring into existence *La Società Italiana per la Costruzione e il Commercio delle Automobili Torino*, simplified as Fabbrica Italiana Automobili Torino, better known by its acronym, Fiat.

Any contemporary commentator would be forgiven for dismissing this venture as a pipedream. The white heat of industrial revolution that swept nineteenth-century Britain, France and Germany had yet to make much impact south of the Alps. Nothing about Italy in the 1880s suggested it was a viable base for a motor manufacturer. For one thing, there was little in the way of coal or iron ore deposits. Its heavy industry was tiny in comparison to that of its northern neighbours, and metalwork was the preserve of small family workshops with skills handed down through the generations. Nor was there much prospect of change. The nation's semi-feudal, agrarian economy was riven with income disparities and farming methods in much of the country had changed little since medieval times. Conditions got even worse in the 1870s with the arrival of cheap grain from America, which impoverished the rural population. Between 1876 and 1914, 14 million Italians emigrated, two thirds of them men.

None of this materially touched Bricherasio's set, who enjoyed all the benefits of land ownership and lucrative positions in the judiciary, banking and government. But he and his fellow signatories feared for the future of their city and its prosperity. The Risorgimento – the unification of Italy in 1861 – was born in Turin but turned out to be a mixed blessing for the city. For 300 years it had been the administrative and military capital of the ancient kingdom of Savoy, but after unification and his coronation as the first king of Italy, Victor Emmanuel moved his court and government to Rome. Shorn of its bureaucratic and military *raison d'être*, culturally overshadowed by Venice and Florence, Turin had become a backwater. In the 1890s the city's only highlights were the premier of Puccini's *La bohème* and the founding of Juventus football club. As one of the Fiat signatories put it, 'Grass grew green and beautiful in our main streets. Turin had become "a city of silence".'

Bricherasio and his friends were all early adopters of motor cars and cycles on which they sped about the city and parked outside their favourite meeting place. The Caffè Burello was known to them as 'La Pantalera', Piedmontese dialect for a canopy that shielded patrons from the sun. There may have been some irony to this name since the canopy was long gone, the gilt on the décor was chipped and the premises looked distinctly run-down. What it had going for it was its central location at the junction of Corso Vittorio Emanuele II and Via Urbano Rattazzi, close to the Porta Nuova railway station. This made it an advantageous position for trading horses and carriages and watching the traffic go by. Of the small number of motor vehicles that passed, almost all were imports from Germany or France.

A few doors down from La Pantalera was the workshop of Giovanni Ceirano, the watchmaker's son who appears in Delliani's painting. 'Clever, energetic and obstinate to a marked degree' was how Biscaretti di Ruffia described him. Ceirano started out importing British-made Rudge bicycles but he dreamed of making his own motorised machines. He took on a qualified engineer: Aristide Faccioli, according to Biscaretti 'one of the few men in Turin capable of designing an automobile'. Count Bricherasio had enthusiastically backed the venture with 6,000 lire and in March 1898 a small 3.5hp car emerged from the works. Ceirano gave it the incongruous and, to his ears, English-sounding name Welleyes, a mash-up of 'well' and 'yes' but with an Italian 'e' in between. Perhaps he hoped to channel some of Britain's reputational credibility which had helped him sell those Rudge bicycles. Biscaretti described it as 'a small car of unique design, graceful and fairly well sprung, which greatly raised the hopes of its producers'. Ceirano entered it in a 90km trial on the outskirts of the city. It came second, impressing in particular a spectator at the event who had also recently joined the Pantalera motoring set.

Lieutenant Giovanni Agnelli had just resigned his commission in the elite Savoia Cavalleria. Born in 1865, he had grown up in the splendid baroque Villar Perosa on his family's estate south of Turin. His aspirant father had bought the property with the proceeds from an investment in the silk business that had underpinned the region's wealth for centuries. But Agnelli's father died when he was six and, although wealthy, young Giovanni was nevertheless a commoner without the noble status that would allow him to mix with the likes of Bricherasio. To secure her son's entrée into Piedmont society, his mother decided he should become a cavalry officer. In his biographer's words, he would be 'taking revenge against those schoolmates of his who since they were nobility did not have permission from their parents to speak to someone from a different social class like him'.

But for all its status, the cavalry bored him. The routine was filled with ceremonial duties many of which had changed little over the centuries. Stationed in Verona, he found extracurricular amusement in the cavalry workshops experimenting with a Daimler internal combustion engine. But his attempt to rig it up as an electric generator was a disaster, injuring his batman whom he had roped into the venture.

Still only twenty-six, Agnelli dismayed his mother by abandoning the calvary, but back on the family estate, he was still bored. In search of inspiration he moved to Turin, into an apartment on the Corso Valentino. Opposite was the premises of Luigi Storeo, who was selling French-made motor tricycles. He soon bought one for himself, also made in Paris but by a Piedmontese émigré, Giuseppe Prunello. Impressed by Storeo's business, Agnelli thought about going into business with his neighbour. But first he embarked on a fact-finding visit to Prunello's workshop in the French capital. It was a revelation.

Paris in the 1890s had become the world's first 'Motown'. Although it had been born in Germany, *l'automobile* had been christened and nurtured into a commercial proposition by the French. At their factory on the Avenue d'Ivry, Panhard et Levassor employed over 800 craftsmen, boasted a machine shop with 350 lathes and its own foundry. The firm had also pioneered the Système Panhard, the automobile template that would become the industry standard: an engine in the front driving the rear wheels with two rows of passengers seated in between.

With nine more car makers in the capital and half a dozen more in the provinces, France had launched an entirely new industry. Agnelli realised that Italy was in danger of being left behind.

Back in Turin, Agnelli digested what he had seen. His friend Michele Lanza's thriving candle-making business allowed Lanza to pursue his dream of making his own cars from scratch, building them one by one and improving as he went. But after what he had seen in Paris, Agnelli was no longer impressed with his chandler friend's sideline. 'When you realise he builds his cars piece by piece and throws away the dies that cost him a tremendous amount for every new car he manufactures, you can imagine the sort of balance sheet he has at the end of the year.' Forthright despite his relative youth, Agnelli warned Lanza: 'you'll go bankrupt making cars in your candle factory.'

Ceirano's backers were coming to the same conclusion about the Welleyes. Although better realised than Lanza's efforts, its development had rapidly gobbled up Bricherasio's 6,000 lire. Much, much more would be needed to turn the venture into a viable business. So the count rounded up his wealthy acquaintances and obtained a further 80,000 lire.

When Agnelli heard about this development he was immediately curious. Impressed by the ambition and scale this investment promised, he wanted in, not as an investor but as company secretary, an active participant in the business. For him this was no adventure. 'Here is my signature', he told Bricherasio, 'but on one condition; we take this seriously. We can't waste time ... Hannibal is at the gates. In France even the public sector is starting to use the motor car.'

Soon after Fiat was ceremonially signed into existence, Ceirano decided he would prefer to go his own way, so for 30,000 lire Agnelli arranged for the rights to the Welleyes car design, the services of Ingegnere Faccioli and the small staff of Ceirano's works to be acquired by Fiat. He then organised the purchase of land along Turin's Via Corso and supervised the construction of a brand-new 12,000 square metre factory. To great fanfare, it was opened by Bricherasio's friend the Duke of Genoa, nephew to King Victor Emmanuel.

As to who was equipped to manage such an ambitious enterprise there wasn't much debate, as Biscaretti recalled. 'Instinctively we felt that Giovanni Agnelli was our leader. He made us turn up to all his meetings in which he would give clear indication of the future he envisaged, and of his great ability.' What Agnelli lacked in terms of status or engineering experience, he more than made up for with military training in logistics and strategy. The bored former cavalry officer had finally found his calling. Physically robust, with penetrating eyes under thick eyebrows, he was a commanding presence. He was also usefully devoid of airs and graces. Unlike the aristocrats, he preferred the local dialect, regarding Italian as an affectation, 'unsuitable for one who could still feel the country soil beneath his feet, rather than the city streets'.

Agnelli's position was further secured after Count Bricherasio's association with his creation was cut tragically short. In the autumn of 1904, while staying with his friend the Duke of Genoa in the castle of Agliè, he was found dead with a 'hole in his head'. Details were scarce but rumour suggested it was a 'suicide of honour' due to an affair with another member of the House of Savoy. The suspiciously short obituary in *La Stampa* suggests the possibility of scandal, together with the observance of the nobility's own strain of *omertà*. Strikingly, the Fiat board, meeting just after his death, merely noted him as a 'zealous administrator'.

Bricherasio's demise marked the end of an era. Power had passed from the titled nobleman to a new breed of Italian epitomised by Giovanni Agnelli. By 1903 Fiat sales had swollen to 134, making it Italy's biggest vehicle producer, a position it would maintain ever after. Nevertheless, at the dawn of the new century, Italy was still very much an automotive backwater; France and Germany ruled the roads.

Art of the Car

When the first self-propelled vehicles appeared on Europe's roads, in the late 1800s, they received a mixed reception. The British were particularly hostile, regarding them as an assault on rural tranquillity and legislating that they be preceded by a person carrying a red flag. A gap yawned between devotees of the then-fashionable Arts and Crafts Movement and the mechanics and blacksmiths who were turning their hand to car making.

But in Italy, of all European countries arguably the most steeped in art and culture, no such division existed. As early as 1902, *L'Auto,* the magazine of the newly formed Italian Automobile Club, carried a feature about motoring and art, and on the cover, proudly aboard his own machine, was none other than Giacomo Puccini, celebrated composer of *La bohème* and *Madame Butterfly*. A passionate pioneer motorist, he claimed that the thunder of a powerful engine could move him as much as the sound of music.

This might be dismissed as a somewhat fanciful connection were it not for the example of the teenage son of an esteemed Milanese artistic family who brought together the two seemingly disparate disciplines of art and mechanics. Born in Milan in 1881, Ettore Arco Isidoro Bugatti came from a family at the centre of the city's artistic establishment. At their homes in Milan and Paris, regular guests of the Bugattis included Puccini and Leo Tolstoy. Ettore's father Carlo was a multi-talented painter, sculptor, wood carver and metalworker, who is also credited with developing an entirely new style of furniture drawing from African and Islamic influences. He won prizes for chairs made from walnut and copper, covered in vellum and decorated with silk tassels.

According to Ettore, 'Whether he used the brush, the chisel, whether he carved ornaments for his furniture, whether he engraved metals, whether he made incrustations of mother of pearl and ivory, he had no need of the assistance of any craftsman. When an object left his hands it was he who made it, from the rough block of raw material to the delicate brodery of finished ornament.' Carlo set the bar high.

Ettore was sent to study sculpture at the Brera Art Academy. 'I really tried very hard to be an artist in the real sense of the word ... I had the best possible teachers in painting and sculpture.' But he realised his heart wasn't in it. According to Ettore's daughter, his intimidatingly talented father had warned him that 'artistic effort is of no use unless one is gifted, and that everything is justifiable in an artist except mediocrity'.

Ettore discovered his calling when he was given a chance to try out a motor tricycle built by Giulio Prinetti and Augusto Stucchi, wealthy brothers-in-law who had tried their hands at sewing machines and cork stoppers before graduating to bicycles. Their 'tricar' was one of the very first motor vehicles made in Milan. 'Just by looking at the machine,' said Bugatti, 'I grasped all the intricacies of its mechanism.'

After Stucchi showed him round their premises, Bugatti begged his father to let him leave his studies at Brera for an unpaid apprenticeship at the tricar workshop. As W. F. Bradley, Bugatti's friend and biographer, observed, Carlo Bugatti 'lived in a world of art, of craftsmanship, and the crude machines which had just made their appearance on the streets of Milan were not only foreign to his nature but abhorrent in the clumsiness of their manufacture'. Carlo's resistance might have been sharpened by the memory of his own father's squandering of his savings on trying to solve the mysteries of perpetual motion. But he gave in and in 1898, aged seventeen, Ettore began his apprenticeship.

In 1898, he entered a Prinetti tricar in one of Italy's first ever motor races, a 119-mile round trip from Turin to Asti and Alessandria and back. Riding another Prinetti was Torinese motor pioneer Giovanni Ceirano. Neither finished, but the following year Bugatti entered nine more events and claimed five first places, in one event beating Giovanni Agnelli.

'I very quickly thought of modifications that could be made to the tricar; some of them proved to be valid,' Bugatti wrote. But what he had in mind went far beyond the capabilities of the Prinetti works, which was limited to simply adding a second engine.

On 12 March, he drove in the 100-mile Verona–Mantua event. Bugatti won on a Prinetti, Count Biscaretti was second and the four-wheel class was won by Agnelli on a Fiat. Emboldened, Bugatti entered the Paris–Bordeaux. Alone, and without any backing, the 18-year-old was one of seventy-eight competitors, up against Louis Chiron, Charles Jarrott and Selwyn Edge, the top rank of motor racing's pioneers. Despite inexperience, choking dust and a route littered with early casualties, Bugatti finished the first stage in third place. On the second day he had to retire after a collision with a dog damaged his machine. But he returned to Milan determined to build a car of his own design. Stucchi was showing signs of tiring of their precocious apprentice and the multi-talented Prinetti had gone to Rome to become Italy's foreign secretary.

Still in his teens, untrained and with no qualifications, young Ettore persuaded two wealthy brothers, the Counts Gulinelli, to examine his drawings. He briefed them with such conviction and enthusiasm that they agreed to back him. Even Carlo at that point agreed to help.

Ettore made all the technical drawings, deployed the wood-carving skills he had learned from his father to make all the patterns for the foundry, supervised the forgings and did all the finishing and fitting. The car ran perfectly on its first outing, easily exceeding 40 mph. What fired Ettore's imagination, according to his daughter, was 'having something to create, to model, to perfect, and the joy of seeing the machine come into existence, as a work of sculpture did in the hands of his father and his brother'.

In May 1901, Milan held its first international automobile show. Ettore's design, a 12hp, 3.4-litre machine won a fine silver cup 'for the car of private construction proving to be the fastest among those exhibited and which joins to speed the requirements of simplicity, solidity, optimum functioning and of clever construction'.

But for the prize, Bugatti might have gone on to be a leading light in Italy's nascent motor industry, but the award brought his car to the attention of an industrialist from Alsace, Baron Eugène de Dietrich. Since the outcome of the Franco–Prussian War had cut de Dietrich off from his main customer, the French railways, he was looking to diversify. He examined Bugatti's design and not only decided to buy the rights but made the 19-year-old an offer he couldn't refuse. Still a minor when the contract arrived, Ettore had to get Carlo to sign it for him. The terms were spectacular given Bugatti's age and inexperience: a royalty equivalent to £16 for each car of 10hp, £20 for a 15hp car and £80 for a racing car.

Bugatti departed with de Dietrich for Alsace. A few years later he set up his own business there and after the First World War, when Alsace was reclaimed by France, Bugatti's celebrated competition cars sported that country's blue racing colours. Although his role as a leading light in Italy's motor industry seemed to be over before it had started, he never renounced his Italian citizenship and his designs were a fusion of art and engineering that owed much to his Milanese heritage.

Bugatti was always regarded as an exception, occupying his own personal space in the global story of the automobile. Jean-Albert Grégoire, a French auto engineer and pioneer of front-wheel drive, said of him, 'Bugatti was an artist pure and simple; his only scientific knowledge stemmed from ever-growing experience plus a natural mechanical bent supported by the gift of observation. He did not believe in calculations, formulae and principles. He joked about pages covered with figures. This lack of scientific grounding enabled him to take mechanical liberties, although he made mistakes at times. Nothing seemed impossible to him . . . he sometimes achieved solutions which no ordinary engineer would have dared to attempt.'

What Bugatti lacked in the way of technical education he more than made up for through the artisanal skills and aesthetic imperative of the world in which he had grown up. Like his brother Rembrandt, a gifted observational sculptor of animals, Ettore Bugatti could *see* a car as a whole rather than the sum of its components.

Famously, Bugatti never allowed the aesthetic purity of his designs to be compromised by mundane engineering considerations. But this trait is by no means unique among his fellow Italian automotive pioneers. And as we shall see, for the rest of the century Italian cars, no matter how basic or practical or cheap, always bore some imprint of art and style.

3

Know Thine Enemy

Bugatti and Giovanni Agnelli, beyond a shared enthusiasm for cars, were polar opposites when it came to building their businesses. Agnelli did not aspire to be an engineer; what he brought to the table was an understanding of organisation and strategy acquired at military college. He saw engineering as a means to an end. 'A car is not a poem; it's a product for sale', he is reputed to have said. In the Ceirano works, before it was bought out by Fiat, there had been no division of labour between development, production, servicing and repair. Everyone had pitched in, including a pair of teenage recruits, Vincenzo Lancia and Felice Nazzaro, whose elastic roles covered everything from sweeping to bookkeeping to development testing, while Aristide Faccioli, the Welleyes designer, ruminated about improving his creation. Once Agnelli was in charge, clear demarcations and lines of authority were imposed. He introduced cost accounting and piece-work pay rates with bonuses for foremen.

Also drilled into him from his time in the cavalry was Chinese military strategist Sun Tzu's famous dictum: 'know thine enemy'. As 1900 drew to a close, while Faccioli prepared the first in-house Fiat, Agnelli made his second trip to Paris. The city's Salon d'Auto was the world's showcase for all new car designs, where he could see first-hand what his future competitors were doing.

At the turn of the twentieth century, the automobile had yet to shake off its 'horseless carriage' connotations. For most of the

1890s, the efforts of automotive founding fathers Daimler and Benz (their merger was two decades away) still resembled their horse-drawn forebears, with wooden frames tottering on tall wooden wheels, their passengers perched above spluttering, temperamental machinery.

At the Paris *salon*, one new model was about to change all that. After Gottlieb Daimler's death the previous year, Wilhelm Maybach, assisted by Gottlieb's son Paul, had seized the initiative. The new model, the first to be called Mercedes, bristled with new features that signalled the metamorphosis of the horseless carriage into a fully fledged motor car. Mounted on a pressed steel frame, with the same size wheels all round, it made all the other exhibits look dated.

In particular, Agnelli was impressed by its cooling system. Until then, engines relied on a primitive stack of brass tubing through which water was pumped and somewhat ineffectually cooled. Maybach's innovation featured a honeycomb network of 8,000 tiny 6mm brass capillaries, which dramatically increased the cooling surface area. This radiator was integrated into the bonnet assembly and a fan mounted directly behind it kept the airflow moving when the car was stationary. Other innovations included mechanical inlet valves, electric ignition and a carburettor that enabled the driver to keep far more accurate control of engine speed. Its gear selector even boasted an 'H' gate that can still be seen on manual-change cars 120 years on.

For the first time the dominant French manufacturers had some serious competition. Paul Meyan, writing in *La France Automobile*, urged the nation's car makers to catch up 'before it's too late and Mercedes becomes the fashion of the day'. For Agnelli, it meant Fiat might yet be doomed.

Back in Turin he advised Faccioli that they should purchase a Mercedes for evaluation – and adopt Maybach's radiator. Italy was an inhospitable place for the motor car. Not for nothing was their region called Piedmont – the foot of the mountain. As well as largely unmetalled, under-maintained roads, its many forbidding hills pushed engines literally to boiling point. But Faccioli, a proud and accomplished engineer as well as a purist, was piqued. He felt that he should be free to innovate through his own expertise and experimentation. Copying was beneath him.

The dispute reached its climax in the Fiat boardroom. Agnelli argued he had seen the future and warned his fellow board members that they could not afford to burn through capital while their chief engineer mused over his next innovation. The directors were dismayed; Faccioli after all was one of very few Turin engineers known to be capable of designing a viable automobile. But Agnelli's view was that the fate of their new business could not be reliant on the vision of one man. The industry was blossoming in several countries, with innovations bursting from all quarters, all of which needed to be absorbed, either by imitation or licence. Faccioli had to go. Agnelli told the Fiat board that if they gave him the mandate, he would handle it.

The Fiat board acquiesced. Carlo Biscaretti, son of one of the Fiat founders and one of the first to record the increasing influence of the company secretary, noted Agnelli's 'steely reserve', combined with 'a power of persuasion and of imposing his will which we could almost call hypnotic'.

'You are too intelligent for us,' Agnelli told Faccioli when it came to letting him go. Wounded, the proud engineer designed Italy's first aero-engine. But it failed to take off and Faccioli died a bitter, penniless recluse.

On the face of it, Agnelli's choice of replacement seemed eccentric. Giovanni Enrico, already fifty, had no automobile experience at all. An engineering graduate, he was best known for his installation of electric lighting in Turin's Teatro Regio. He had worked on railway development and designed steam turbines for power stations. Elegant, with a long, waxed moustache, high collars and white tie, always with a pencil in hand, he was attentive to the dictates of his new boss. Agnelli bought a Mercedes for him to learn from and Enrico's first effort did indeed bear a strong resemblance to the groundbreaking German design.

In June 1902, Agnelli put the new car to the test. The Superga Basilica, the burial place of the Savoy royal family, sits atop the most prominent of the hills that rise around Turin. A drive up the switchback track to the summit provided a short, sharp proof of concept. Pitted against the Mercedes, Enrico's 7.2-litre four-cylinder 24hp

Fiat beat the German car by forty-five seconds. Enrico had achieved exactly what he wanted. Possibly this influenced Agnelli's subsequent choices of engineer for he often picked generalists, perhaps because they were less fixated and more pragmatic than automobile specialists.

A few commented on the resemblance between the Fiat and the German machine, but the Mercedes was also to become the template for most of its competitors. Under Enrico's direction, Fiat began to seize the initiative on innovation, pioneering major advances such as pressurised lubrication, friction shock absorbers, a multiplate clutch and, most significantly, hemispherical combustion chambers with the inlet and exhaust valves positioned directly above the cylinders. Bringing the valves as close as possible to the combustion chamber meant the gases had the shortest distance to travel in and out of the chamber on each stroke, enabling the engine to run faster and produce more power.

By the end of 1902, the company was showing a profit and already beginning to diversify. But as it grew, threats to its future began to emerge. There were limits to how much Fiat could rely on outside suppliers of raw materials and components. To expand, it had to grow its own industrial infrastructure. Over time Agnelli took control of steel making, ball-bearing manufacture, carpentry and coachbuilding. Demand for cars was still limited to the wealthy few, and, compared to other Western nations, the Italian wealthy were even fewer. So in 1903 Fiat began making trucks. Engines for ships, submarines and aircraft followed. Agnelli's grip on the business was also tightening. That same year he stepped up from company secretary to managing director.

4

The Littlest

The Fiat project was not merely the whim of the affluent indulging in their new-found passion; there was another element. The prominently displayed copy of the Karl Marx tome on Count Bricherasio's palazzo library desk wasn't just for show. The Fiat venture was envisaged as a philanthropic gesture, a means of bringing employment to the beleaguered province of Piedmont. Although the north of Italy was far better off than the southern Mezzogiorno, no part of the newly unified country escaped the crippling agricultural depression that followed the euphoria of the Risorgimento.

In 1898, just as Agnelli and his well-heeled associates were planning the creation of Fiat, a poor, illiterate agricultural labourer and his wife decided to abandon their lodgings in the municipality of Cortanze and move their eleven children 30km away, to Turin. The Farina family had nothing to lose; even in the good years, labouring in the fields and vineyards brought in only starvation wages. Two decades of depression in Europe in the late nineteenth century had stalled economic progress. Cheap wheat from Russia and the United States forced down local agricultural prices. Not only did it impoverish labour, banks, whose solvency depended on agrarian revenue, became insolvent, which in turn crippled investment. To add to the new nation's woes, an internecine tariff war with France further undermined exports. For the Farina family, the move to Turin was an attempt to escape from poverty.

The youngest, Battista, had just turned five. He acquired the nickname Pinin, Piedmontese dialect for 'littlest'. He would never grow taller than five feet.

They settled on what was then the outskirts of the city, on Via Canova. 'There were grey fields, dusty kitchen gardens,' recalled Pinin, 'the houses were rather skewed, put up in a hurry and not built to last.' His father took on whatever work he could find, from mucking out stables to bottling wine. Ever resourceful, he brought in empty wine kegs from Cortanze and sold them on in the city, while his wife ran the household, distributing tasks to the children, which included finding a baker to sell them two- or three-day-old bread that they revived by dipping in soup. They also drank watered-down milk and on rare occasions there were hard-boiled eggs and salad. There is something poetic, even in translation, about the way Farina describes his parents' gift for making the best of their meagre earnings: 'They weighed income against expenditure using a precision scale, managing at the same time to feed all those ever-open mouths.'

The first pair of shoes his mother got him were two sizes too big so he wouldn't grow out of them; she also urged him to take longer strides in the hope they would last longer. She assigned him tasks, to fetch water and polish her few fine copper pots, her only wedding presents.

Despite the hardship, for Pinin the city would become his playground and his inspiration. Errands for his mother took him further into the centre, to the Porta Nuova, where he was awed by the mansions he passed and for the first time inhaled the heady brew of smoke and fumes that wafted out of the workshops clustered around the railway station. He peered through gates into courtyards where metal was being machined by men in overalls. There he got his first glimpse of a motor car 'playing hide and seek amongst the carts and carriages'. Enthralled, when the first showrooms opened he 'hung around those windows more than the cake shops'. He also observed how the motor car was starting to influence fashion: 'women in long outfits of heavy vicuna, fustian jackets and calf length furs in the winter with wool lined muffs. Hats were always large with stiff brims covered with thick veils gathered at the neck. Others wore long dust coats of grey silk. They all wore single-lens goggles.'

The first signs of upward mobility for the Farina family came when Giovanni, one of Pinin's older brothers, became apprenticed to a coachbuilder. From a premises on the Via Orto Botanico, Marcello Alessio had carved out a successful business supplying the first generation of Torinese car owners with grand bespoke coachwork. Pinin used to go and wait for his brother at the gate so he could glimpse more cars. 'My first impression was that they were like monuments; I liked them better than the equestrian statues in Turin.' But soon he was developing a critical eye. 'What really annoyed me was the very fact that they looked like carriages that had lost their two or four in hand [horses]. It was easy to see that those cars were not made for speed but for the trot of the four-legged animals.' When he began to draw cars, his mother encouraged him. She bought him a pair of compasses in a handsome box. The boy was thrilled, 'It was a grand unforgettable day.' He never forgot his mother's encouragement, as he reflected later. 'How could a person like that without the slightest formal education be possessed of all wisdom?' As it turned out, he might as well have been talking about himself.

At school he struggled with Italian, preferring the Piedmontese dialect he spoke at home. He survived by bartering drawings for essays with his classmates. He drew prodigiously, radiators which looked like medieval shields and fan-shaped bumpers. 'I was looking for something, a line or a shape that would transform these cars ... I was drawing things which might have come out of Jules Verne ... Afterwards came my period for drawing low smooth cars with almost hidden wheels. I was already savouring the pleasure of running contrary to the norm, a very pronounced characteristic in Piedmont folk.' The keen-eyed youth found pleasure and inspiration wherever he looked, from his father's wine-making tools to the boats on the River Po with their 'slim, elegant simplicity. The rich world of all these things made with the experience of centuries is there for the taking: just keep your eyes open, no other school has as much to teach.'

As Turin's new motor industry grew, it spawned other businesses to supply and service it. In 1905 when Giovanni Farina left Alessio to go it alone, repairing carriages and car bodies at no. 12, Corso Tortona, Pinin left school and became his apprentice. He was just twelve.

Business was brisk. One early commission was on the Fiat racing cars. These had no actual bodies, just a rudimentary bench for the driver and mechanic. Farina developed a speciality for bespoke, figure-hugging 'baquet' seats, to help driver and mechanic stay in position while being thrown about by the fast corners. Through this work, Pinin met Felice Nazzaro and Vincenzo Lancia. Brimming with curiosity and confidence, the teenager made every effort to befriend their customers.

As well as repairs, some also ordered cosmetic modifications. Pinin was disparaging of those 'who wanted to complicate the lines of already complicated cars, they demanded junk and knick-knacks ... I knew practically nothing about style, but I was increasingly convinced that everything in coachwork needed to be turned upside down.'

'It was a question of the car's anatomy that had to change, erasing the idea of a carriage drawn in the traditional style. It had to take into account the change in speed, the function of the driver, who was certainly no longer a coachman. In fact it was a different kind of dynamics – and we had not yet got to aerodynamics.'

At home, Pinin was still in charge of fetching water from the pump but at Stabilimenti Farina, barely into his teens, he was now in charge of design and publicity.

Florio and the Targa

G iven his fanatical concentration on the business side of car making, it might seem surprising that Agnelli wanted Fiat to go racing. Motor sport could be a punishing drain on resources, and early cars were high-maintenance, prone to failure. Drivers required both superhuman stamina and determination bordering on the demented to stay on the supposedly closed public roads, strewn with hazards from slippery cobbles to deep ruts and potholes to choking clouds of dust. Charles Jarrott, Britain's first racing driver, recalled the start of the 1903 race from Paris to Madrid. 'Hundreds of cars of all sorts, shapes and sizes. Some unsafe, unsuitable and impossible. Some driven by men with every qualification as drivers of racing cars; others with drivers having no qualifications – all let loose over that long broad road to get there.'

The race claimed several lives, including that of Marcel Renault, brother of Louis and founder of the eponymous company. It was halted at Bordeaux by order of the French prime minister and all the surviving vehicles impounded. For a time it looked as if motor racing could be banned altogether. But the pioneer European manufacturers Peugeot, Renault, Panhard and Daimler, with their Mercedes, had established their brands through competition.

At home Fiat faced an existential problem – there simply weren't enough Italians who could afford a car. To survive at all, Agnelli would have to market it abroad – and that meant racing.

Fiat had already suffered a very public near-humiliation. Over dinner at a restaurant in Monte Carlo in 1901, Garibaldi Coltelletti, a devotee of France's Panhard et Levassor, boasted to the Duke of Abruzzi, grandson to the Italian king, that his 24hp Panhard, which had just come third in the Paris–Berlin road race, could beat the duke's recently ordered Fiat. Abruzzi, an accomplished explorer and adventurer and also a passionate patriot, was in no mood to let Coltelletti's claims about French supremacy stand and made a bet of 5,000 lire that over a 300km route between Turin, Villanova d'Asti and Bologna, his untried Fiat could beat the Panhard.

When news of this duel reached Agnelli, he was aghast. As he told motoring journalist W. F. Bradley, 'If we lose money, it does not matter very much because we can always find means of making more. But we cannot always remake a lost reputation.' Such a high-profile challenge was bound to attract press interest, but he was in no position to persuade the duke to withdraw. So, on 24 November 1901, despite terrible weather, a crowd of the aristocrat's friends, including the president of Italy's Chamber of Deputies, Tommaso Villa, gathered to see the combatants off.

So bad were the conditions, the start had to be moved a few miles down the road to Villanova d'Asti. At 8.30 a.m. Coltelletti's Panhard roared away, with his wife and a mechanic aboard. Ten minutes later, the duke set off with Agnelli and the young Vincenzo Lancia sharing the wheel. The Fiat seemed to be gaining on the French car but outside Alessandria, the duke, travelling at a top speed of nearly 50 mph, skidded on wet paving and struck a milestone, which broke the front axle. The occupants were lucky to survive.

The duke lost the race and his 5,000-lire wager, but Agnelli had arranged for another Fiat, a 12hp model – with half the power of the Panhard – to shadow them. The little Fiat finished the route at an average of 35 mph, four minutes faster than the much more powerful Panhard. The driver, not yet twenty, was Felice Nazzaro, the son of a village coal merchant, en route to becoming one of motor racing's first superstars.

When Agnelli secured control of Ceirano's workforce, Nazzaro, who had joined the company at thirteen, was already on the payroll. Initially his menial tasks included sweeping, but, being a willing and fast learner, he rapidly absorbed the ways of the workshop and graduated to mechanic. Agnelli also noted how patient and attentive with customers Nazzaro could be, at a time when the successful sale of a car needed to be accompanied by driving lessons and instruction in basic maintenance. It helped that Nazzaro was also a fastidious dresser which belied his humble origins, and unfazed by the airs and graces of wealthy, demanding customers. So when an order for a car arrived from Sicily's wealthiest family, Agnelli gave Nazzaro the job of supervising the delivery.

Vincenzo Florio, still in his teens, wanted for nothing. From a humble general store, his forebears had built a formidable commercial empire that included fisheries, wine, shipping and banking and the supply of most of the world's sulphur. They also financed the construction of Palermo's Teatro Massimo, then Europe's largest opera house. Cosmopolitan and cultured, the Florio family slipped easily into European high society; their visitors included the German Kaiser and the Prince of Wales, the future Edward VII.

But if mainland Italy was still struggling to drag itself into the modern world, Sicily had barely begun. In the 1880s, when a British traveller, Frances Elliot, attended a party at the Florio family's Palermo palazzo, she noted a table in the lobby 'literally covered with all sorts of weapons: handguns, revolvers, knives, sticks and daggers left by people together with their hats'.

When Vincenzo was just eight, his father died, leaving his elder brother Ignazio, twenty-three, in charge of the family's vast interests. Educated at home by a retinue of English tutors, he led a pampered life. The art nouveau Villino Florio was Vincenzo's bachelor pad. Designed by Ernesto Basile, it sat in parkland which included a private menagerie. From an early age, Florio was fascinated by new forms of transport. He accumulated a fleet of bicycles and experimented with hot air balloons, nearly setting fire to a nearby convent when one got caught in the nuns' washing line.

He was doted on by Ignazio, who brought from Paris a De Dion-Bouton tricycle, the island's first motor vehicle. On Sicily's roads, where the main form of transport was mule cart, the latest Florio toy was not well received; Vincenzo found himself being pelted with tomatoes by affronted road users.

Undaunted, he wanted to race the De Dion, but against what? He recruited two friends, one on a bicycle and another on a horse, but the cyclist got cramp and the De Dion overheated, so the horse won. Florio needed a better car.

In 1901, when Felice Nazzaro arrived in Palermo to deliver the Florios' new Fiat, the two young men developed an instant rapport. Florio persuaded Nazzaro to stay on, ostensibly as his chauffeur and mechanic, but more as a sidekick with whom to share his latest passion. Among Italy's nascent auto enthusiasts, position took second place to passion. The Fiat was joined by more cars, each bigger and faster than the last and he roped in more friends to join him in races round Palermo's Parco della Favorita, stipulating that no one should give way to him. Smitten by the thrill of competition, he took the plunge and put his name down for a 10km race on the mainland, from Padua to Bovolenta, scheduled for October 1902. Still a teenager, he approached Fiat about buying a car for racing, but Agnelli turned him down. He didn't want to see the scion of Sicily's most important family come to grief in one of his cars. Indignant, and with just a few weeks to go before the race, he sought help from Panhard in Paris, but their only available racing model was in pieces. Florio persuaded them to assemble it while he waited. As soon as it was ready, he tried it out in the Bois de Boulogne where he found it would do well over 100 kph. He handed over 40,000 francs and had it shipped straight to Padua with instructions to Nazzaro to collect it and prepare it for the race.

To his delight Florio won easily, beating two Fiats. His average speed was 112 kph, the first time that more than 100 kph was averaged in an Italian race noted *La Stampa Sportiva* approvingly. 'Very seldom do we see a young man from one of the wealthiest Italian families whom life could dispense every indulgence attempting such a difficult and dangerous task with so much enthusiasm.'

Emboldened, he put his name down for the 1903 Paris–Madrid race and ordered an even faster Panhard. But when his brother Ignazio got to hear about it, he was furious. It happened that Vincenzo's departure coincided with Sicily's infamous *Mattanza* (slaughter), when migrating tuna en route to spawning grounds were lured into a series of ever narrowing pens, trapped and harpooned. Such was the family's grip on Sicily's affairs, Ignazio ordered that no boats could leave while the *Mattanza* was under way. Vincenzo, too, was trapped, which, given the tragic outcome of the Paris–Madrid race, may have been a blessing. The next year, he turned twenty-one and was finally free to fully indulge his passion for motor sport. And in the northern city of Brescia he found like-minded young men of means keen to organise their own events.

Back in 1899, the city had held a four-day automobile festival, the first of its kind in Italy, combining an exhibition of new machinery and a road race on a triangular route taking in Cremona, Mantua and Verona. It was such a success that a group of local industrialists got on board, seeing an opportunity to show they could compete with the likes of Milan. They backed plans for a bigger event in 1905. But when Milan's Auto Club announced their own show for the same year, the Brescians pulled their event forward to September '04, which would include a 370km race they called Circuito di Brescia.

Fiat driver Vincenzo Lancia won the race but Florio came second on a 60HP Mercedes. He was so impressed with the event that for the next year's race he offered to put up 50,000 lire in prize money. And to show this wasn't just a one-off whim, he commissioned a cup, the Coppa Florio, to go to the manufacturer who secured the most wins in the *seven* subsequent races. But then state officials started to throw spanners in the works. Crossing railway lines, which had so far been informally agreed with local station masters, was now blocked by their superiors further up the line. And the Ministry of War vetoed the use of troops to help police the route. This all went down very badly with the citizens of Brescia, so much so that when the 74th Infantry Regiment arrived to perform their regular Saturday concert in July 1906, the crowd began to whistle and jeer and clashed with carabinieri in what was arguably the first recorded protest *for* the motor car. The press took notice and more demonstrations followed until the premier himself, Giovanni Giolitti, intervened to cool passions and ask for alternative solutions. A volunteer force of 500, drawn from fire brigades, forestry and local carabinieri, was raised and an underpass beneath the Brescia–Verona railway line was dug and on 1 and 2 September 1907, the first Coppa Florio race was waved off.

Florio himself was starting to realise that his enjoyment of racing was as much to do with the spectacle as the driving. He met Henri Desgrange, editor of France's *L'Auto* and founder of the legendary Tour de France cycle race, who surprised him with the question – why was there no race in Sicily? 'Because there are no roads' was Florio's reply.

Florio wasn't entirely wrong. Away from the coastal plateaux, the Sicilian interior relied on tracks and paths dating back to the Punic Wars. A young man of Florio's privileged background would have had little idea about life up in the hills or if a circuit could be navigated, so he recruited a team of scouts to see if they could come up with one. The result was the Madonie, named after one of Sicily's main mountain ranges. Ninety-two miles long (150km) it would have 2,200 corners, far and away the world's most daunting circuit.

The first few miles seemed relatively welcoming as the route ran flat along the coast, the road bordered by orange and lemon groves with cascades of geraniums. The long straight was to be taken flat out, but then the route plunged inland, climbing towards San Calogero's 5,200-foot summit and looping through mountaintop villages such as Petralia, 3,000 feet above sea level, its dwellings carved into the rockface. Parts of the route were no more than ledges let into the cliffs with sheer drops below; many were little more than mule tracks past shepherds who had never before seen a car. To W. F. Bradley, the first British journalist to recce the route, it was 'writhing as a tortured soul, freed from remorse for a few hundred yards, then again stricken with rage and fury which caused it to twist back on itself, to dash forward in despair, only to find there was no outlet in that direction and once more to double on itself'. As well as sheer drops, drivers were warned they might have to contend with bandits and wolves. Carrying a gun was recommended. But the greatest challenge was to the endurance of the driver faced with 2,200 bends to negotiate with heavy steering and brakes only on the rear wheels. As Lancia, one of the first to attempt the Targa put it, 'the first condition for winning a race is to stay on the road'.

To help lure in entrants, Florio ordered from Paris a gold *targa* – a plate or plaque – as the trophy and offered prizes of 30,000 lire for the winner, with 10,000 and 5,000 for the runners-up. The first race in May 1906 was three laps covering 277 miles. To spread the word, *Rapiditas* ('speed' in Latin), a lavish magazine, was specially launched to celebrate Sicily's new latest craze with soaring hyperbole. 'Here is the new goddess . . . in the fever of wonderful annihilation of the distance, the automobile will be honoured as one of the greatest achievements of the human genius, the most fruitful bringer of material advantages and spiritual passions.'

Excitement gripped the island. From three in the morning, special trains with tickets discounted 75 per cent departed from Palermo crammed with passengers. All of Sicily was caught up in Targa fever. Gentlemen in boaters and ladies swathed in veils to keep out the dust mingled with peasants, all hoping to glimpse the starters leaving at timed intervals from six o'clock. A network of telegraph stations around the route kept spectators informed of the race order. Three and a half thousand carabinieri were deployed around the circuit. Astonishingly, the race ran without catastrophe. Cars approaching the start/finish line were announced by cannon fire and a trumpet blast. The only mishap occurred when two cars were accidentally refuelled with water instead of petrol.

Six out of the ten entrants finished. Despite the number of corners, many of which had to be negotiated at walking pace, average speeds exceeded 40 kph. Alessandro Cagno won in an Itala, after nine and a half hours of racing, his victory almost upstaged by the revelation that French driver Hubert Le Blon had taken along his wife as his riding mechanic – wearing trousers.

Sceptics at the time wondered whether the race could be repeated. Few of them would have lived to see the last Targa Florio – in 1974. Goaded on by Vincenzo Florio, Sicily had been thrust into the forefront of the automotive revolution. No road race in the world would survive as long – but one event a year later did very nearly overshadow it for complete and utter madness, with the Italians once again in a starring role.

Pechino–Parigi

I t was more of an adventure than a race, and, given its audacious scope, could well have sprung from the mind of Jules Verne. Indeed, it became the subject of a bestselling book by one of the winning crew. Translated into eleven languages, *Pechino–Parigi* (*Peking to Paris*) by Luigi Barzini remained in print for most of the twentieth century.

The call to action emblazoned across the front page of *Le Matin* on 17 March 1907 was to the point: *Will anyone agree to go, this summer, from Peking to Paris by motor car?* Big-name manufacturers stayed away, fearing high-profile failure in the trackless steppes of Mongolia.

No such doubts afflicted one Italian aristocrat. Scipione Luigi Marcantonio Francesco Rodolfo Borghese, Prince Sulmona, Prince Bassano, Prince Aldobrandini, the holder of four Italian dukedoms and four marquisates, a duke of France, a grandee of Spain, could also have sprung from fiction. Even more of an aristocrat than the founder of Fiat, Borghese could trace his ancestry back to thirteenth-century Siena. Among his illustrious ancestors he could claim Camillo Borghese, who became Pope Paul V.

Born in 1871 on one of his family's many estates, educated by private tutors, Borghese's gilded life shuddered to a halt when his father lost the family fortune in a banking crash. Their palatial state apartments in Rome's Piazza Fontanella di Borghese were leased out while the family retreated to the rooms once occupied by the tutors.

His parents dispatched him to Paris to find a rich wife who could restore their position in Roman society, and he duly married the daughter of one of Genoa's ruling families.

But Borghese was no feckless noble. Military service had brought him into contact with other classes, which gave him a loathing for what he regarded as the provincial ignorance of the nobility and their indifference to business and technology. He stood for parliament as a radical and founded a political journal. Thin and wiry and unfashionably clean-shaven, his nose permanently askew after being nearly severed by a horse's kick, he stood out in a crowd. He was a man of few words who smiled little, whose passion was exploration. In 1900 he had crossed Asia from the Persian Gulf to the Pacific on foot and by camel. He enjoyed mountaineering – always alone, navigating himself. His daughter, Princess Santa Hercolani, was always at a loss as to what gift to give him. 'His habits were extremely frugal ... He did not drink, gamble or smoke. He had to spend a lot, to be sure, to live as a prince in Rome, prepare for his expeditions to climb high mountains or explore little-known countries ... but always with a clear sense of moderation and a precise purpose of mind.'

Peking–Paris was a challenge Borghese could not refuse and, as a proud patriot, he had to have an Italian car. Since no one took the venture seriously, no one was about to offer him a drive. The car Borghese eventually chose was a 7.4-litre model from Itala, winner of the previous year's Targa Florio.

The origins of Itala demonstrate the breathlessly peripatetic nature of Turin's first-generation motor engineers. After Giovanni Battista Ceirano sold his business to Fiat, he set up another car-making venture, Fratelli Ceirano, with his brother Matteo, but it failed so Giovanni set up a third company, Società Torinese Automobili Rapid (STAR), while Matteo set up his own, Itala, then left to form another, Società Piemontese Automobili (SPA). Meanwhile, Giovanni Battista then founded Ceirano Fabbrica Automobili with another brother, Giovanni Ernesto, before taking over Fabbrica Anonima Torinese Automobili (FATA), built by a Turin firm founded by Matteo Ceirano in 1903, in the Via Guastalla. Battista 'Pinin' Farina observed that the Ceiranos operated like 'the shock troops when it came to business. No sooner had they given life to a firm than they moved on to something else, often in competition with the original one.'

Indeed, by the time Borghese settled on the Itala, the Ceiranos had departed. The prince specified a number of modifications including a sixty-gallon tank, reinforced chassis and springs and minimum bodywork. To look after the car and share the driving was his faithful chauffeur Ettore Guizzardi. Ettore had made a dramatic entrance into the Borghese household. As a boy he assisted his engine driver father until the locomotive came off the rails near a Borghese villa and rolled down an embankment, crushing Ettore's father and injuring the boy. Borghese took Ettore in, nursed him back to health and, on discovering his mechanical aptitude, sent him to technical college and put him in charge of maintaining the family's cars.

Also aboard was a reporter from the Milanese newspaper *Corriere della Sera*. Luigi Barzini's task was to send back by telegraph reports of the Itala's progress. For Italy this threesome was as much a novelty as the motor car itself. As Barzini's son Luigi Jnr observed, 'the three men all represented "la nuova Italia", in revolt against the provincial mediocre, prudent life of their ancestors'.

Although *Le Matin* received several dozen expressions of interest, on 19 June only five competitors made it to Peking for the start. The race had no rules. The first team home would win a magnum of Mumm champagne. The route took them from the Chinese capital across the steppes to Outer Mongolia and Ulan Bator, past Lake Baikal in Siberia. A train of camels carrying fuel cans set up stations along the way. There were no maps; the route roughly followed telegraph posts from which Barzini could report their progress. A team of coolies carried the vehicles across rivers and hauled them over mountain tracks with mules. Such was the interest that Barzini's dispatches were shared with the London *Daily Telegraph*.

The journey took them into worlds that had never seen a European, let alone a motor car. To pay for provisions, acquired from whoever they encountered, Borghese travelled with the internationally recognised currency of silver ingots, shaving off pieces which he weighed with scales to the satisfaction of the nomads and herdsmen in exchange for food, water and help. Several times the car was bogged down in desert or marsh and near Lake Baikal it slipped between the planks of a bridge and had to be hauled out of a deep ravine.

Barzini admitted that the enormity of the challenge overwhelmed him, but he was reassured by Borghese's measured calm. He 'always made it his rule to impose upon himself short easy tasks and not to consider the difficulties lying beyond it. He often said to me during the trying despairing days of slow difficult advance: "All I wish for is to reach the next village." And he suppressed all the rest from his mind.'

Also impressive was their tireless chauffeur Guizzardi. When Barzini encountered him lying under the Itala, motionless, arms folded, he observed: 'This is one of his favourite pastimes, a way he has of taking recreation. When he has nothing special on hand he stretches himself out under his motor car, and contemplates it piece by piece, bolt by bolt, screw by screw, in a long strange colloquy with the machine.'

On the final leg of the voyage, Borghese felt confident enough to detour from Moscow to to dine with friends in St Petersburg before returning from the capital to rejoin the route. Thanks to the telegraph, news of their approach preceded them; as they approached Paris they were met at each town and city by ever-increasing throngs of spectators. From Berlin they were accompanied by a trio of Italas keen to milk the publicity value of the venture, along with a cohort of journalists. The Italians' triumphal entry into Paris's Place de la République, after their two-month voyage of 9,000 miles, was three weeks ahead of the runner-up. Astonishingly, all the entrants but one finished, which disappeared into the sands of the Gobi Desert, its crew rescued by tribesmen.

Barzini's son wrote, 'It seemed to confirm qualities (mechanical capacity, moral determination, adventurous spirit) which foreigners, who thought of us mostly as mandolin strummers, refused to believe we possessed.

'The crew somehow gave Italians the idea that the country was not condemned to be a dusty museum of past greatness, an itinerary of crumbling ruins for foreigners to gape at, but could compete in the modern world with other countries, no longer over-burdened by the past.'

As it turned out, the Italian crew aboard the Itala were not quite *la nuova Italia* that Barzini's son imagined. When the prince's aristocratic friends threw a dinner for him at Mons, the night before they reached their destination, Barzini, the journalist, was not invited and ate alone in his hotel room. And although the prince wrote to him, saying, 'these two months together I will preserve a lively admiration for you and a deep feeling of friendship which will resist time', after Paris they never met again. The motor car as a democratising force in Italian history still had a way to go.

It was easy for detractors to dismiss 1907's Peking–Paris as hardly a true competition given its paltry field and limitless time allowed for completion. But that year would see Italian cars take their place on the front rank of motor racing, a position that would last for the rest of the century.

Three-card Trick

Unlike its European neighbours to the north, Italy could only draw a comparatively small clientele for its cars. To survive, Fiat would have to concentrate on exports, which meant raising its profile internationally. Motor racing was already a proven route, but it was fraught with danger. Success required competitive, reliable machines and talented, fearless drivers. Daimler and Benz from Germany, Panhard, Renault and Darracq from France had already shown how it could be done. Typically, Agnelli rose to the challenge with his customary confidence. The story may well be apocryphal but, having passed into Fiat folklore, it deserves repeating.

In Turin the Caffè Allaria had replaced La Pantalera as rendezvous for the city's motoring fraternity. Legend has it that on one occasion early in 1907, Agnelli spread three cards on a marble-topped table marked 20B, F2 and 8B. 'These establish our supremacy without question,' he told the onlookers. They were the racing numbers of Felice Nazzaro's Fiats for the Targa Florio, the German Kaiserpreis and that summer's French Grand Prix. Surely no one driver, let alone one make, could win all three of the season's top races?

Sicily's uniquely demanding Targa Florio had aroused international attention and the second event in 1907 saw its entry list double to forty-five. Established stars of the motor racing world included the American-born Arthur Duray, Germany's Fritz Opel and French luminary Louis Wagner driving for Darracq.

Alexandre Darracq was a founding father of France's automobile industry. A canny and sometimes impetuous entrepreneur, he designed a sewing machine which won a gold medal at the 1889 Paris Exposition Universelle. He then started a successful bicycle business which he sold on and with the proceeds built his own factory in the Paris suburb of Suresnes. But a fatal attraction to unconventional engineering was almost his undoing. A five-cylinder rotary-engined moped and a belt-driven motor car both flopped before he hired a more sober designer who produced a series of successful machines.

In 1904 he launched himself at the Gordon Bennett Trophy. Rules at the time stipulated that, as at the Olympics, nations rather than individuals competed. Darracq tried to circumvent this by entering identical cars built in Britain, France and Germany. None of his 11.3-litre monsters finished. But that year a 200 bhp V8 machine developed by combining two of his Gordon Bennett race engines broke the land speed record at 104.53 mph (168.22 kph). Although Darracq himself neither drove nor even liked riding in cars, his star driver, Frenchman Louis Wagner, had made the company's name in America, winning the Vanderbilt Cup in 1906 on New York's Long Island.

For Florio, it was something of a coup that his next Targa would be joined by Wagner and the Darracq team, going head-to-head against Italy's Fiats. W. F. Bradley, the British journalist at the event, was in no doubt that the Fiat team were the stars. 'The drivers who stood out most prominently were [Vincenzo] Lancia and Nazzaro, the former bulky, jovial, dominating his car by brute force, the latter slim, elegant, distinguished, delicate of touch, burning with enthusiasm.'

Wagner drove furiously, clawing his way up from sixth place to second. But on the last lap, just three minutes behind Nazzaro and closing in fast, his engine suddenly raced as if it had slipped out of gear. In fact, a half-shaft had sheared; there was nothing Wagner and his mechanic could do. Nazzaro was the winner, having covered his distance in the shortest time with Lancia second, eleven minutes behind. Third place went to an Itala. A measure of how much faster and better the cars' handling had become was the fact that one hour and fourteen minutes had been cut from the previous year's winning time. Wagner's disappointment was sharpened by the reaction of company boss Alexandre Darracq: 'We shall have to announce that our drivers ran off the road.'

Wagner was not going to stand for that. He knew that the other Darracq, driven by René Hanriot, had suffered the same fault. 'If you state that I ran off the road, you are damaging my reputation,' Wagner told his boss. For Darracq, the reputation of the car came before the driver. Wagner stood his ground, warning him: 'If you put the blame on me you will regret it.'

Wagner knew his value. As well as his victory on the Long Island race course, he had gained further publicity in New York after an impromptu sprint down Broadway in his winning car earned him forty-eight hours in The Tombs, the city's infamous jail.

Agnelli, alert to Wagner's despondency, approached him with an offer to drive for Fiat, at double his Darracq salary. But Wagner's contract with the French team carried a heavy penalty if he broke it. Agnelli offered a *pont d'or* – a golden hello in modern parlance – to smooth the transition. Furious, Darracq appealed to the Automobile Club de France, threatening to retire from racing altogether. All over the sports pages of the French press a lively debate ensued as to whether a man was entitled to sell himself to a foreign firm. All this was grist to Agnelli's mill, since it gave the arriviste Fiat more profile as a serious contender. Wagner signed with Fiat.

The action moved to Germany and another new event. Initially, Kaiser Wilhelm had been unimpressed by his subjects' invention, insisting that he would never step into an automobile as long as there was 'a warm horse left in the stable'. But after losing a race between his carriage and a Benz, he was transformed into an ardent supporter, sponsoring his own Kaiserpreis to be held on a 117km circuit in the Taunus Mountains north of Frankfurt. In an attempt to contain the vogue for ever bigger engines and encourage more production cars, engines were limited to eight litres and 1,165kg.

It worked: ninety-two entrants applied, forcing the organisers to split the event into two heats and a final. Nazzaro triumphed again, with new Fiat recruit Wagner coming fifth, just in front of Lancia. Mercedes were ninth and eleventh and a solitary French Lorraine-Dietrich thirteenth. Not to miss out, Vincenzo Florio filled Wagner's empty seat in the Darracq, which failed to finish. The Kaiser himself presented the trophy. To rub salt in Darracq's wounds *Le Figaro* condemned French car makers for their lack of vision and failure to combat the growing threat from Turin.

Nazzaro's triumph on German soil put both driver and Fiat on the front of Europe's sports pages and heightened anticipation of the last big race of the season, the French Grand Prix in July at Dieppe. This would be a ten-lap race on a triangular circuit of closed public roads, totalling approximately 500 miles. Again, the organisers sought to keep speeds under control. The restrictions for this race applied to fuel consumption, 30 litres per 100km, but not to engine size. So Fiat responded with a monstrous 16.25 litres. Of the estimated 200,000 spectators, 10,000 Italians are believed to have made the journey to Dieppe. Thirty-seven cars were entered from six nations.

The cars were flagged off at one-minute intervals. This time Wagner, in front of his home crowd, led the field for the first three laps, only to crash out. Fellow Fiat driver Lancia then fought a battle with Duray in a Lorraine-Dietrich. The French car seemed to be beating it and only three of Lancia's four cylinders were firing, but the Lorraine's gearbox seized and brought Duray to a halt out on the course. Lancia then ran out of fuel. Having bided his time, on the penultimate lap Nazzaro took the lead. Despite the monstrous proportions of his Fiat, he managed it with his now customary style. As Bradley observed, 'He handled his cars as a violinist his instrument – perfectly attuned but brought to life by a hidden fire.' Nazzaro won the French Grand Prix at a spectacular 70.5 mph and the hat-trick was his and Fiat's. And for good measure he also set the fastest lap at 74.6 mph.

'Never in the history of the motoring movement has France's industry suffered such humiliation as the defeat it suffered yesterday,' pronounced London's *Morning Post*. Fiat had claimed all three of Europe's top motor racing trophies. Agnelli had served notice: the Italians had arrived. Fiat, the youngest car maker from the country with the least developed industrial infrastructure, had triumphed against experienced firms more than twice its age from countries with a substantial industrial and technological infrastructure.

The reasons for Fiat's surprising success are by no means obvious.

Passion and commitment play their part, but the same could be true of all the other entrants. Luck mattered for the best cars as crews faced innumerable hazards on the road. Mercedes, Renault, Panhard were already highly experienced engineering firms. But the upstart Fiat's triumph on the circuit over France's and Germany's established brands in the 1907 season's three major races underlined Agnelli's strategy of concentrating resources on quality of engineering and proven design. However, Fiat's racing cars were bespoke machines. To grow, the company needed to raise its output. Italy was still an automotive backwater when Agnelli made his first trip to the USA in 1906; the year before, it had produced a mere 850 units compared to France's 20,500. He went for the opening of Fiat's first American showroom on New York's Broadway. It was his first time in the United States and he was dazzled by what he saw, not so much in Manhattan as in Michigan's unglamorous industrial hub, Detroit. Paris may still have been the place to view all the latest designs and innovations, but he wanted to see the American automobile industry at work. What he found was an enterprise that owed nothing to the French pioneers, that was on an altogether different trajectory from anything in Europe. And for Agnelli, it was not about the product but the entire manufacturing process, which one man was about to revolutionise.

That year, Henry Ford's output would be 1,599 cars, a surprisingly similar number to Fiat's. The moving production line was still a decade away and Ford's first giant factory, Highland Park, had yet to be built. The term 'mass production' would not be coined until 1926 when Ford came up with it in an article he was invited to write for the *Encyclopaedia Britannica*. But what Agnelli saw was how the American was putting together all the ingredients to make products in vast numbers as efficiently as possible. Ford's cars were lightweight, unadorned, utilitarian devices, designed to function in a rural environment, the opposite of the bespoke seven-litre chassis that was then Fiat's bestselling model. But appearances were deceptive. The components that went into Ford's humble products were made of the highest quality metal, using the most sophisticated precision tooling Agnelli had ever seen.

The pioneer car makers he had seen in Paris like Panhard et

Levassor, had workshops full of general-purpose machine tools with skilled fitters hand-finishing each part so they would fit together. Ford demanded all parts be made to a standard gauge. His precision tools could cut hardened steel produced parts more accurately than any human hand could achieve, in a fraction of the time. All his designs were drawn up with ease of assembly in mind. Where Panhard's cylinders were individually made, Ford's were cast in a single block. The supposed virtue of 'hand finishing' left no room for economies of scale. Production at Panhard could only be increased with the employment of more fitters.

On the face of it, Ford and Agnelli could not have been more different. The self-taught American, born into rural poverty, who showed an early aptitude for repairing watches, had more in common with the Ceirano family of craftsmen whose business Fiat had bought out. Once Ford was satisfied with his car's design, he focused all his creative energies on the production process, learning lessons variously from American arms manufacturers and the vast industrialised meat-packing operation in neighbouring Chicago.

Nothing in Italy was made this way. It went against the customs and principles of the skilled craft culture and tradition that had underpinned European manufacture for centuries. Henry Ford came with none of that baggage. His mission was simplification of design and manufacture for precision and speed.

Agnelli was looking at Ford's operation not with the eyes of a dismayed craftsman, but as a graduate of military college, with its emphasis on organisation and logistics of supply. He recognised immediately how economies of scale could be achieved with superior tooling to machine precision parts that did not need hand-finishing. If a craft-based manufacturer wanted to increase production, the only option was to invest in more machines and more skilled staff. Ford's method enabled higher productivity from a less skilled workforce and – in turn – a cheaper product.

What he saw excited Agnelli enormously. 'We are at the beginning of a very large movement of capital, people and labour ... I am convinced that the motor car will bring fundamental change in human society. I am following the trend and I intend to take my part in it when the time comes.'

But Agnelli very nearly didn't get to take any part; not long after his return from Detroit, Fiat would face an existential crisis that threatened to destroy the firm and put him in jail.

Cavalier Attitude

For the first five years of the twentieth century Fiat's growth as a business had been nothing short of spectacular. In 1904, it paid its first dividend of 6 per cent; in 1905 it made a profit of 2 million lire on capital of 800,000 lire and declared a 200 per cent dividend. Agnelli then split the firm's 200 lire shares into eight shares of 25 lire each. By March 1906, the price of these new shares had rocketed to 2,300 lire. He then announced to the shareholders that the original company would be dissolved and a new one formed with Agnelli and just two of the original founders as the major shareholders. They raised the share capital to 9 million lire in 100 lire shares and distributed two and a half of these shares for each 25 lire certificate so the holders of an original 200 lire share now each had twenty 100 lire shares.

A year later Fiat announced profits for 1906 of over 5 million and paid 40 lire per new share in dividends. A sequence of stock splits and intense demand drove one 25 lire Fiat share up to an astonishing 4,625 lire. But then the market crashed. By mid-1908, shares had plummeted to a fraction of their value. Fiat's losses the previous year had amounted to more than 7 million lire and Agnelli had to call on shareholders to pay in over 60 lire per share to keep the business afloat.

The Turin prosecutor's office accused Agnelli of stock manipulation. It claimed he had published erroneously optimistic news about the business's financial health, doctored the balance sheets and accounts and enriched himself and his board at the expense of small investors. Agnelli was forced to step down from the Fiat board while a trial ensued.

Despite his initial success as an industrialist, Agnelli was still a comparative newcomer. The scandal could have finished his career, but he was far from done; in fact, he seemed to thrive on adversity. Unofficially he continued to manage the company while prosecutors struggled to prove their case. A retrial dragged on until 1913. And by the time he was acquitted he had acquired most of the remaining shares at bottom-of-the-market prices and emerged from the crisis in an even stronger position.

Proof, however, of Agnelli's capability was that while numerous smaller car firms were eviscerated by the financial crash, Fiat not only survived but by 1909 it was profitable again. By 1914 it was one of Europe's biggest producers, turning out over 3,000 vehicles, more than any British firm and a thousand more than former role models Daimler and Panhard. And he achieved this in part by a fundamental rethink of Fiat's product.

At the time of Agnelli's 1906 Detroit mission, Fiat's bestselling car had been an expensive seven-litre model for an exclusively wealthy clientele. After his audience with Henry Ford, Agnelli prioritised ever smaller and more affordable models made of standardised parts to appeal to a wider group of less affluent buyers. The 1908 Tipo 1 was a modest 2.2 litre, conceived with an eye to the taxi market, and not just in Italy. Cheap, sturdy, its wheels suspended with half-elliptic springs all round, its four cylinders cast in a simple, single block, the Tipo 1 earned a reputation for rugged reliability and found buyers as far away as Paris and London.

But the Tipo 1 was just a precursor for an even smaller car, the 1800cc Zero of 1912. Priced initially at 8,000 lire, by 1913 it had dropped to 6,900 lire, half the price of its rivals. It embodied everything that Agnelli had learned in Detroit: it was a single standardised design to be built in numbers and sold at a price that brought it within reach of an expanding clientele. But unlike Henry Ford's wilfully utilitarian Model T, the Zero appearance boasted groundbreaking styling – from the pencil of a self-taught teenager.

By 1911, Stabilimenti Farina was making cabs for Fiat's trucks.

This brought the Farina brothers into regular contact with Fiat's engineering supremo Guido Fornaca and his deputy, Enrico Marchesi, at the Corso Dante plant. The relationship was working well and when they asked Giovanni to come up with a design for the Zero's body, he replied, 'Pinin is our designer, let him take care of it.'

Pinin was in awe of the dour and formidable Fornaca, whom he regarded as an 'automotive virtuoso', and was all too aware of the big boss's apparent dismay that Farinas had sent such an 'extremely callow youth' to their meetings. But he found they shared a distaste for poor design when he overheard him say to a foreman who was showing him a new part, 'Does it have to be ugly to be useful?' Pinin was eighteen. By now he had six years' experience working for his brother and was as keen as mustard to develop that new aesthetic he felt the motor car needed. Most car coachwork began at the bulkhead, a vertical division between the engine bay and the passenger compartment that stood proud of the actual engine cover. Pinin's design did away with that step and smoothed the way for a continuous line to run from the apex of the radiator to the rear of the body. Like all distinctive body styles of the day, it was given a name, in this case torpedo, suggesting a smooth-sided projectile. It wasn't entirely new; it had already been seen on some racing cars, but this was the first time the design had appeared on an everyday road car, let alone an economy model.

Getting the body right was only part of the process. 'There is nothing more risky than designing a radiator,' he recalled, finding them frequently laden with unnecessary ornamentation. But as car designs became more uniform, radiators started to be a key distinguishing feature. Fiat's designers were also tasked with coming up with their own ideas. Pinin agonised over what he feared were his own 'provincial tastes'. It was his mother, clearly wise beyond her education (she could not yet read) who urged him to 'Do the opposite of everyone else.'

As a result, Pinin's own radiator was a model of understatement, a simple sloping shouldered design completely devoid of any decoration, but it was up against twenty-seven other renderings. The mock-ups were laid out for inspection and Agnelli himself was summoned to make the choice while Pinin looked on. Agnelli lit up half a Toscano cigar and began his review of the designs.

'Suddenly he turned to me and invited me to go to his side.' Pinin, rooted to the ground at first, but noting that Agnelli spoke the same Piedmontese dialect, found the confidence to join him. One by one Agnelli eliminated the designs.

'Not that one, nor that one either, it looks like a church window.' Suddenly he turned to Pinin: 'What do you think?' Pinin was tongue-tied.

'Say what you think.' Agnelli whittled them down until eventually there were just two, one of them Pinin's. He turned to Marchesi, who usually erred on the side of caution.

'One of the radiators does have some advantages, but the other is not bad at all,' he hedged.

Agnelli, evidently irritated by his caution, said: 'Well, we can't put two on the same car.' He turned to Pinin, '*Ca Ciancia un po'chiel* [You say something]. Which radiator do you prefer?'

'I like this one best because I made it,' replied Pinin. Agnelli's face was obscured by a cloud of cigar smoke. 'Well, then, we have chosen.' And with that the boss departed. 'It was the test that determined my life,' Pinin recalled. A few weeks later, he was put in charge of the whole operation of turning out the Zero's body and radiator shell, the youngest in the workshop apart from a few apprentices. The Zero was a runaway success. Over 2,000 were made between 1912 and 1915, most of them with Pinin's body design. Agnelli rewarded him with his own dark red example. 'He gave it to me like a decoration on the battlefield.' Only very few teenage boys from extremely wealthy families like the Florios in Sicily owned their own cars.

In little more than a decade, Pinin had risen from a peasant boy in shoes two sizes too big to being the designer of Italy's most successful car, in a transformation that was nothing less than spectacular. 'In those days taking the wheel and being the centre of attention, and having the approval of girls, felt to me as if I had achieved a unique and complete conquest.' Seemingly Turin, the backwater former capital of Savoy, was willing to break all convention and embrace the new.

Pinin Farina's elevation brought him within sight of a whole new world of style as Turin emerged not only as Italy's 'motor city' but also as the driving force of European cinema. It was in the same city that Giovanni Pastrone, who, like the Farinas, had migrated from a village in Piedmont, pioneered the epic movie with *The Fall of Troy* in 1910. Pinin was entranced by Pastrone's groundbreaking *Cabiria*, which liberated film from the proscenium arch. He was enthralled at how the camera 'did not stay fixed in one place in front of the scene but moved nonchalantly and inquisitively in front of everything'. He supplied cars to stars and producers and even acted as a driver. He identified with the producers who 'all lived and behaved like pioneers' and compared their lively competitive spirit to that of the city's motor industry. 'I suddenly found myself in another planetary system.'

The Futurists

For all the challenges facing Italy's nascent motor industry – the lack of raw materials, an established industrial infrastructure, even a decent road system – the nation more than made up for in enthusiasm. In September 1908 when a metal fabricator from Modena took his sons to watch the Coppa Florio, a race around a 50km circuit of closed roads outside Bologna, there were fewer than 3,000 cars on Italy's roads. France at the time had ten times that number. For many of the spectators it was their first sight of a car, a sight that could fire ambition.

For the younger of two boys, age ten, standing among the thousands who had swarmed to the event, it would be a defining moment. Up until then his ambitions were to be an opera singer or a sportswriter. After watching Felice Nazzaro, who had come from a similarly modest background, triumph in his red Fiat, covered in muddy spray thrown up by the charging machines, ten-year-old Enzo Ferrari's mind was made up. 'From that moment I knew my life would never be the same; motor racing would be my destiny.'

'Modernity bursts onto the streets, kicking up dust around the telegraph poles,' proclaimed the Bologna newspaper *Il Resto del Carlino*, 'devouring kilometres on four wheels.' The motor car gripped the Italian imagination; rich or poor, educated or not, the excitement was universal. And no one felt this more acutely than poet and theorist Filippo Tommaso Marinetti.

An impatient critic of what he dismissed as the stifling, reactionary forces of religion and tradition holding Italy back, he saw in the automobile a means of liberation from the dead weight of the past which had oppressed his countrymen. Mythology, he claimed, would be overtaken by technology. For him the new beauty was to be found in speed.

In 1909 he published *The Futurist Manifesto*. In it he eulogised the racing car, with its bonnet 'embellished with great exhaust tubes like snakes with explosive breath', more beautiful, he insisted, than the Winged Victory of Samothrace, second-century BCE masterpiece of ancient Greek sculpture.

Marinetti was by no means alone. Giacomo Balla's 1912 painting *Velocità d'automobile* is a heady abstraction of a speeding car merged with the landscape. *Dinamismo di un'automobile* by Luigi Russolo of 1913 depicts a car fragmented into arrow shapes to give the sense of high speed and in the same year Italian poet Luciano Folgore published an anthology of poems entitled *Il canto dei motori* – the Song of the Engines.

The triumphs of Nazzaro, in the foremost international races at the wheel of an Italian car, were a huge vote of confidence for a country whose prestige until then had lain only in its distant past. Bastions of Italian culture were seduced. Composer Giacomo Puccini, an early adopter, owned eight cars at one time. Flamboyant man of letters Gabriele D'Annunzio celebrated the liberating promise offered by machines of the petrol age. After making the pilgrimage to Brescia for the 1907 Coppa Florio, D'Annunzio immediately bought himself a 90hp Florentia, which he filled with roses when he took women out for a high-speed drive.

And although there was never any direct association between the Futurists and the car industry, their work celebrated a synergy they detected between the transformative power of the motor car and their own desire to break with the stultifying feudal and papal order that had kept the nation in check. Their agenda was complicated by its subsequent connections to the Fascist movement, but at the end of the twentieth century's first decade they identified the motor car as a liberating force, a means to freedom, even though few could yet afford one. This impetus was in stark contrast to what was happening in England, where the pastoral idyll and traditional crafts celebrated by the likes of John Ruskin and William Morris were still in vogue. In a speech he gave in London in 1910, Marinetti berated Ruskin for his 'morbid dreams of a rustic life' and his 'hatred of the machine'.

Italy's embrace of modernity was influenced by a change in its fortunes that the new century had brought. Although it missed out on the first industrial revolution driven by coal and steam that was enjoyed by its northern neighbours, it thrived on a second wave, powered by electricity, the internal combustion engine, the telephone. The absence of coal had spurred the development of vast hydroelectric power stations that carried electricity from the Alps down to the northern cities. But for all the enthusiasm for the automobile, Italy was still a diminutive player in terms of production. By 1913, France still led in Europe with an output that year of 45,000, followed by Britain's 34,000, Germany's 20,000 and Italy trailing with just 6,800. Of that, more than three quarters was from Fiat, its plants by now bursting at the seams.

The greatest shrine to the Italian futurist impulse was not the work of an artist in the conventional sense. Giacomo Matte-Trucco, a civil engineer by training, had honed his skills designing foundries and workshops. In 1905 he had been hired by Agnelli to plan the expansion of Fiat's overcrowded Corso Dante plant. But when Agnelli made a second visit to Detroit for further investigation of Henry Ford's operation, he now came away convinced that what Fiat needed was a greenfield factory designed to accommodate the specific demands of motor car construction. Matte-Trucco was set the challenge. Agnelli stipulated that the plant should be 100 per cent functional. 'Don't expect to be invited to the [architectural] Biennale,' he warned the designer. 'The factory must have no aesthetic preoccupations.'

In construction it owed nothing to Italian tradition, nor had there been anything in Italy built on such scale. It dwarfed all the palaces and cathedrals built by the dukes of Savoy. Seventeen thousand workers would be accommodated in 16 million square feet of floor space. It used 40,000 tons of concrete reinforced by 20,000 tonnes of iron, a form of construction which was still a novelty in Europe, with 10,000 square metres of glass windows to maximise daylight.

Superficially it resembled the Detroit car factories designed by the Prussian-Jewish émigré Albert Kahn, a pioneer of steel-reinforced concrete, but Matte-Trucco's five-storey design included several bold and unique features. He designed the factory around the production process, beginning on the ground floor, where the heaviest presses were placed. As each vehicle began to take shape, it ascended to the next floor, then the next, via helicoidal ramps like those later adopted by multi-storey car parks. Finished vehicles emerged into daylight on the roof, where there was a test track, complete with banked corners like the Indianapolis raceway, and made world-famous decades later by its starring role in the film *The Italian Job*.

Despite Agnelli's prescription, Matte-Trucco's creation instantly became a design icon. The architect Le Corbusier praised its 'most acute elegance and economy' and pronounced it 'one of the most important spectacles of industry'.

For most of the world's first generation of car makers who made the pilgrimage to Detroit, Henry Ford's model was too ambitious and too radical. The prohibitive up-front costs of machine tools, which could only be recouped by rapid acceleration of production, helped deter the fainter-hearted. But not Agnelli, who grasped the logistical imperatives behind Ford's vision and set Fiat on course to become one of Europe's biggest car makers. No other Italian company would come close in terms of output. But the drive towards mass production demanded standardisation and simplification. These were laudable engineering principles but did not leave room for the sort of heroic experimentation that would make Italy's automotive products so endearing, like those of Agnelli's great protégé, his former test driver and racer, Vincenzo Lancia.

'I Would Have Remained a Nobody'

'To anyone who drives many different cars, it soon becomes apparent that in one or two cases a machine possesses something akin to what in a human is termed a soul. How otherwise is it that one can sit down at the wheel and at once feel in sympathy with the car, at once know that it will do exactly what one wants it to do? Such a car, undoubtedly, is the Lancia Lambda.' This was the verdict of *The Autocar*, after an extensive road test for its 11 January 1924 edition.

Until the early 1920s, the reputation of Italian cars had been built on their racing exploits and their durability. With such a small home market, success depended almost wholly on exports to more developed markets like France, Britain and the United States. Competitive pressures and an increased focus on price tended to suppress innovation and experimentation. In this climate of increasing convention, Lancia's Lambda stood out as a beacon of innovation, boasting features that were decades ahead of the competition, most of which had sprung from the mind of its extrovert creator.

Vincenzo Lancia was exuberant, hard-charging, a vivacious joker, a talented if erratic racing driver whose passion for cars was almost matched by his love of opera. Like Ettore Bugatti, he had abandoned the path set out for him by his father and like Agnelli, who would become his sometime mentor, he was alert to the expectations of customers and the vital importance of marketing.

Lancia's association with the Italian motor industry started at the birthplace of Turin's motor industry, on Turin's Corso Vittorio Emanuele II, where the pioneering Ceirano brothers built their first Welleyes. Those two ground-floor rooms belonged to the Lancia family's townhouse. As Lancia observed later, 'If my father had not had the brilliant idea of renting the place to Ceirano I would have remained a nobody.'

Vincenzo's father expected his son to join the family firm. Giuseppe Lancia had prospered supplying canned food to the troops in the Crimean War. He then founded a thriving business in Buenos Aires, a popular destination for entrepreneurially inclined Italians in the nineteenth century. When he returned to the newly unified Italy, he was a wealthy influential whose honorifics included adviser to the king on guns and game.

As well as a house in Turin, he acquired a family retreat – a pitch-roofed alpine villa up a steep track near the tiny hamlet of Fobello beneath the south face of the Monte Rosa. It was there on 24 August 1881 that Vincenzo, the youngest of Lancia's five children, was born and spent his formative years. The villa's lands were the boy's playground where his irrepressible fascination with all things mechanical emerged. A particular passion was damming streams and constructing waterwheels. He also contrived to make his father's ornamental cannon fire live rounds.

Having detected his son's aptitude for mathematics, Giuseppe decided he should be prepared for the position of bookkeeper in the family business. But at school in Turin the boy showed no interest in study. He frequently played truant and was once brought home by a policeman after falling into the river. He also took to hanging around the Ceirano brothers' workshop on the ground floor of the family house, fascinated by the cycle business with its lathes and forge. His despairing father warned him that if his behaviour didn't improve he would be sent to boarding school seven miles from Turin in Varallo. It didn't, so off he went. On his first day he discovered some pupils had hired a bicycle – still a very new fad – but had no idea how to ride it, so he showed them, which made him an instant hit. His academic performance showed no improvement, but he was put in charge of school sports.

Still fixed on Vincenzo becoming a bookkeeper, his father enrolled him when he turned seventeen in Turin's newly opened Giuseppe Lagrange technical school. But on his way to and from college the Ceirano workshop proved even more of a distraction now that their chief engineer, Aristide Faccioli, was developing the Welleyes car. Soon he was helping them out, even on Sundays after Mass. Exceptionally sociable and willing, he endeared himself to Faccioli who recognised the boy's natural aptitude. Eventually, with Ceirano and Faccioli's blessing, Vincenzo proposed a compromise: Ceirano would take him on as an apprentice bookkeeper. His father wearily agreed.

It's uncertain how much bookkeeping was actually done. Faccioli soon noted Lancia's uncanny talent and troubleshooting, pronouncing that he had 'the ears of a blind man', capable of detecting the slightest fault by listening to the sound of the drivetrain. Despite an age gap of more than thirty years, Faccioli and Lancia developed a close rapport. As well as their shared passion for mechanics they both loved music; in any spare moment, Faccioli would accompany Lancia at the piano while the young man belted out their favourite operatic arias.

Word of his seemingly supernatural capability got round; when Carlo Biscaretti di Ruffia's Benz broke down, Lancia – with no prior knowledge of the machine – fixed it, and made a lifelong friend.

As the Ceirano business was being absorbed into the new Fiat enterprise, Lancia, still only nineteen, made a similar impression on Agnelli. For one of the first race meetings Fiat entered, from Padua to Vicenza and back, Lancia inspected the course and advised that negotiating the particularly steep hill at Breganze would necessitate the fitting of a lower gear ratio, but Agnelli vetoed the proposal. Lancia was then disqualified for having to push the car up the hill. It was a lesson learned. Shortly after that, Agnelli appointed him chief inspector, watching over Fiat's planning and development testing.

He and fellow Ceirano alumnus Felice Nazzaro also became the nucleus of Fiat's works racing team. Nowhere was Lancia's fearless exuberance more in evidence than behind the wheel, his driving style dramatically different from his teammate's. When the two drivers came into the Farina workshop in Via Canova to be fitted for the seats of their racing machines (there was no bodywork as such on these early racers), the teenage Pinin Farina got to observe them at close quarters, even riding with them on test runs 'as ballast'. Where Nazzaro – reserved, measured, slim, as immaculate in his dress as in his driving – handled his car 'with the precision of a surgeon', Lancia showed no such restraint, 'throwing everything into the first corner as if it was the last ... He paid no attention at all to method.'

While the pair enjoyed considerable success as Fiat's in-house driving stars, Lancia's ambitions lay elsewhere. He was impatient to go it alone and build cars of his own design. Like Lancia, Claudio Fogolin had been led astray from his studies by a passion for machines, abandoning agricultural college in the north-eastern town of Udine to go racing. In November 1906, 'so as to think and create in freedom', they presented themselves at the Turin office of the Royal Notary to sign an agreement. Each invested 50,000 lire and took on the lease of Itala's recently vacated premises on the corner of Via Donizetti and Via Ormea. Lancia e C. Fabbrica Automobili was born. Lancia was still a mere twenty-five. Agnelli must have been endeared to his irrepressible protégé as he allowed him to remain on the payroll for two further years and continue to race for the Fiat works team.

Lancia recruited a small team of engineers, to whom he was an exacting and tireless leader. Neither volatile nor overbearing, he was nevertheless a stickler for quality and when displeased would whistle a Piedmontese 'romance' as a warning of trouble ahead.

Lancia was nearly put out of business before he had even started. One evening in February 1907, oil dripped from a lamp onto a stove, setting fire to the workshop. Everything was destroyed: the prototype, all the patterns and tooling. His sister Maria said it was the only time she had ever seen her little brother in tears. But the following evening he was out playing boules with friends and the day after started to recreate his car in an adjoining building. When he discovered the doorway was too narrow for the finished article to pass through, he ordered his team to take sledgehammers to the stonework.

Superficially, the first Lancia, a 12hp four-cylinder, seemed relatively conventional, but subtle features betrayed its understated sophistication. By paying close attention to the load-bearing points of the chassis Lancia was able to reduce the thickness of the steel on some sections, while increasing torsional rigidity by deft positioning of the cross members.

On the road, the machine showed remarkable promise. Lighter and lower than the competition, its modest two-litre engine willingly revved up to 1,450rpm when most cars of the time could manage little more than a thousand. And instead of chain drive which was still the convention, power was delivered to the wheels via a prop shaft. Commentators were sceptical but customers loved it.

But launching some seven years after Fiat, Lancia faced a much more crowded market. With fifty workers in the Via Ormea works producing an average of two cars a week, he would have to export from the get-go. Within a year he had set up agencies in London and New York. His racing career helped. In America he was known for his performances in the Vanderbilt Cup races. His slogan there was 'The man who knows'. He made the most of his celebrity as a racing driver to promote the name abroad, winning races on Long Island against the more powerful, locally made Buicks and Maxwells.

Although the glamour of racing helped with recognition it only went so far. Being around Agnelli at Fiat, Lancia had learned that fundamental to any success in export markets was a dependable spares service. He commissioned his friend Carlo Biscaretti, who had also designed the shield-shaped Lancia badge with its vertically pointing lance, to produce an illustrated spares catalogue. This mundane measure went down well with influential commentators like *The Autocar*: 'We have never seen anything of the kind more completely or satisfactorily done. The possession of such a ready means of ordering spares without trouble and with the utmost certainty should be a great comfort to every Lancia owner.'

Lancia also supplied detailed technical drawings for the coachbuilders with instructions translated into English, French and German. An added advisory note betrays the detail-mad Lancia's frustration with having to outsource such a key element of his car: 'Our experience had proved beyond doubt that it is possible to considerably reduce the weight of bodies hitherto built without affecting their strength and durability. We therefore urge bodybuilders to carefully consider every part to be fitted to the chassis so as to ensure the finished car is as light as possible which is advantageous for the reputation of the body builder and for us in the satisfaction derived by the owner.'

Lancia's output of 150 cars in 1909 doubled the next year. And in 1911, bursting out of the Via Ormea works, the business moved across town to a 30,000 square metre factory on Via Monginevro. When Italy joined the Great War in 1915, Lancia was well placed to bid for lucrative military contracts for trucks and armoured cars, and even staff cars for the British Admiralty. The company thrived on its reputation for refinement and durability, which it maintained into the 1920s. It was the first in Europe to introduce a standardised wiring system and electric starters. While nothing like the size of Fiat, Lancia seemed to ride out the febrile post-war social and economic climate, while the similar sized Alfa Romeo, despite being dazzling in competition, seemed never far from management turmoil or financial doom.

But Vincenzo Lancia was by temperament an impatient innovator. After the early period of frantic trial and error during its birth, the automobile industry had settled into risk-averse convention where survival came before innovation. In 1922 Lancia turned that on its head.

First seen at the Paris Salon d'Auto in November 1922, the Lambda caused a sensation. Lancia himself was on hand to introduce his new machine. He had just married his secretary, Adele Miglietti, and their honeymoon consisted of visits to the Paris and London shows. Its slimline silhouette gave it a lean, athletic style that made the competition look ponderous and encumbered.

Its most startling feature was the absence of a separate chassis. The body structure was itself a frame. He had got his inspiration when on a sea voyage, ruminating on the structure of a ship's hull. Dispensing with the chassis not only saved weight, it also enabled the body to sit nearer the ground. Today this would be recognised as a 'monocoque' or 'unibody', but in 1922 there was no word for it in any language. Gone, too, were the traditional dumb irons – a legacy of the horse-drawn carriage – which supported the leaf springs and protruded beyond the front wheels. In their place was an ingenious system of independent suspension. Strikingly simple and effective, it involved a pair of telescopic tubes, the narrower lower one moving inside the larger upper one with a spring inside it. The lower tube also acted as the kingpin around which the wheel assembly could turn for steering. It was the brainchild of one of Lancia's devoted engineers, Battista Falchetto, who drew up fourteen different designs for him to choose from. Also fitted were brakes on all four wheels, a novelty then, with aluminium drums and shoes.

The engine was equally innovative: a four-cylinder engine arranged in a tight thirteen-degree V formation, narrow enough for a single overhead camshaft to operate both banks of cylinder valves. From its wooden two-bladed cooling fan to the rear of the flywheel, the engine assembly measured a mere 22 inches. *The Autocar* opined that 'With an almost perfect suspension the car when driven at ordinary speeds gives no indication of the state of the road surface', and found the car 'altogether exceptional in its performance'. Another feature *The Autocar* picked up on was 'a large felt-lined compartment for luggage'. So ahead of the curve were Lancia that the English term 'boot' had yet to gain currency.

These features would remain on Lancia models for decades to come and underpinned the marque's engineering flair. While Lancia would never approach the scale of sales achieved by Fiat, from an output of 472 cars in 1922 to 2,220 two years later, Lancia had proved that innovation was not the enemy of profit but, rather, the reverse.

Lancia's business powered steadily forward under the benevolent and all-embracing stewardship of its founder, who ran it like a classic paternalistic Italian family business. Pinin Farina, who observed him at work, noted his loyalty to his team of engineers; he 'transmitted his electricity to all these collaborators and to others too so they worked at high voltage'.

Lancia's other passion never dimmed. He befriended the Torinese composer Alberto Franchetti, and admired his *Cristoforo Colombo* and *La figlia di Iorio*, whose librettist was Gabriele D'Annunzio. Lancia used to take Franchetti on alpine drives on which they argued the merits of composers and operas as if they were discussing racing drivers. He joined the board of the Teatro Regio and would sneak into rehearsals and sit alone near the back. Director Giovacchino Forzano said, 'I am more frightened of Lancia's opinion than the audiences.'

But with Lancia, family always came first. Before work each morning he would drive his mother to Mass at the church of Sant' Antonio in Via Claudio Beaumont, frequently following her in for a short time. Pinin Farina marvelled at how cleverly Lancia juggled his duties to family and factory. 'When the lunchtime hooter went he raced home with the happy face of a schoolboy coming back from lessons. The world could burn down for all he cared, he was Lancia the father and husband', and then back at the factory he would regain 'all the vitality of a commander, demanding to the point of despotism'. Company co-founder Claudio Fogolin recalled a visit to the family retreat at Fobello one Sunday morning. 'I found him busy in the workshop, making tiny chairs and tables for his two little girls, Anna and Eleanora, who was three. Gianni was helping him. I waited with them until their work was finished . . . Just like his father, his concentration was marvellous to see. He knew the name of each tool and was ready to give it to his father when requested.' Gianni would need everything he learned at his father's elbow – sooner than he expected.

Although Pinin Farina was an admirer of Giovanni Agnelli, it was Vincenzo Lancia who became his mentor and role model. 'I behaved like a pupil before a master when I was with him and no other man has occupied a place in my life as he did . . . Lancia was always my compass.' When Pinin struck out on his own he used Lancia's business as a template.

Although they were from very different backgrounds, they were both self-taught, mixing keen observation with their own intuition and vision. Both men shared an appetite for the original, for pushing the boundaries of their craft. And while Lancia was creating the visionary Lambda, Pinin Farina was fretting over conventions and compromises that undermined the progress of automobile styling, which had yet to evolve from nineteenth-century coachbuilding traditions. Pinin dismissed car designs of the early 1920s as 'a cross between a motorcycle and a puppet theatre. The wheels themselves were the real enemy, the wheels which prevented the closure of the shape and of the whole vehicle.' As Farina were suppliers of bespoke bodies, Pinin's personal quest for a new automobile aesthetic was on hold as they responded to exacting customers. He bridled at unnecessary adornment 'masquerading bonnets and false radiators, it was the kingdom of false appearances ... There was no tradition to which we could appeal, our occupation was brand new and we paid for mistakes we made in person. I had to be alone for that experience, I could not look for hand holds anywhere outside myself.'

But before Italy's car industry could re-establish itself after the Great War, it would be engulfed by another existential crisis as revolutionary fervour swept across Europe.

The Years of Blood

One of the leading Marxist theoreticians of the twentieth century, Antonio Gramsci might seem a surprising name to find in this story; however, Italy's emerging motor industry and Fiat in particular would have a defining impact on his thinking. He in turn would also leave an indelible mark on the direction in which Agnelli would take Fiat in the post-war era.

Gramsci was born in Sardinia in 1891. A gifted pupil, he had to give up his education to support his family after his father, a minor official, was jailed for embezzlement. His early years were also plagued by health problems. He suffered from severe curvature of the spine which stunted his growth so that he never reached five feet. Despite this, he managed to secure a scholarship to the University of Turin in 1911, but soon got distracted from his studies. The industrial metropolis that the city had become was a world apart from the grinding poverty of rural Sardinia. Here he saw how working people could be a mobilising force for their own liberation. In 1915 he gave up his studies to write for a left-wing paper, *Il Grido del Popolo* (The Cry of the People), and in 1919 founded *L'Ordine Nuovo* (The New Order).

The Great War would be a bonanza for Italy's nascent car industry and the scale of growth during the war years was mind-boggling. Fiat's capital leapt from 17 million lire in 1914 to 200 million lire by 1919, and steelmaker Ansaldo's from 30 to 500 million. Fiat's workforce of 4,300 in 1914 mushroomed to over 40,000 by 1918, by which time it had become the largest vehicle maker in Europe. In Milan, Nicola Romeo was another beneficiary of government contracts for vehicles and armaments. But for the rest of the country the war was a disaster, especially for the troops, who entered into it with nothing like the patriotic fervour that had motivated the British to sign up so eagerly and nothing like as rigorous a training.

The fighting on the northern frontier with Austria was as brutal as anything on the Western Front. At Caporetto in 1917, 11,000 Italians were killed and over a quarter of a million taken prisoner; 350,000 deserted and 400,000 became refugees. More are believed to have died of cold and hunger than battle. As a proportion to its population of 35 million, its losses of 689,000 were higher than that of Britain, with 745,000 dead out of 46 million. Back home in Turin, seventy-five-hour working weeks became the norm as factories ramped up production for the war effort. Strikes were banned and wages tightly controlled. Fiat's swollen workforce stretched Turin's food supplies to the limit. Pinin Farina, conscripted into making arc lights and bowsers for the military, recalled 'a growth of moral tiredness' that accompanied the return of the wounded, and the blank spaces in newspapers from censorship. By the end of the war over a million men were charged with desertion before an amnesty was declared. Italy's eventual victory was more a result of the collapse of the Austro-Hungarian Empire than their prowess on the battlefield. It left a bitter legacy, and a divided, vengeful society.

In August 1917, with the war still raging, industrial strife erupted in Turin after police killed two people during a march for 'peace and bread'. The widespread strikes that followed combined demands for better wages with a revolutionary anti-war fervour. Women joined in and the carabinieri were exhorted not to fire on their comrades but to join them. But the protest was brutally put down. Armed troops are believed to have killed over fifty protesters and injured hundreds more.

For Gramsci these were formative times. For the industrialist Giovanni Agnelli, the tumultuous months that followed would define his and Fiat's place in post-war Italy.

In August 1920, exasperated by inconclusive negotiations with the unions, Nicola Romeo locked his Milan factory gates and shut the workers out. When news of this reached Turin, on 1 September Fiat workers responded by staging a factory occupation. They hoisted a red flag over the building and Fiat striker Giovanni Parodi, a war veteran and Socialist Party activist, appointed leader of a factory workers' council, was photographed seated at Agnelli's desk. Inspired by Gramsci's writing and the revolutionary workers' soviets in Russia, Parodi's aim was to show that the factory could be run without the bosses. He arranged with rail workers to keep supplies moving, appointed guards to keep watch for police or armed forces and enforced a ban on alcohol inside the plant. When rumours spread that the military were about to attack, wives and children barricaded the gates. In the first week of the occupation they did manage to keep production going, albeit at a little over half the regular output.

For Gramsci, the Fiat workers were an inspiration: 'Social hierarchies have been smashed and historical values turned upside down,' he wrote in *L'Ordine Nuovo*, but, presciently, he warned that there would be one of two outcomes: 'either the seizing of political power on the part of the revolutionary proletariat ... or a tremendous reaction on the part of the property classes and governing caste.'

The scene looked set for revolution. The wartime government had printed money to pay for munitions which drained the lira's value. By 1920, the lira was worth one sixth against the US dollar of what it had been in 1913. Big firms faced bankruptcy, unemployment passed 2 million. Riots and looting became common as people struggled to survive.

But unlike their comrades in Russia, Parodi's workers' council had no political organisation supporting it. Italy's Communist Party had yet to be formed, the Italian Socialist Party kept its distance and the metalworkers' union, the Federazione Impiegati Operai Metallurgici, refused its support. That summer of 1920, Premier Giovanni Giolitti, on his fifth term as Italy's prime minister, a liberal centrist leading a fragile coalition, took a benign view of the action, rejected calls to intervene with force and went on vacation in France.

Agnelli tracked him down and exhorted him to act. Giolitti refused to put troops into positions where they could be fired on by workers from the roof of Fiat's five-storey plant. He told Agnelli that if he really wanted the strike broken he would have to bombard Lingotto with cannon. But Agnelli did not want his brand-new factory destroyed.

After eleven days, the workers' resolve dissolved. Gramsci gave voice to their bitterness: 'There is no shame in the surrender of the workers of Fiat. That which had to happen implacably did happen. The Italian working class has been flattened beneath the steamroller of capitalist reaction.'

On 20 September 1920, Agnelli returned to his office, running a gauntlet of boos and jeers, only to find the portrait of the king that hung above his desk replaced with one of Lenin and a hammer and sickle. What Agnelli did next would come to symbolise the Fiat boss's shrewdness and cunning. Apparently stung by the humiliation of the workers' occupation and exasperated by the government's failure to take a stand, or perhaps calling everyone's bluff, Agnelli announced his resignation and advised the board that Fiat had become a workers' cooperative.

Shortly after that, on 31 October, Agnelli's beloved mother, Aniceta, died. Out of respect, all fourteen Fiat works closed and an estimated 3,000 workers turned out for the funeral. As the coffin left the church en route to the burial, a member of the workers' committee called out, 'come back to us'. Agnelli uttered no response but the duration of their handshake was taken as a signal.

Not surprisingly, the shareholders who had already voiced their opposition to Agnelli's departure unanimously voted him back in, his position now stronger than ever. But there were no reprisals or witch-hunts of the agitators, rather the opposite. Agnelli, it appeared, had not forgotten the philanthropical element to Fiat's founding fathers' original mission – to bring employment to Turin – nor was it his style to behave like the vengeful capitalist. For all his power and glory, he avoided attention. Austere and formal, he was only ever seen in a dark suit, starched shirt collar and Borsalino hat. He always spoke in the Piedmontese dialect, with as few words as possible. Pinin Farina described Agnelli's dialect as 'like a language fit for stone tablets, reduced to the essential'. When the councillors of his birthplace, Villar Perosa, renamed the town square after him he insisted the signs be removed and replaced with Piazza della Pace.

According to Pinin Farina, when anyone tried to pay him a compliment 'he used to cut them off with the proverbial phrase "Ca lassa perde": Drop the subject.'

In the coming years Agnelli put in place a number of workers' benefit initiatives, including a mutual society to help fund medical bills and a summer camp for their families. These measures evolved into a cradle-to-grave welfare system for all Fiat employees. For the steady stream of job-seeking migrants in flight from the grinding poverty of the south, such benevolence was undreamed of.

The time of strife became known as the '*Biennio Rosso*' (the two red years) but the speed with which the action petered out suggests it fell far short of a workers' revolution. Gramsci had yet to found the Italian Communist Party; there was no figurehead to provide revolutionary leadership – at least not on the political left. Nevertheless, the *Biennio Rosso* had sent a shockwave through Italian society and spooked business owners.

Unnerved by what they saw as widespread anarchy, with a weak-willed centrist government promoting compromise, together with the fragility of social order, the business owners began to look elsewhere for political protection. They found what they believed was their salvation under the spreading wings of Benito Mussolini. His initially progressive platform of universal suffrage – confiscation of war profits and an eight-hour day – had hardened into a violently anti-left movement, with its own armed '*squadristi*' militia. The ever-amenable premier Giolitti tolerated the Fascists, eventually forming an electoral bloc with them, easing their entry into the heart of Italian government, over which Mussolini would soon take total control.

Agnelli did not fall into step behind Mussolini like some of his fellow industrialists; he didn't need to. Fiat was becoming a power all its own. By 1924 it had twenty plants including steel mills and foundries. As well as cars and commercial vehicles it produced aircraft, diesels, tractors, tanks, ocean-going ships, railway rolling stock, ball bearings, tools and armaments. The emphasis on exports ensured that Fiat was never dependent on its small and comparatively impoverished home market – or on government contracts. Ever the pragmatist and survivor, Agnelli carved out a modus operandi with the Fascist government that was in both Fiat's interests and his own. It's a measure of Fiat's strength as a powerful entity in its own right that Mussolini, also something of a pragmatist, did not attempt to dominate it. Soon after his rise, to flatter the agnostic Turin business elites Mussolini made Agnelli a member of the Italian senate. But the Fiat boss did not exactly throw his weight behind Il Duce.

In October 1923, Fiat prepared to receive the new Italian dictator for a tour of its futuristic new Lingotto factory. Agnelli gathered representatives of his workforce and told them there were three ways they could respond to Mussolini's visit: to applaud, stay quiet or sabotage it. 'I will be comfortable with either of the first two.' They chose the second; Mussolini was received by the Fiat workforce in contemptuous silence. His lieutenant in Turin, Maria De Vecchi, was one of his most fervent supporters who had joined the Fascists' decisive march on Rome in 1922. Furious at the muted welcome, he took Agnelli to task in front of Il Duce for his workers not showing more support. But Agnelli was not to be cowed by the upstart De Vecchi. In 1925, when a Fascist-backed union tried to organise Fiat, Agnelli saw them off, negotiating a pay rise with communist-supporting officials. De Vecchi was removed and shipped off to Africa as governor of Italian Somaliland. From then on, Agnelli and Mussolini maintained a peaceful, if distant, coexistence.

As Pinin Farina observed, 'Nearly every family in Turin had a member or more than one, who worked either directly or indirectly for Fiat. In this way Turin was his personal city.'

Tears in the Park

Sometime in the winter weeks after the Armistice, a recently demobbed soldier made his way to the Fiat factory in Turin. He was not alone. The city was crammed with like-minded former conscripts, all in search of work. But with the end of the war came the end of the lucrative military contracts that had kept factories busy. Fiat wasn't hiring; it was laying people off.

The young soldier had dodged the bullets, but, like thousands of others, he was in poor health and low spirits. He had also lost his beloved elder brother and his father during the conflict, through illness rather than battle. Armed with a letter of recommendation from his commanding officer, from the 3rd Mountain Artillery, he managed to get an audience with Fiat engineer Diego Soria, but the skills he could boast amounted to little more than reshoeing horses. Soria gave the young man short shrift: Fiat could not possibly absorb the shoals of veterans washed up in the city.

Stung by the rejection, with no job, nowhere to sleep and no apparent future, Enzo Ferrari, the ex-conscript, found himself in Parco del Valentino next to the Po River. He swept a layer of snow off a bench and lay down. 'I was alone. My father and brother were no more. Overcome by loneliness and despair, I wept.'

He had to act. The small inheritance he had from his father on which he had been subsisting was dwindling, but he hung on in Turin and made his way to the bars and cafés of the Corso Vittorio Emanuele II, where, twenty years before, Giovanni Agnelli had met his fellow Fiat founders. There in the Bar del Nord he rubbed shoulders with mechanics and racing drivers and even caught sight of his great hero Felice Nazzaro.

Ferrari could drive and managed to talk his way into a job with a firm that was converting war surplus trucks into cars. Ferrari delivered the bare chassis to a *carrozzeria* where they were fitted with torpedo bodies. It was a matter of pride to him that his licence number was 1363, making him one of Italy's earliest drivers. It was menial work, but it was a start behind the wheel and his deliveries took him to Italy's other motor-making centre – Milan. There he befriended former bicycle racer Ugo Sivocci, who had become a test driver for a small car firm, CMN. In November 1919, they entered the Targa Florio. They drove all the way to Naples, through a blizzard in the Abruzzo hills, fending off wolves with a pistol, before boarding the Florio's ferry, the *Città di Siracusa*, for the night voyage to Palermo.

Their car, a stripped-down production model, looked crude beside the pure-bred racing machines from Fiat and Peugeot. The weather in Sicily was terrible with snow in the mountains and mud on the roads that caked the cars so they were virtually indistinguishable. The road surfaces were so rutted that Ferrari's petrol tank was shaken loose and he lost an hour while he and his mechanic struggled to fix it. Outside the village of Campofelice the police flagged him down to a halt while the Italian prime minister gave a speech in the square. When the entourage departed, Ferrari had no choice but to follow along behind. It was dark by the time he reached the finish. All the officials had gone home, but for a solitary policeman armed with an alarm clock. Furious, Ferrari went in search of Count Florio who grudgingly classified him with ninth place.

Ferrari's dogged performance did not go unnoticed; it helped to give him an entrée into the racing team that was poised to overtake the all-conquering Fiats.

By the 1920s, Alfa Romeo had already experienced several changes of ownership.

French industrialist Alexandre Darracq, Agnelli's aggrieved rival in the early years of competition, decided to challenge Fiat in its own home market, with his 'voiturette', in Milan. Isotta Fraschini, founded there in 1899, was making cars under licence from Renault, Darracq's great rival. He chose a site in an as yet unnamed suburb and christened the plant Il Portello after a nearby trattoria which he frequented.

The facilities were state-of-the-art but the cars he started making there in 1908 were emphatically not. Underpowered and under-braked, the delicate 'voiturettes' were no match for Italy's forbidding hills and rough track roads. By 1909, bankruptcy loomed; Darracq beat a hasty retreat, offloading Portello onto his Italian creditors, the Banca Agricola di Milanese.

The bankers, recognising its potential as a manufacturing site, put together a consortium of local industrialists to keep it running. Keen to distance themselves from the failed French venture and to boost their local credentials, they commissioned a trademark combining the city of Milan's coat of arms with the Visconti family's alarming heraldic emblem of a viper devouring a small child. They also came up with a new name, Anonima Lombarda Fabbrica Automobili. As with Fiat, the initials soon gave way to the acronym. In June 1910, Alfa was born.

To deliver the first new in-house-designed Alfas they hired Giuseppe Merosi as technical director. A trained surveyor, he preferred to be addressed as 'Geometra' Merosi.

Unusually tall at 6 ft 1 inch, his first passion was cycle racing and after an unrewarding spell in Lombardy's department of public thoroughfares he moved on to building bicycles of his own design. Inspired no doubt by the Ceiranos' Welleyes, he adopted another surprising English name: Endless. Then, after a spell at Fiat, he was working at the Milanese motorcycle makers Bianchi when the invitation came to join Alfa.

Merosi's designs owed nothing to Darracq's efforts. They were solid and reliable, and by 1914 output had risen to 200 cars a year. After one finished third in the 1914 Coppa Florio, he was inspired to create a Grand Prix contender, but the First World War put the brakes on it. Not only that, Alfa had yet to turn a profit so its bankers began the search for an exit.

Nicola Romeo was in almost every way Merosi's opposite. Short, bald and excitable, with a sprawling moustache perched beneath shining eyes, Romeo was both extremely clever and very persuasive, nicknamed 'the siren' in later life when he became a senator. Usually a fastidious dresser, he favoured three-piece suits and celluloid shirt collars and camouflaged his bald head with a broad-brimmed golfer's cap like that beloved of the Prince of Wales. The attire belied the hardship of his southern upbringing. Born in 1876 to an impoverished elementary school teacher near Naples where over 80 per cent of the population were illiterate, he worked his way through high school to university in Naples, tutoring other students to make ends meet.

He excelled in maths and English and graduated with a degree in civil engineering. Further studies followed in Belgium, France and Germany, before he tackled the job market. Despite his brilliance, his southern origins were a barrier and he was about to settle for a post as a provincial station master near Rome when he was approached by a British company selling equipment for electric railways, looking to set up a base in Milan. The job set Romeo on his way, playing to his natural ability as a salesman and giving him an entrée into Milan's commercial life.

In 1905, he married the musically gifted daughter of a Portuguese admiral, who gave up her studies at La Scala to bear him seven children and in 1907 he struck out on his own. Within a few years he and his banking partners had amassed a portfolio of businesses from air compressors to tractors to mining machines. He also acquired a property, the Villa Castiglioni on the shores of Lake Como, as his family retreat.

The timing of Romeo's swoop on Alfa could not have been better. He saw opportunity in Portello's well-equipped but underused facilities by turning it over to the manufacture of artillery shells. He added a foundry and forging shop and even a workers' village. Capital of 1.8 million lire in 1915 mushroomed to 10 million by the end of 1917 as production expanded to include aircraft engines and generators. War contracts were a goldmine for Romeo, who rewarded himself in 1917 by acquiring a dramatic art nouveau-style villa in the centre of Milan, which dismayed his older, less flamboyant business partner Ugo Ojetti with its friezes of nude women on the façade. Romeo, a fugitive, was determined to flaunt his fortune. The future, it seemed, was full of promise.

As for most Italian industrialists, Nicola Romeo's good war was followed by a very fraught peace. By the end of hostilities his empire had grown spectacularly. Although he was by no means the only shareholder, as head of the company he took home 35 per cent of net profits, far in excess of the 6 per cent earmarked for interest on capital. But almost all his output had been geared to the war effort. Since 1915, no cars had been built. But with the Armistice, all military contracts were cancelled, a crisis compounded by the economic downturn that followed.

In 1921, the Banca Italiana di Sconto, Romeo's main creditor, collapsed. The government hastily created the Banca Nazionale di Credito, to help keep struggling businesses like Romeo's afloat, taking a closer interest in how they were run and where savings could be made. Romeo was a gifted mathematician and salesman but by nature an expansionist, adept at building businesses, not pruning them. But as he was also smart and stubborn, his grip on the business remained tight.

One casualty of Romeo's arrival at Alfa in 1915 had been its chief designer and general manager, Giuseppe 'Geometra' Merosi. Romeo wanted the general manager role for himself and exiled Merosi to one of his railway factories in Naples. This move cannot have endeared Merosi to his new boss as after hostilities ceased and Romeo's profits from war contracts came under scrutiny, Merosi actually gave evidence against him. But Romeo was a pragmatist and experienced motor engineers were hard to find. After a failed attempt to build American tractors under licence, Romeo invited Merosi back to Portello, albeit in the lowlier role of 'technical consultant'.

Initially, the product was no different from pre-war output. The cars' big 6.3-litre engines were antiquated and only fifty-two were built in 1921. All that had changed was the name: Alfa Romeo; the boss wanted it known he wasn't going anywhere. Merosi's replacement RL model, with an engine half the size, saved the business from oblivion and in 1922 800 were built. Romeo was keen to go racing, even though he had nothing like the resources of Fiat to develop competition machines. But Merosi's designs were robust and reliable, which helped Alfa to impressive first, second and fourth places in the 1923 Targa Florio, which spurred them on to an attempt at

Grand Prix. The 1923 twin-cam two-litre P1 looked the part but failed to perform as hoped. It was handed to the experienced racer Ugo Sivocci, Ferrari's original driving partner. It was Sivocci who had won the Targa for Alfa after painting a *quadrifoglio*, a green four-leaf clover, on his car. But in practice for the Italian Grand Prix, and without his lucky emblem to protect him, he crashed and was killed outright. The P1 never raced again. The message was clear. Grand Prix racing needed resources that were beyond those of Alfa Romeo and its foray into the top level of motor sport might have ended there. As it turned out, it was just the beginning.

Garibaldino

B y the 1920s Grand Prix racing cars were no longer multi-litre monsters like the Fiats with which Nazzaro had swept the board in 1907. Smaller, lighter, faster-revving engines had taken their place and moved them further away from conventional road cars in the relentless quest for higher speeds, faster cornering and better brakes. Supercharging – forcing the fuel mixture into the engine – dramatically boosted power but added technical complexity, as designers were pressed to squeeze more speed from less weight. Grand Prix racing car design was becoming a speciality of its own.

Giorgio Rimini, from Catania in Sicily, had followed Romeo north to Milan. Possibly because of his familiar southern roots and his own comparative lack of flamboyance, Romeo regarded him as a kindred spirit and let him operate with a good measure of autonomy. Rimini's amorphous brief covered sales, testing and racing, where he soon realised that Alfa would need to raise its game to have any hope of competing with the giant Fiat.

It was Rimini who saw potential in the 22-year-old Enzo Ferrari as both a driver and something of a fixer. Their first contact proved to be a useful life lesson for Ferrari. It began when a car he had ordered from Alfa failed to materialise. Ferrari's complaint was passed to Rimini who responded by pointing out a usefully ambiguous clause in the contract stating that his car would be delivered 'as soon as possible, or even sooner'. Ever after, Ferrari made a point of reading the small print. In spite of this, the two men, comparative outsiders in the rarefied world of Milan, struck up a good rapport. Ferrari recognised in the wily Catanian a kindred spirit, 'swarthy of complexion, with staring eyes and a cigarette permanently hanging from his lips'.

Despite his modest provincial origins, from his early years Ferrari was a commanding presence. Almost six feet tall, he stood head and shoulders above the Italian crowd, with his striking looks: a large nose and half-hooded, reptilian eyes that sloped down towards his temples, and a thick shock of hair. Driven, persuasive and calculating, as his confidence grew he became adept at mastering whatever situation he found himself in. He confessed to feeling 'so provincial, so Emilian', but he projected a determination and cunning which got him past the forbidding airs and graces of the better-heeled.

In 1920 he was back in Sicily for the Targa Florio, part of a three-car Alfa works team led by Giuseppe Campari, a 16-stone extrovert racer and operatic baritone, who had played Alfredo in Verdi's *La traviata at* Bergamo's historic Teatro Donizetti. Before the race began, several days of rain had reduced the 67 miles of mountain track to a tree- and boulder-strewn assault course. Of the seventeen starters, only seven made it to the finish. Campari retired with a waterlogged magneto. But, aided by a pair of incongruously large improvised front mudguards, Ferrari slogged on and finished second. This success in the prestigious Sicilian race boosted Ferrari's reputation and helped launch Alfa Romeo as a brand. But in the top tier of motor racing, Fiat dominated with its groundbreaking Tipo 805. The first supercharged car to compete in a Grand Prix, its straight-eight, twin-cam could not be matched by any of the competition.

Since the return of the Grand Prix series, Fiats boasted features that made the competition obsolete. Smaller, lighter, lower, their full-length undertray aerodynamically encased the drivetrain. The exhaust was enclosed, and the driver's and riding mechanic's seats staggered to shave centimetres off the width of the body, which narrowed to a vertical wedge at the rear. Under the direction of Agnelli's formidable technical lieutenant, Guido Fornaca, the design was the joint effort of Fiat's best and brightest.

Romeo was ambitious for his company. He wanted Alfa to take on Fiat in the top tier of motor racing. And Rimini knew that to have any chance they would need fresh blood. He summoned his new driver and quizzed him. 'Ferrari, where are the competent people? Carry them off by all tolerably legal means.' Fiat had amassed a vast pool of engineering talent. Luigi Bazzi had fallen out with Fornaca and jumped ship to Alfa. Ferrari consulted him and he suggested he approach Vittorio Jano, 'a man of great worth, who is being treated as a bit of a subordinate'.

Ferrari, never one to pass up an opportunity for revenge, relished the chance to get back at Fiat for turning him down after the war. In September 1923, he travelled to Turin and sought out Jano in his Via San Massimo apartment. There he encountered Jano's wife, Rosina. After he revealed the reason for his visit, Rosina insisted there was no possible chance of the Piedmontese Jano leaving Turin for such foreign pastures as Lombardy and Milan.

Born Viktor János in 1891 to Hungarian immigrants in Turin, his father the technical chief of the city's historic arsenal, Jano had grown up with a passion for machines. At eighteen, having graduated from the Istituto Professionale Operaio di Torino, he was already working as a draughtsman for one of the Ceirano brothers' many short-lived firms. Snapped up by Fiat, after two years he was already head of a department and, at the time of Ferrari's visit, seemingly very satisfied with the way his career was developing.

Jano listened to Ferrari's overtures, but told the young emissary he would need to hear the proposal from someone more senior. Romeo's deputy Edoardo Fucito was dispatched to Turin with an offer Jano couldn't refuse: double the salary Fiat was paying him, plus his own apartment in Milan – even more important, complete freedom to design his own racing car. A week later, he, Rosina and their 2-year-old son Francesco were installed in an apartment on Milan's Corso Sempione. Starting in September 1923, his first act at Portello was to find a draughtsman who was prepared to work on a Sunday; Luigi Fusi said he would come after 6 a.m. Mass. By that Sunday lunch-time Fusi had completed the first cross-section drawing of the new racing engine, drafted as Jano, standing behind him, reeled off the dimensions. Ten days later the rest of the engine had been drafted.

Back at Lingotto in Turin, Jano's former boss, Fornaca, was incandescent. The year before, two of Jano's fellow Fiat engineers,

Vincenzo Bertarione and Walter Becchia, had defected to Sunbeam in Britain. The design they came up with was nicknamed the 'Green Fiat', since beneath its British racing green paintwork it bore a striking resemblance to their erstwhile employer's machine. Fornaca dispatched a carabiniere to Jano's new apartment in Milan with a warrant to search for any blueprints that he might have brought with him from Turin. There were none. All that Jano needed was in his head.

Jano's impact at Portello was dramatic. Where Merosi would run test-bed engines on full power for less than a minute, Jano would have them run for hours on end. He treated his team much the same. Within months of his arrival at Alfa's Portello plant, Jano produced his P2. Although encouraged to rework Merosi's troubled P1, what Jano produced was an entirely new machine.

There were similarities with Fiat's racing engine. But there were also critical differences. Jano knew the Fiat's weak points, some of which, under the imperious Fornaca, he had not been given the opportunity to change. Fiat's cylinders in two blocks of four could distort under intense heat so Jano made his Alfa engine with four blocks of two cylinders which would each be more solid. He improved the magneto by building in a manual spark advance. Instead of high-precision bevel gears driving the camshafts, he chose bigger cogs that were more robust. Where the Fiat's supercharger was attached directly to the crankshaft, obliging it to turn at the same speed as the engine, Jano introduced gears to vary the drive ratio. The valve springs were prone to breaking on the Fiat, so for the Alfa Jano had them made from a thicker gauge steel and lightened the spring loading so the engine could run 1,000rpm faster without them breaking. Jano's innovations were typical of him; they were practical and straightforward, prizing simplification over sophistication.

Rimini had also brought another inspired newcomer to the Alfa's racing team. Antonio Ascari only started racing seriously after becoming Alfa's sales agent for Milan and Lombardy, but he showed immediate promise. Ferrari regarded him as a *garibaldino* for showing a reckless spirit that echoed the revolutionary general's red-shirted comrades. But there was more to Ascari than pure drive. Rather than the brute force and superhuman endurance demanded of Nazzaro and Lancia, racing drivers increasingly needed preparation and precision to find that edge and get the best from their finely tuned machines. Ascari and Alfa would be a game-changing combination.

In June 1924, the P2 was barely finished when it was entered for a 200-mile race at Cremona, in Lombardy. Its aluminium bodywork had not even received its coat of red paint when Ascari blasted away from the start with Bazzi riding as mechanic. Journalist Giovanni Canestrini likened it to a silver bullet, 'the singing of the engine giving the impression of uncommon power'. Ascari pushed the P2 to over 120 mph and averaged over 100 mph for the whole race, which he won with ease.

Cremona was just a taster. In August, at the European Grand Prix outside Lyons, Alfa went up against the cream of international motor sport. There were twenty-two entries, including the previous year's winner, Sunbeam from Britain, no fewer than six Bugattis, a pair of Delages from France and four Fiats from Turin led by their perennial star Felice Nazzaro. Jano's preparation was exhaustive. He used one of Merosi's P1s as a test bed to work out which gear and axle ratios best suited the circuit. Among these thoroughbreds, Alfa Romeo was an interloper, but all that changed soon after the flag dropped. In an intense and unusually close race, Sunbeam, Fiat and Alfa each held the lead with Delage not far behind. Ascari's Alfa died on the last lap and his mechanic Giulio Ramponi collapsed trying to push the car to the finish, but his Alfa teammate, the baritone opera star Campari, romped home first. Never before had a brand-new car triumphed in its first Grand Prix.

For Nicola Romeo it was the ultimate validation of all his engineering ambition. Having sprung Jano from Fiat, he had given the young engineer his head and been amply rewarded. As Pinin Farina observed: 'It was curious to see them together, Romeo and Jano, during the races in front of the Alfa pits, because they made a strange pair of engineers: the former looked upon races as an operation in logarithms, the latter as a derby run between thoroughbreds. But as a pair they were as tightly bound together as skeins of wool.'

For Agnelli and Fiat, this was a double humiliation. Not only had Alfa triumphed thanks to the skills of one of their former engineers, none of the four Fiats had even finished. Also, Ascari was emerging as a driver with real star quality. 'On several occasions he made the crowds scream with horror when he came off the banking, with the car fishtailing,' reported *Corriere della Sera*. 'Four times he reached the rim of the banking – a few centimetres more and he would have flown off. However, the heart and hands of the racer do not tremble. The car is under his control, and all that is left of the danger is a puff of yellow dust.' But Ascari's apparently aggressive racing style masked a calm and precise car control that came from meticulous preparation. He developed a knowledge of the track that enabled him to exploit it better than his rivals.

Realising that Ascari and Alfa were an unbeatable pairing, after nearly twenty years on the front line of motor sport Agnelli took the decision to quit. Never again would Fiat compete in a Grand Prix motor race.

Ferrari was also making headway as a competitor. For the Coppa Acerbo at Pescara, he was entered as a backup to Campari, in an older and heavier sports model. But early in the race, Campari retired with a broken gearbox which put Ferrari in the lead, ahead of a pair of German Mercedes. Cunningly, Campari had moved his stricken car off the track, out of view of his competitors on subsequent laps. The Mercedes drivers – and Ferrari – could only imagine that Campari was far ahead and therefore would not attempt to go all out and chase him down. The track was a treacherous mixture of fast straights and tight, narrow corners through a trio of villages. Ferrari managed to stay ahead of the more powerful Mercedes and brought the Alfa home first.

Ready to congratulate him when he stepped out of his car was a formidable trio: Mussolini's Air Marshal Italo Balbo, the Duke of Abruzzi and Baron Giacomo Acerbo, another of Il Duce's close associates. It was Acerbo's dead war-hero brother after whom the race had been named. Ferrari was rewarded with a silver cup, a cheque for 5,000 lire and the title of Cavaliere della Corona d'Italia – Knight of the Crown of Italy.

But while his place in Alfa's driver line-up was now assured, Ferrari faltered. At Lyons for the French Grand Prix, after a few practice laps he abruptly pulled in, left the track without explanation and boarded a train back to Italy. Giovanni Canestrini, *La Gazzetta dello Sport*'s motor racing correspondent, speculated in print that Ferrari was afraid in the face of such formidable competition – causing a thirty-five-year-long rupture between the two men. As Canestrini saw it, Ferrari did not have the *garibaldino* killer instinct he had identified in Ascari.

But perhaps Ferrari was coming to realise his real skills lay off the track. As well as admiring Ascari's verve behind the wheel, Ferrari was also impressed by his business sense. Having got himself made Alfa's exclusive dealer for Lombardy, Ascari found that the publicity from his success on the track translated into sales. This gave Ascari an independence that Ferrari craved, but for now his future lay with Alfa Romeo.

Nineteen twenty-four had been the company's breakthrough year. At the Italian Grand Prix at Monza, Ascari led four cars home. Not since Nazzaro's triple triumph for Fiat in 1907 had an Italian team enjoyed such stellar success. Evidently Ferrari's flight from the French race had not damaged relations with his employers. He is present in the euphoric group photographs after the company's triumph at Monza, standing alongside Rimini and Romeo. Ferrari's real contribution to Alfa's success had come not from driving so much as headhunting the talent that had brought Alfa such triumph.

Another change in Ferrari's life, which may have had a bearing on his step away from racing, was his marriage. On one of his trips to Turin for Rimini, in one of the city's bars, he met Laura Garello, a native of the Piedmontese village of Racconigi. She was eighteen and working as a dancer and, like Ferrari, living away from home. Although they didn't marry until 1923, he began to go around with her in a manner that was unconventional for the times, even referring to her as Signora Ferrari. After the couple moved back to his native Modena, his widowed mother and Laura vied for his attention as he focused on laying the foundations for his own business. Its original name, Carrozzeria Emilia Enzo Ferrari, suggests he had plans to build bodywork but, following Ascari, he also became the exclusive dealer for Alfa in Emilia-Romagna, trading on his reputation as a driver. In six short years Ferrari had gone from a nobody to a somebody, a player in the automotive world. But the best – the very best – was yet to come.

14

Fallen Hero

In the run-up to the 1923 Italian Grand Prix, Jimmy Murphy, America's most famous racing driver, was in the Monza paddock working on his Duesenberg. Two years before, he had gained international fame by winning the French Grand Prix (it would be forty-six years before another American in an American car won a Grand Prix). At first he paid no attention to a couple of onlookers until one stepped forward with an invitation to lunch the following day – with Benito Mussolini. 'I didn't sleep a wink that night,' recalled Murphy, who was worried 'because I might pick up the wrong fork or something like that.' As it turned out there was no cause for alarm. Mussolini was already a fan of motor sport and rather in awe of Murphy's talent. 'He made me feel like I could have had the whole of Italy if I'd wanted it.' He gave Murphy a rather tasteless watch made from an old Italian gold coin and, because Murphy loved dogs, two German shepherds.

Unlike his future protégé Adolf Hitler, Mussolini was a keen driver, always ready to wrestle the wheel away from his chauffeur, Ercole Boratto, who said of his boss 'he drove fast but badly', scaring passengers by drifting around corners. When Mussolini travelled through Modena in 1924, en route from Milan to Rome in his brand-new Alfa three-seater roadster, he was at the wheel with Boratto and his secretary beside him. For a parade lap through the streets of Modena, Ferrari was detailed to lead the way. Boratto urged him to drive slowly as it was wet and Mussolini was apt to get into hair-raising skids.

Alfa's rise to international stardom coincided with Mussolini's own ascent and made him a great fan of the marque. Although none of the drivers expressed their outright support for him, Il Duce was always ready to exploit their success as symbolic of Fascist Italy's prowess. He conferred on Enzo Ferrari the title Commendatore, for his services to motor sport.

The 1925 Grand Prix season was the first to offer a world championship prize to the most successful car constructor. With Jano's triumphant P2 plus Ascari, arguably the world's most promising driver, this seemed to be Alfa and Italy's time to shine. At the inaugural Grand Prix d'Europe at the Spa circuit in Belgium, on 28 June, all of the rest of the field retired, leaving Ascari and Campari with the track to themselves. And since Ascari had a twenty-minute lead over Campari, they weren't exactly racing. Feeling short-changed, the Belgian spectators began to boo so Jano called his drivers into the pits, where there was food and drink for them to enjoy while the cars were cleaned and polished, then sent out for the closing laps. It was a rare display of hubris on Jano's part. He was otherwise noted for his almost military discipline and introspection. Although he could be distant and preferred to spend as much time as he could with his wife and young son, he inspired fierce loyalty in his staff.

Not surprisingly, when Ascari arrived at the French Grand Prix, scheduled for 26 July, he was the firm favourite. It would be the inaugural race at France's newly built Montlhéry Autodrome, just outside Paris. Ever thorough, Ascari had visited earlier in the year to learn the circuit and expressed his disapproval of the wooden palisade posts threaded with wire that bordered the outside of much of the track. He asked for them to be removed but his request fell on deaf ears.

Despite this, on race day Ascari showed his dominance, jumping straight into the lead from second row on the grid. By lap fifteen when he pitted for fuel and new rear tyres, he was ahead of the next Alfa by seven minutes. Jano suggested he back off a little since he had such a margin, but Ascari was having none of it. He grabbed a couple of bananas and his Thermos of champagne and water and screamed out of the pits. By lap twenty-three, when Ascari failed to appear, it had started to rain. The loudspeaker reported the crash of car number 8. Spectators reported that as he entered a fast corner at what would have been well over 100 mph, he clipped one of the wooden posts with a wheel hub. Ascari corrected – a fraction too much, for he hit several more posts, uprooting them for 50 metres along the track and trapping them under the car which rolled twice. It landed upside down in the ditch that separated the track from the spectators. Trapped underneath, Ascari struggled to extricate himself but he was horribly injured. One leg was almost severed, the other broken, as was one arm. There was an agonising wait for help as mechanics who rushed to the scene tried to stop the profuse bleeding from his leg. En route to hospital in Paris, he died.

In Italy, *Il Popolo d'Italia*, the paper founded by Mussolini in 1914, heaped praise on Ascari for giving so much of himself to his country, and likened him to one 'who had died on the battlefield like a soldier who is hit by an unknown sniper in the midst of battle'. As the train carrying his remains crossed the Italian frontier at Bardonecchia, a wreath from Mussolini was placed on his coffin with the inscription 'To the intrepid one'. As it passed through Turin en route to Milan a delegation of dignitaries, including Fiat boss Giovanni Agnelli, stood on the platform in silent tribute. When it reached Milan's central station, a motorised procession escorted the coffin to the Alfa Romeo factory at Portello. According to *Il Popolo d'Italia*, the procession took over twenty-five minutes to pass with the wreaths alone occupying two trucks and nine cars.

It was a foretaste of how much European motor sport was about to become engulfed by the rising tide of nationalism. While it was still a comparatively niche interest as a spectator sport, new circuits like Monza near Milan and Montlhéry brought paying spectators closer to the action, and, by the end of the decade, radio and the telegraphing of photographs and newsreels all helped spread the word. No other sport promised such jeopardy. Inevitably, drivers killed on the track would continue to be likened by Mussolini's propagandists to fallen soldiers.

Despite the traumatic loss of Ascari, Alfa Romeo easily won the constructors' championship, a spectacular achievement for a relatively underfunded newcomer. On the team's return to Milan from Monza after clinching the prize, Mussolini ordered the procession to be showered with flowers by the air force and ever after he used Alfas as his official cars. To commemorate the achievement, a laurel wreath was added to the Alfa badge. All this ought to have been a great compliment to Nicola Romeo, under whose command Alfa had in less than a decade gone from complete obscurity to world fame. Unfortunately, his creditors didn't see it that way.

The cover story was that, out of respect to Ascari's memory, Alfa was stepping back from Grand Prix motor sport. The truth was far more prosaic: despite all the glory on the track, the business was not thriving. Racing was expensive and did not automatically translate into sales. Although it neared a dizzy 1,000 units in 1925, Alfa's output was tiny compared to the upwards of 40,000 vehicles now being mass-produced by Fiat on automated lines at the Lingotto plant.

The Banca Nazionale di Credito (BNC) charged with keeping afloat Italy's increasing number of failing companies, was growing increasingly impatient with Alfa's mercurial boss, and fought a tug of war with Romeo over downsizing his sprawling operation. By the end of 1924, the sale of a locomotive works at Saronno and a pair of rolling stock plants in Rome and Naples put Alfa's balance sheet temporarily in the black, but by now the bankers had concluded that Romeo was wholly unsuited to running a tight ship and had to go. They unseated the titular company president Ugo Ojetti, and gave the post to Romeo so that they could bring in their new managing director, Pasquale Gallo. Like Romeo, he was a southerner but there the similarities ended. A hard-headed mechanical engineering graduate, he already had form dealing with distressed automotive marques, having rescued Itala, of Peking–Paris fame, a few years before. His clear-cut mission was to either save the company or close it down. But in late 1926, the BNC's functions were taken over by yet another entity with the no-frills title of Istituto di Liquidazione Industriale (the Liquidation Institute) which brought Alfa a step closer to Fascist government oversight – and also found the means to dispose of Nicola Romeo. In exchange for the forgiveness of his debts, he was persuaded to sever all connections with the company. Although Mussolini rewarded him with a seat in the senate, and for his charitable work he was made a Knight of the Great Cross of the

Crown, Romeo could not see the move as anything other than an unwarranted punishment. Tormented by the humiliation for himself and his family, he insisted that anything to do with Alfa Romeo should be wiped from their lives and the company never mentioned in his presence ever again.

The new regime at Alfa put a stop to all competition. Desperate to cut back on expenditure, they sold off all the remaining racing P2s. For now, Jano was directed to focus only on road cars.

15

The Scuderia Assembles

The idea of a private racing club was not a new one. Several others launched by wealthy amateurs had come and gone. What Ferrari envisaged was something more businesslike – a club that both raced but also tuned and sold cars, independent from the mood swings of a manufacturer. Despite his contribution to Alfa Romeo, as a driver and a headhunter, Ferrari was never going to be a team player – unless he was running the team. The volatility of Alfa's internal politics was a needless distraction for him as he honed a vision of his career independent of corporate influence.

To finance his new venture, Ferrari knew where to go. In the febrile economic climate of post-First World War Italy, there was one source that seemed to have remained remarkably stable despite the nation's upheavals – old money. The first generation of the Italian motor industry's customers were wealthy, almost all of them from established families whose affluence went back generations, if not centuries. Their offspring showed just as much enthusiasm for spending lavishly on cars – and racing them. Given the further economic upheavals ahead, securing such support was an astute move. It also no doubt helped that one of those first regular drivers was Luigi Scarfiotti, a Fascist member of parliament.

Officially launched on 1 September 1929, Scuderia Ferrari secured backing from two wealthy customers who had bought Alfa Romeos from Ferrari for racing. Alfredo Caniato was a textile manufacturer from Ferrara and Mario Tadini was from a wealthy Bergamo family.

On 1 December 1929, at the office of Modenese lawyer Enzo Levi, the joint-stock company Società Anonima Scuderia Ferrari was signed into existence. Tadini and Caniato each put in 130,000 lire, which Ferrari topped up with 50,000 and a further 5,000 from local vet and drinks distributor Ferruccio Testi. Ferrari then enrolled Milan's tyre makers Pirelli, while Alfa Romeo agreed to a token 10,000 lire investment. Armed with this backing, Ferrari then approached Bosch and Shell, suppliers of spark plugs and fuel respectively, pioneering the type of sponsorship arrangements that would become the bedrock of motor sport financing in the future. He also recruited Bolognese carburettor manufacturer Edoardo Weber, and persuaded Shell to co-operate with him on improving engine combustion, an association which would make Weber the pre-eminent supplier of carburettors for all racing makes.

It was with the formation of the Scuderia that Ferrari adopted the legendary 'prancing horse' emblem. Back in 1923, after winning a race at Ravenna, he was approached by Enrico Baracca, whose son Francesco was Italy's most feted First World War fighter ace, having downed thirty-four enemy aircraft before being shot down over Montello in June 1918. It was the dead hero's mother, Countess Paulina, who told Ferrari he should adopt her son's 'cavallino' emblem, the black prancing horse which had graced the fuselage of Baracca's Spad biplane. Ferrari added the initials SF and la cavallino rampante has graced the bonnets of Ferrari cars ever since.

Ferrari had by now decided that driving was ultimately not where he got his thrills and that finding backers and spotting talent both behind the wheel and under the bonnet was where he excelled. What made him different from the other private racing teams was that he could make hard-headed commercial decisions that playboy enthusiasts overlooked, but he was adept at using their money. Giuseppe Campari, by now one of Italy's best-known and loved racing drivers, had led a double life as both driver and baritone. Like many of his fellow racers he had a passion for opera, though probably his enthusiasm ran ahead of his ability. Booed during a performance in Bergamo, he reportedly stopped mid-aria. 'What am I to do?' he asked his stunned audience. 'When I race they tell me to sing, when I sing they tell me to go race.'

Campari had already made no secret of his frustration with Alfa Romeo's on-off commitment to racing. The deal with Ferrari was concluded over dinner at Campari's home in Milan's San Siro district. An accomplished cook, he produced his speciality *ricciolini al sugo* for Ferrari and his backers, after which he and his wife sang a duet from *La traviata*. Securing the services of a big name served notice that Scuderia Ferrari was a serious operation.

When the Scuderia became too ambitious for his original backers, Ferrari arranged for them to be bought out by another amateur racer, whose family happened to own a provincial bank, the Banca Sella. Count Carlo Felice Trossi, better known as 'Didi', was born into extreme privilege and determined to make the most of it. 'Tall, fair-haired, loose-limbed, he brought a unique tone of carefree aristocracy into the team.' A stint at Leeds University to study textiles (the family's original business) turned him into a lifelong Anglophile and devout pipe smoker. A talented driver, he lacked the single-minded focus to be truly competitive. He was, in Ferrari's eyes, 'a great dilettante all his life, flitting from flower to flower, sipping at his pleasures: speedboats, planes, cars, collections of rare birds, the rebuilding of his castle in Gaglianico, a marina at Paraggi and his wool factory'. Pinin Farina observed that, like many drivers, Trossi was superstitious; in dramatic contrast to his considerable wealth he always wore the same ancient, shapeless shoes he had on when he won his first race. 'When a car was written off in a race they used to say: "It's worse than Didi's shoes."'

Based in a former machine tool workshop on Modena's Via Emilia, Scuderia Ferrari began preparing cars for their first event, the 1930 Mille Miglia. Ferrari's premises in Modena became the headquarters and soon acquired more than sixty employees. To help keep the operation afloat, he also sold Ford cars and tractors. For a man who ten years before had found himself homeless and unemployed in the midst of a bitter Torinese winter, Ferrari had come a long way. His modest origins were no barrier to the wealthy and privileged whom he drew into his web. As Pinin Farina had discovered, in the car industry at least, humble origins or lack of qualifications were no barrier to success where talent, whether for business, speed, engineering or style, was concerned.

This leap into the unknown did not mean the end of his relationship with Alfa. If anything it deepened it, for Vittorio Jano was about to produce a series of career-defining cars, ones that were particularly suited for a new event, one that would bring motor racing quite literally to the door of thousands of Italians.

Back to Brescia

Back in 1922 the automotively inclined city of Brescia had suffered a serious humiliation. The previous year it had proudly hosted Italy's very first Grand Prix, but it was also to be Brescia's last, for the event was snatched away to a brand-new, purpose-built circuit at Monza. Brescia, with some justification, still considered itself the spiritual birthplace of Italian motor racing. Not only had the Coppa Florio become a semi-annual fixture, in 1909 local enthusiasts had added an air show, the first in Italy. With the Wright brothers given top billing, the event attracted such diverse luminaries as Giacomo Puccini, Gabriele D'Annunzio and the then little-known Franz Kafka.

But after the 1921 Italian Grand Prix at Brescia, the Automobile Club di Milano, which organised the event, found themselves out of pocket. After a post-race audit, they discovered that the high cost of staging the event and policing the circuit of closed public roads overwhelmed the paltry revenue to be extracted from spectators, who didn't need to pay to stand beside what was a public road. Their solution, they concluded, was a permanent gated circuit like Brooklands in England or Indianapolis in the USA. And the site they settled on was 80km away from Brescia, in the royal park at Monza, just to the north of the club's home city of Milan. The cornerstone was laid in February 1922 by Italy's pioneer racing stars Vincenzo Lancia and Felice Nazzaro and, at a breakneck pace, a workforce of 3,500 armed with thirty trucks and three miles of light railway completed the track in time for that September's Grand Prix. Engineered by Piero Puricelli, the visionary behind the nation's *autostrade*, the design was outrageously ambitious, with banked corners like Brooklands and Indianapolis and subways and overpasses to give paying spectators access to the infield. Facilities were lavish: it boasted four restaurants. The venue was a success from the outset. A hundred thousand paid to attend the first event. After that, with only one exception, Monza was the home of the Italian Grand Prix.

For one young Bresciani nobleman, the loss of the Grand Prix was a slap in the face. Having tried his hand at racing and even developing his own machine, Count Aymo Maggi now devoted himself to restoring his beloved city's wounded pride. Since 1923, twenty-four-hour endurance races had been running on closed roads just outside the French city of Le Mans. Brescia, he thought, could do something similar, but with one spectacular difference. Rather than closing a triangle of roads near to the city like Le Mans, Maggi envisaged something more along the lines of the vastly popular Giro d'Italia cycle race, Italy's answer to the Tour de France, a one-lap race passing through as much of the country as was practically possible.

Appropriately, his first move was to book a table for dinner and invite three friends to join him. Franco Mazzotti, 'Kino' to his friends, born in 1904, was even younger than Maggi, but just as wealthy. He had grown up on his family's estate, tearing around the grounds on motorbikes and staging slaloms between the marble columns of his family's art nouveau palazzo at Chiari in an Austin Seven. He launched Italy's first amateur motor-racing team, the amusingly named Scuderia per Dilettanti. Renzo Castagneto, having helped organise the Giro d'Italia, knew something about staging road races. The fourth member of the group (Maggi soon started to refer to them as the four musketeers) was Giovanni Canestrini, of *La Gazzetta dello Sport*.

After dinner they repaired to Canestrini's apartment, where they argued into the night. What they agreed was that despite Monza, Italian appetite for motor racing was faltering. Monza and other dedicated circuits had taken the sport out of the public eye. Fiat had retired for good, Alfa was taking time out and Bugatti was now an expatriate, his cars painted French blue.

The four companions concluded that this was Brescia's opportunity; the crucible of Italian motor sport should lead the revival by taking it back to the people, as many of them as possible, outside their very doors. Legend has it that when Castagneto suggested 1,500km was a good distance, Mazzotti, a seasoned pilot used to working in miles, exclaimed, '*Sono mille miglia!*'

As well as having a near-homonymic ring to it, Mille Miglia had other handy resonances. Roman soldiers had measured their vast marching distances in miles and, as it happened, anything that invoked the nation's glorious imperial Roman past was very much in favour with Italy's current regime.

By the end of the night they had agreed on a figure-of-eight circuit, starting and finishing in Brescia. The route would go via Piacenza, inland to Parma, then Modena and on to Bologna. From there it would cross the Apennines to Florence, down through Umbria to Rome. The return route would go east across the Abruzzi mountains to Ancona on the Adriatic then north up the flat coastal strip to Pesaro and Rimini, back to Bologna and north again via Vincenza and Verona to Brescia. The total was 1,004 miles. Cars would race against the clock starting at timed intervals, the slowest first to limit the time the roads had to remain closed. Faster drivers would have the added challenge of getting past the back markers on what was a circuit of narrow two-lane roads, most of them untarmacked. And with an entrance fee of just one lira, it welcomed all comers.

Days later, Canestrini, via the pink-hued *Gazzetta*, broke the news to the world, billing it as 'the greatest manifestation ever of Italian motor sport'. But the notion of turning half the country into a race track was widely ridiculed. How could it be policed? Mounting such a venture would require the deployment of a vast army just to control the spectators alone. And it might well have never got beyond its genesis as a diverting dinner conversation were it not for the prevailing political conditions of the time. Although the Italian Automobile Club's officials were equally doubtful, its president Silvio Crespi made an inspired suggestion that they write to Augusto Turati, secretary general of the Fascist Party. As well as number two to Mussolini, he was a passionate advocate for Italian sports. He had founded the sports paper *Lo Sport Fascista* and would also be remembered for devising *volata*, a home-grown alternative to the pervasive 'English game', which, despite energetic government support, got absolutely no traction in a nation of football fanatics. Crucially, Turati was also born and bred in Brescia, so it was decided that Maggi should travel to Rome to deliver the letter himself.

Crespi's intervention was a master stroke. The meeting between Maggi and Turati was a great success. The ambition, the hint of Roman heroics and the revival of Brescia's fortunes all worked for Il Duce's *numero due*. Maggi emerged from the meeting not only with official approval for the race but also the means to marshal the thousand miles of public road. The army and police, Mussolini had agreed, would be put at their disposal.

At 8 p.m. on 26 March 1927, in Brescia's Parco Rebuffone,Turati flagged off the first of seventy-seven entrants. On board an Isotta Fraschini was Maggi, with Isotta engineer Bindo Maserati beside him. The route was not actually closed to traffic, so to keep their path clear, 25,000 soldiers had been stationed along the course, twenty-five for every mile, to shoo away spectators and livestock. *The Autocar*'s continental correspondent, W. F. Bradley, who rode as a passenger, vividly recorded the experience. 'Running over dusty roads often with a stream of water on each side, the competitors made their way through village after village, with the natives ensconced in doorways, at windows, on ledges, in the trees or occasionally in the more important centres, behind a rope.' Fifty-one of the entrants made it back to Brescia. Giuseppe Morandi was the fastest, finishing in just under twenty-one hours and five minutes. *Corriere della Sera* hailed the achievement: 'It took just under twenty-four hours, not even a day and a night, to complete almost 1,700km at an average speed of more than 77km an hour. The automobile has passed over the roads of half of Italy like a ruler of time and space. The success of this mechanical creation is astounding.'

After twenty-two and a half hours, with eleven stops for fuel and three for tyres, Maggi and Maserati came home sixth. Exhausted but triumphant, Maggi, job done, was looking forward to a long break. But then came an order from Rome. So focused had he been just getting the event off the ground that it simply hadn't occurred to even think of a follow-up. But Mussolini was enthralled. This was just the sort of showcase to display the new vigour of Italy under his rule. As far as Il Duce was concerned the Mille Miglia was now an annual fixture.

17

Extraleggera

Alfa Romeo's retirement from Grand Prix racing could have signalled the end of Vittorio Jano's career in competition. But since Giuseppe Merosi had followed Nicola Romeo out of the company, from 1926, Jano – at thirty-five – was now in overall charge of engineering all future Alfa cars.

Before the axe fell on the racing programme, Jano had been developing a small six-cylinder engine in anticipation of the new Grand Prix rules that stipulated engines no larger than 1.5 litres. The convention was that small capacity road cars had four cylinders; Jano ignored that. He pressed on and the end result was the 6C, essentially a domesticated version of his aborted six-cylinder GP engine.

At the time, production sports cars which dominated races like Le Mans were big beasts such as Britain's Bentleys and German Mercedes SSKs with hefty six- and eight-litre engines that owed their inspiration to pre-Great War racers. But the Mille Miglia, with narrow, twisty roads and literally thousands of corners, demanded something nimbler and more manageable.

The attention the inaugural race had attracted was enough to convince Jano that it would be a great showcase for his new model. For the 1928 event he entrusted Campari with a twin-camshaft, supercharged version of the 6C as it was now known, which won comfortably.

A feature of Campari's Mille Miglia-winning Alfa was a revolutionary new type of bodywork, first seen on his 1928 winner. It was extremely light, more like the fuselage of an aircraft, and that was no coincidence because its creator, Ugo Zagato, had honed his trade building aeroplanes in the Great War.

Born in June 1890, Zagato was the youngest of six boys in a family of impoverished farmers from the Veneto. His parents hoped he would become a priest, but Ugo had other plans. At fifteen he left home to look for work and got a metalworking job in a foundry in Cologne. Four years later he came back to Italy to join Milanese coachbuilder Cesare Balli, who was just branching out into automobile bodywork. Balli soon detected Zagato's promise, taught the boy technical drawing and even made him his workshop manager. In the evenings Zagato attended night school at Milan's Royal Santa Marta Technical Institute where he studied industrial design. Conscripted for the war effort in 1915, he was sent to Turin to a factory building the first Savoia-Pomilio C2 biplanes, where he soon became head of wing and tail component production. But a special project would launch him into a world even further removed from his humble peasant origins.

Gabriele D'Annunzio, poet, fanatical *automobilista* and now war hero was a vociferous advocate for an Italian air force. In 1918, he got the go-ahead to lead what would be one of Italy's most celebrated aerial missions of the war, a 1,200km round trip to Vienna. But the payload was not bombs, it was leaflets, 50,000 of them, printed on three-coloured cards, green, white and red, the colours of the Italian flag, exhorting the Austrians to surrender.

To go the distance and make it back was an immense challenge for any aircraft of the time. Zagato's team modified the Ansaldo SVA biplanes, adding 300-litre fuel tanks and making them as light as possible so as to clear the alpine peaks. On 9 August 1918 seven aircraft made the round trip in ten hours. D'Annunzio was feted by the London *Times* and awarded a Croix de Guerre by the French.

For Zagato, it was another achievement but far more important was an introduction to one of D'Annunzio's pilots, Aldo Finzi. As soon as the war was over, Zagato was raring to get back to Milan and start building car bodies. When Finzi heard about this he offered to invest in the business. An early supporter of Mussolini, Finzi was one of nine Fascist members of parliament of Jewish heritage, and held the position of under secretary of the interior. He used his influence to help Zagato secure commissions from figures such as General Emilio De Bono, governor of Tripolitania, and for an Alfa Romeo destined for Il Duce himself.

Stubborn, tireless and exacting, Zagato swiftly developed a burgeoning trade and a payroll of eighty and soon caught the attention of Vittorio Jano. The Alfa engineer was among the first to focus on weight. His 1925 6C 1500 was one of the smallest six-cylinder cars designed at the time and every kilo counted if it was to be truly competitive. Jano asked Zagato to use his aircraft experience to develop an *'extraleggera'* (extra-light) body for Alfa's assault on the 1928 Mille Miglia. In a field led by cars with much bigger engines than Jano's, power to weight ratio could mean the difference between victory and ignominy.

At the time, *carrozzeria* convention dictated wooden frames with either metal or wooden panels. Zagato applied his aircraft fuselage experience to build a body entirely out of beaten aluminium, held together by a web of metal tubes. The result was a slim, neat two-seater roadster body, known ever after as the Zagato Spider. (The term 'spider' was originally used for a lightweight sporty carriage, with wheel spokes so thin they were likened to spiders' legs.)

The Zagato-bodied Alfa set new standards of both performance and style. Alfa Romeo test driver Gianbattista Guidotti heaped praise on the Zagato-bodied cars. 'Even on gravel roads the car seemed glued to the surface. Driving it gave a new sensation of extreme safety. Seeing it was like being in the presence of a work of art.'

For 1929, Jano increased the engine size and added a supercharger. The car became known as the 1750 Gran Turismo, the first time that name was used, creating a whole new category of car. In the Mille Miglia Campari triumphed again, leading a field of which a quarter were Alfas. The next year, the team took the first four places, but what stole the show would be a historic duel between two of Alfa's drivers, Tazio Nuvolari and Achille Varzi, both on the threshold of international fame.

18

The Rivals

With its entry list swollen to an astonishing 223 starters, the send-off for the 1930 Mille Miglia from Brescia's Viale Rebuffone began in the middle of the night. The slowest cars leaving first, it was dawn by the time Achille Varzi took off, a minute ahead of his Alfa teammate, Tazio Nuvolari, both in identical machines, each fitted with a distinctive trio of headlights. Visibility was poor, and Nuvolari's mechanic Guidotti was terrified by conditions on the unmetalled Raticosa and Futa mountain passes, which were also shrouded in cloud. Nuvolari's only refreshment throughout the race was a flask of sweet tea with a tube to drink through as he drove and pieces of orange and barley sugar handed to him by Guidotti.

At Florence, Nuvolari was ahead but, by Rome, Varzi had retaken the lead. Nuvolari delighted the crowd by passing through the checkpoints and getting his time card stamped without actually coming to a halt, but on the faster sections of the return stretch north, Varzi opened up a two-minute lead. From Venice, the next leg took them back onto loose-surfaced rural roads on which Nuvolari excelled and by the time they reached Lake Garda, he had narrowed the gap between them to half a minute and was chipping away at Varzi's lead until it was no more than a few seconds. Somewhere between Verona and Peschiera, as daylight faded, Nuvolari caught sight of Varzi's tail lights. After the Peschiera checkpoint, leaving the illumination of the town's streetlights, they were shrouded in darkness.

Because of the staggered start, Nuvolari could have just hung on to Varzi's tail to be sure of a win, but to Guidotti's dismay, Nuvolari doused his three headlights and closed right in, navigating by Varzi's own beams. Nuvolari's aim was to use his apparent disappearance to encourage Varzi to relax and ease off. Then, with the finish in Brescia only 3km away, Nuvolari struck. Varzi was completely surprised when Nuvolari switched his lights back on and blasted past him. At the finish, Varzi had to watch, humiliated, as Nuvolari was plucked from his car and carried aloft to the winners' podium. His average speed over the thousand-mile course was 62.51 mph, which he completed in sixteen hours.

Nuvolari and Varzi were opposites in every way. Where Varzi was unemotional and methodical, never appearing to be going as fast as he usually was, Nuvolari always drove as if his pants were on fire. Pinin Farina observed that 'Varzi operated the wheel like it was a pair of compasses, Tazio like a roulette wheel'. Beside Varzi, the well-bred, dapper dresser Nuvolari, short and swarthy with a labourer's tan, came over as the sort of daredevil who would break as many hearts as cars, yet he had married his teenage sweetheart Carolina Perrina and remained a solid family man devoted to his wife and sons. Meanwhile, Varzi's scandalous love life would devastate an otherwise stellar career.

Nuvolari was born in November 1892 in Castel d'Ario, a village near Mantua, the last of four children and so feeble he was at first not expected to live. His father and uncle were farmers who had done well enough to find time to enjoy the late nineteenth-century fad for cycle racing. Tazio got his first bicycle at eight, but by then he had also mastered horses, riding with neither saddle nor bridle, which must have helped hone his superhuman capacity for balance as well as daredevilry. Like the young Enzo Ferrari, he was taken to Brescia to see his first race, a Coppa Florio, starring the inspiring Vincenzo Lancia and Felice Nazzaro.

Yet he came to motor sport relatively late, at twenty-eight. From the beginning, he stood out. Diminutive at just 1.65 metres (5 foot 5 inches) and skinny, he looked more like a jockey, unlikely to have the physical stamina to control the brutish racing cars of the early twenties. *The Autocar*'s W. F. Bradley, who witnessed Nuvolari at work, wrote that it reminded him of 'a jockey whipping a tired horse'. To compensate, he developed a driving style all his own, one that looked so ragged and dangerous that most expected his racing career to be a short one. He justified it in his own inimitable way by asking, 'Do you expect to die in bed? Then how do you have the courage to get into it every night?'

Nuvolari's cornering technique appeared to be completely reckless. As he made his approach he would throw the car into a full skid then, arms and elbows furiously gesticulating, fight to keep it from spinning. But there was more to it. Only by chance, when riding with him during practice for a race in 1931, did his team boss Enzo Ferrari finally learn the secret. Unnerved that Nuvolari was approaching a corner too fast, Ferrari ducked down beneath the dash. 'I noticed he never took his foot off the accelerator, but kept it flat on the floorboards.' His strategy, Ferrari realised, was not to use the brakes at all but to point the nose of the car at the inside edge of the corner, keep the power on, controlling the skid so that by the time he reached the apex of the corner the car was already facing in exactly the right direction for him to make his exit. For spectators it was a tremendous sight. Ferrari concluded that, 'Nobody quite matched the flat-out attack of Tazio Nuvolari, for there was probably no one who combined so high a degree of driving sensitivity with an almost superhuman courage.'

The death of Antonio Ascari had left a big hole in the Alfa driver line-up. Ferrari suggested to Rimini and Nicola Romeo that Nuvolari be given a test at Monza in the run-up to the Italian Grand Prix. Jano, wary of the Mantuan's reputation for driving right on the limit, warned him not to exceed 5,400 revs. But on his first lap Nuvolari flew off the track when the gearbox seized on a downshift, locking the rear wheels and pitching the car and driver into the trees.

In hospital, Nuvolari was told it would be a month before he could be discharged, but ten days later he was back at the track. He had talked the doctors into strapping him into a rigid position with a mixture of bandages and plaster so he could ride a motorcycle. Lifted onto his Bianchi, he proceeded to win the Italian Motorcycle Grand Prix, frozen in the same position for 500km.

But a works drive with Alfa was unforthcoming. After the incident at Monza, when Jano sent his mechanics to collect up the remains of Nuvolari's car from the woodland, they found the rev counter, its face smashed, the needle jammed at 6,200rpm – 800 over the limit he had been instructed to keep to.

Achille Varzi came very much from the opposite side of the tracks. He was born in 1904 in Galliate, near Milan, the privileged son of a successful textile manufacturer. Like Nuvolari, he started on motorbikes, which is where they began their great rivalry. But they also became good friends, and after Nuvolari persuaded his family to sell enough land to buy him a Bugatti the pair joined forces, forming their own private team. But after several ferocious battles on the track, Varzi, sensing he was overshadowed by Nuvolari, left mid-season and went off on his own, buying from Campari one of the P2 Grand Prix Alfas that Jano had been forced to sell off.

Three weeks after his humiliation in the 1930 Mille Miglia, Varzi met Nuvolari again at the Targa Florio. Sicily's event had become a permanent fixture in the racing calendar, attracting international support as drivers and teams came to do battle with the forbidding Madonie mountain track. With fame came folklore, how the German driver Rudi Caracciola had his white Mercedes painted red after locals in the hills pelted it with rocks, how Campari supplied a local musician with a throttle cable to replace a missing string so he could accompany the opera singer-driver in a rendition of 'O sole mio'.

Varzi got his own back by winning the Targa in under seven hours while Nuvolari only managed fourth. But Varzi instead came under pressure from Frenchman Louis Chiron. Since 1925 the cars of Italian émigré Ettore Bugatti had enjoyed an astonishing five consecutive Targa wins and looked set to secure a sixth. Varzi's duel with Chiron's Bugatti would go down to the finishing line.

Rather than the rugged and proven Alfa 6C, Varzi elected to drive his ex-Grand Prix Alfa P2. Given the rutted tracks and sheer gradients of the mountainous Targa route, this seemed like a mad choice. In an attempt to match the P2's lightness, to fill the seat of the mandatory riding mechanic, Chiron recruited the smallest local boy he could find on the island. But when it came to the race, the young lad was overcome with fear, became violently ill and spent most of the race curled up on Chiron's lap.

Varzi, in a similarly desperate quest for lightness, wrenched off his spare wheel mid-race, damaging the fuel tank in the process, leaving his mechanic Canavesi no choice but to top it up while still in motion from a spare onboard can. As they neared the finish, he spilled some on the red-hot exhaust, turning the car into a virtual fireball. Spectators were treated to the sight of Varzi powering past in the flaming car while his mechanic struggled to smother the flames with his seat cushion. By the time he reached the finish line Varzi's clothes were on fire, but he beat Chiron by under two minutes.

19

Scandal in the Desert

T he rivalry between the cool, aloof Varzi and Nuvolari, the clownish extrovert, magnified their fame far beyond their homeland. In 1933, on his way to the Belfast Tourist Trophy race, ordering shirts in an Italian-run shop in London's Piccadilly, Nuvolari was amazed to be mobbed by English fans. They peppered him with questions while the obliging tailor translated and then refused payment for the shirts. The reach of this new-found celebrity had a lot to do with the revolution that was under way in reportage. Photographs no longer needed to be couriered to newspapers. The *Daily Mail*'s 'phototelegraphy' service wired images in an instant, and cinemagoers were now treated to newsreels with sound. Racing drivers were international celebrities. And much of that glory was shared by their winning cars.

Varzi eventually got his own back at Monaco where the stage was set for one of the most epic battles in the history of the sport. By 1933 the principality was well established as the most glamorous – and most unlikely – venue for Grand Prix racing. The circuit provided a bewildering number of challenges to both car and driver. The route was picturesque, running alongside the sea (where some casualties ended their race) with a steep climb to its famous casino. Then a chicane awaited them when they emerged from an unlit tunnel. Drivers managing all the sudden changes could look forward to severely blistered hands from all the gear changes and rapid steering moves from which there was no let-up anywhere on the circuit. Spectators filled the balconies of the houses and hotels that bordered the course as it snaked its way past palaces, casinos and nightclubs. Spectator stands squeezed between the buildings swept down from the Casino Square to the tightest 180-degree bend, the gasometer right-hand hairpin.

For nearly a hundred laps, Varzi's Bugatti and Nuvolari's Alfa, entered by Scuderia Ferrari, swapped the lead. On lap eighty Nuvolari opened up a five-second lead and looked like he might have the race in the bag, but Varzi fought back and narrowed the gap to less than a second, at the same time becoming the first driver ever to bring the lap record beneath two minutes. Two laps from the end, Varzi finally inched ahead. Spectators were treated to the spectacle of Nuvolari, apoplectic, thumping the side of his cockpit with his fist as if to force more power from the car. As they hurtled into the Sainte-Dévote turn Varzi went slightly wide, allowing Nuvolari to squeeze into the gap on the inside. But Varzi blocked him mercilessly, pushing the Alfa wide into the rough edge of the track, his tail hanging out so far it brushed the spectators on the steps of the Hôtel de Paris.

The duel lasted for ninety-nine of the race's 100 laps, Nuvolari leading on sixty-six laps to Varzi's thirty-four. Rarely were they more than a couple of car lengths' apart. On the last lap heading up the hill to the casino, Varzi nosed ahead of Nuvolari who responded by flooring his accelerator. But just then a pipe on the Alfa broke loose, spraying oil onto the exhaust and engulfing the car in smoke as they disappeared into the tunnel. When he emerged Nuvolari appeared to be sitting up on the tail of the car which was now wreathed in smoke, using his feet to steer, but when flames shot out from under the engine cover he jumped down and started to push the burning Alfa towards the finish line with the whole crowd egging him on. He got up to the line but not over it, so he was marked down as a non-finisher. Varzi had triumphed and got his revenge but, despite his victory, there was no question who was the hero of the day.

For all their rivalry, the two Italian aces were still friends and, on occasion, collaborators. Their next meeting was at the Tripoli GP in May, a race made famous not so much by the battle on the track as the shenanigans behind the scenes. The event had a special significance for Mussolini, who regarded it as a showcase for his imperial designs in North Africa and he had funded an upgrade of the 13km circuit at the Mellaha Lake.

With its long straights it was reputed to be the world's fastest circuit, cut through date groves fringed with palms and built on a salt basin with a form of tarmac specially designed to stop it melting in the searing heat. It boasted a giant white tower that could be seen for miles, plus a 10,000-seat grandstand. The dedicated track was state-of-the-art, the first to feature electric starting lights. So sumptuous were the facilities that British driver Richard Seaman dubbed it 'the Ascot of motor circuits'.

As a further publicity ploy, motor sport journalist Giovanni Canestrini proposed a lottery along the lines of the Irish Sweepstakes. The first tickets went on sale in October 1932. The closing date was 16 April 1933. Demand in motor racing-minded Italy was immense and it is thought at least 15 million lire was raised. Canestrini reported that 1.2 million covered the Tripoli club's expenses; while 6 million was prize money for the top three finishers' ticket holders – 3 million for first place, 2 million second and 1 million third. The initial draw was held on 29 April 1933, eight days before the race, supervised by the colony's governor, Marshal Pietro Badoglio, sporting several rows of medals.

The draw focused minds, especially those of certain competitors. Canestrini and Nuvolari met up with Varzi and fellow driver Baconin Borzacchini, ostensibly to finalise travel plans to Tripoli. Varzi, however, was more eager to discuss the lottery, and on the Monday evening, before leaving for Libya, he, Nuvolari and Borzacchini met the three ticket holders in Rome's Hotel Massimo d'Azeglio. Canestrini also attended, and negotiated an agreement between them. The group agreed to form a syndicate whereby they would pool the lottery prize money. The three drivers would split half of the syndicate's winnings, plus all their prize money from the race, while the ticket holders would each draw one third of half the lottery money.

Inevitably as they arrived in Tripoli, word leaked out. Campari, incensed, was all the more determined not to let Nuvolari win, even if it meant taking them both out of contention in the process. Mindful of this outcome, Canestrini, it is believed, got the two to toss for which of them would win, which would have constituted match-fixing.

Governor Badoglio got the honour of switching on the fancy electric starting lights. There was a heart-stopping moment when Varzi's Bugatti misfired as they pulled away. Campari's Maserati retired early, leaving the field clear for Nuvolari in the Alfa and Varzi. Twenty-three laps in Nuvolari had to stop to refuel but managed to catch Varzi up. For the final laps they raced almost side by side, when Varzi inched past to win by 0.2 of a second.

Whether Nuvolari backed off was never confirmed. What is sure is that, money or not, it would have been entirely out of character. Because of their agreement it made no difference financially, Borzacchini being particularly happy with the windfall since he was significantly less well off than the other two.

Italy's Fascist government was determined there would be no repeat of such mischief, but the ensuing official inquiry was quietly shelved. From 1934 the lottery draw was made immediately before the race start.

20

L'Auto del Popolo

F iat had disappeared from the racing circuits, but by the end of the 1920s it had captured over 70 per cent of the domestic car market. The multi-storey Lingotto plant now operated full mass production; every day up to 300 cars emerged onto the top-floor track for their final test. By French standards, however, Fiat was still small, building fewer cars than Renault or Citroën. Heavily dependent on exports, these shrank as countries reeling from the aftermath of the Wall Street Crash increased tariffs to protect local producers. Unemployment in Italy, which had stood at 125,000 in 1925 ballooned to 1.3 million by 1934 and in the same period the national debt had swollen from 93 million lire to 148 billion. Agnelli had always prioritised exports, but these shrank from 28,000 in 1928 to just 7,000 by 1933. Fiat was now much more dependent on its home market, and more at the mercy of the government in Rome.

Initially, Mussolini's administration took a relatively laissez-faire approach to industry. During the 1920s, imported Ford tractors and trucks had made inroads into the Italian market. Emboldened by this, Henry Ford sought to open an assembly plant in Trieste, to which Mussolini was receptive. Without compromising his treasured independence from Rome's influence, Agnelli used all his cunning to kill the venture. Knowing which of Mussolini's buttons to press, he argued that Ford's presence, as well as weakening the domestic industry, could even threaten national defence in a time of war. Evidently this worked; Il Duce vetoed Ford's proposal for a factory in Livorno. Agnelli wrote congratulating him on his 'sentiment of justice and political wisdom that always had driven his behaviour in regard to the national industry'. Not yet deterred, Ford then proposed a joint venture with the struggling Milanese luxury car and aero-engine firm Isotta Fraschini, which also appeared to appeal to Mussolini. Again, using his influence in Rome, Agnelli also managed to see this off, leaving exasperated Ford executive Percival Perry to complain that 'these Italians play politics too much with business'.

Although Mussolini championed Italy's motor industry, this did not translate into devoted support for the Fascist administration. Throughout the car factories, there was no stampede to join the party – it was more of a shuffle – nor were there reprisals for non-membership. Agnelli and Pinin Farina and Enzo Ferrari – who signed up in the early 1930s – saw it as expedient, and according to Dante Giacosa, a new recruit to Fiat's design department, when his boss Tranquillo Zerbi 'suggested tactfully that it would be best for Fiat if its executives joined the party I agreed, as did others'.

Ahead of Hitler who had yet to come to power, Mussolini craved a cheap 'people's car' that would motorise the Italian masses. But for most Italians this was a remote dream. By the end of the 1920s, there was one car for every 250 Italians, compared with one in forty for France, one in thirty-seven for Great Britain and in the USA a dizzying one in ten.

Agnelli's response was to commission the utilitarian one-litre model, a conventional no-frills four-seat family car almost indistinguishable from the other boxy sedans being made elsewhere in Europe, but it came with an electrically welded all-metal body, sound-deadening, hydraulic brakes and wind-down windows.

Launched in 1932, for 10,800 lire, roughly the price of a city apartment, it was still beyond the means of all but the well-heeled middle classes, but it would become a staple on Italy's home market for the rest of the decade. In a break with Fiat tradition, the model which had started out with the usual three number identification of 508 was rechristened Balilla, a name rich in contemporary resonance.

In 1925, Mussolini had founded Italy's precursor of the Hitler Youth. It was called Balilla after the nickname of Giovanni Battista

Perasso, a spirited Genovese youth who, legend had it, valiantly started a revolt against the Habsburg forces which occupied the city in 1746. Although in Fiat's marketing there was no overt association with the Fascist youth movement, it was just the sort of arm's-length association with the Fascist regime that Agnelli preferred.

But there was nothing fascistic or even patriotic about the name of Fiat's next and far more revolutionary model. And its designer's impact on Fiat's products would resonate for the rest of the century.

Dante Giacosa, a Turin Polytechnic engineering graduate joined Fiat straight after his military conscription in 1928 and started work at Fiat's vast Lingotto complex. Born in Rome in 1905, the son of a policeman, Giacosa was never going to be a conventional engineer. He attributed his gifts to something quite prosaic – a knowledge of Latin and ancient Greek that he said gave him 'a sense of measure and balance without which I could not have done my job'. He also studied under Filippo Borzio, who combined mechanical engineering with the pursuit of his own brand of philosophy, the doctrine of Demiurge, which aspired to moderate human society by directing its aspirations. Tall and slightly built, ascetic and naturally reserved but with a wry sense of humour, Giacosa claimed he never gave subordinates orders, preferring to enrol them in collaboration through discussion and mutual understanding. Despite being something of a visionary, he tempered a fascination for engineering novelty with a pragmatism that kept him from straying too far from the conservative expectations of his superiors.

In a drawing office on the fifth floor of the Lingotto *palazzina*, his first job was as a draughtsman working on military tractors, with a salary of 950 lire a month. But as a junior, much of his work was filing and writing out instructions since there were as yet no typewriters in the department. In 1930 he moved on to the study of combustion chambers for diesel engines and then in 1932, to aero-engines. His overall boss was Fiat technical chief Tranquillo Zerbi, who had been a key member of the team behind the all-conquering Fiat GP cars before producing his masterpiece, a 3000hp record-breaking sea-plane engine.

Pleased to be in the midst of specialist designers who were not put out by the fact that he had a degree, he was fascinated by the work. 'The problems connected with lightness, functioning conditions at high altitudes and safety, required a familiarity with highly specialised materials and manufacturing technologies completely removed from the mass-produced automobile.' He was also not above conducting his own industrial espionage. He discovered how rivals Hispano-Suiza were mounting cylinder barrels on their engines by posing as an air force officer and getting a guided tour of their works in Paris.

People interested him almost as much as machines. He had his first sight of Mussolini when he visited Lingotto in October 1933. Giacosa recalled him looking awkward. 'He wore a round grey hat with the brim turned up in front, appearing somewhat at odds with the heroic expression on his face and imperious bearing . . . He was absurd and pathetic at the same time and received coldly restrained applause.'

Giacosa was an astute observer of character. He and his immediate boss, Antonio Fessia, a fellow Turin Polytechnic graduate who had joined Fiat in 1925, were total opposites. Fessia did not try to make himself popular. A restless soul, he made no secret of his regret at not having pursued a classical education and dropped Latin phrases into conversation to show off his knowledge of the language. Combative, impatient, arrogant, awkward with his superiors, Fessia could waste valuable time, Giacosa observed, 'especially when he began to expatiate on his prowess as a womaniser'. Despite this he and Giacosa developed a good rapport. 'He was a mathematician, I a designer and we got on swimmingly. He was impulsive and open-minded, calm and reflective. Together we made an efficient pair.'

Their work on aero-engines came to an abrupt halt in 1933 when Agnelli handed Fessia and Giacosa, still only twenty-eight, the task of developing a truly small car, one that would sell for no more than 5,000 lire, half the price of the Balilla. Giacosa could see his boss was wary of the assignment and he knew why. Another designer, Oreste Lardone, had developed a small car with an air-cooled engine and front-wheel drive. When he gave Agnelli a test drive it caught fire. They had a lucky escape, but Agnelli fired Lardone on the spot.

But Giacosa soon learned what a conservative environment Fiat was. Another important figure in the young designer's life would be Agnelli's production director, Alessandro Genero, who had been with the company since 1906, working his way up from the shop floor. Giacosa observed how Agnelli 'liked and trusted this simple, uncultivated man while he had misgivings about designers and their wayward impulses'.

Navigating between the demands and expectations of his bosses, Giacosa developed an almost Zen-like belief that through careful diplomacy, fair play and common sense would prevail.

'This enabled me to keep my distance from the rivalries which often blazed up between the most prominent personalities and also the discontent which often spread through the draughtsmen. My serenity and enthusiasm helped me to disregard the harsh and sometimes overbearing manner of certain departmental heads and works foremen.'

Nonetheless, the small-car project was a daunting challenge, having to reconcile size, weight, performance and price. With space-saving front-wheel drive off limits after Lardone's misfortune, Giacosa reduced the space taken up by the engine by putting it forward of the front-wheel hubs and bringing the radiator inboard between the engine and the passenger compartment. Mounting it higher than the engine also dispensed with the need for a water pump; gravity would do the job instead. Fuel was also fed into the engine by gravity with a high-mounted tank and the oil was circulated by the movements of the engine itself. The chassis was a simple 'A'-shaped frame, drilled for lightness.

Despite these efficiencies, there was nothing rudimentary or compromised about Giacosa's design. It boasted modern independent front suspension, and twelve-volt electrics (the Volkswagen would only have six) and hydraulic brakes. Where two cylinders and three gears could have saved on space, weight and cost, he refused to compromise on performance. Four cylinders and four gears, helped along by a sloped aerodynamic front end, allowed a heady 53 mph (85 kph). It could also carry 50kg of luggage yet consumed a mere 6 litres of fuel every 100km.

Launched on 15 June 1936, it was pronounced a miracle of miniaturisation by a rapturous press. There was simply no other small car so refined or capable. It was called the 500 but its sloping pointy frontal features soon earned it the nickname '*Topolino*', the Italian name already given to a recent import from America – Mickey Mouse. Priced at just under 10,000 lire, it was more than Agnelli hoped, but it was an instant bestseller. Soon, Lingotto was churning out more than a hundred a day.

For Agnelli, who was about to turn seventy, it was a crowning achievement. Receiving an honorary degree from Turin Polytechnic in 1937, he called the Topolino his 'thesis', a leap forward in the democratisation of motoring a decade ahead of Volkswagen and the Citroën Deux Chevaux.

Such was the success of the Topolino, and the Balilla, that by the mid-1930s Agnelli would be planning Mirafiori, a second, even bigger car plant in Turin.

Putting the Clocks Forward

Ever since he had joined his brother's business as a mere 12-year-old, Pinin Farina, restless and determined to grow and learn, had been searching for that elusive automotive aesthetic that would allow the motor car to shrug off its nineteenth-century coachbuilding traditions. As a young man working in the *carrozzeria* his brother had started, he worried that his lack of education was a hindrance. After the war he began frequenting the Molinari restaurant in Piazza Solferino, a meeting place for journalists and actors. 'It was an ambience well worth studying but I did not have the right instrument which in that case was the gloss of an education.'

In 1920 Pinin Farina had made a pilgrimage to the United States and was suitably dazzled. 'America was driving fast and it impressed me. I thought, *They've put the clocks forward half a century*; something similar will happen in Europe when the time is right.' Manhattan, with its vast skyscrapers, steel bridges and elevated railways, he likened to a machine. But he was underwhelmed by the efforts of the American coachbuilders, likening their creations to 'Easter eggs wrapped up in cellophane paper'. He travelled to Detroit, 'an earthly paradise coloured black as smoke'. On a tour of Ford's colossal River Rouge plant he was completely awed. 'In four or five hours the ore is converted to steel, and then into a car. It is as quick as baking bread.' He also managed to get an audience with Henry Ford himself.

The meeting was a revelation. Ford told Pinin that the

coachbuilders in the USA had got off on the wrong foot, 'So we have to do the vast majority of their work.' America's body makers simply could not meet the numbers Ford and co. demanded. Ford pressed Pinin for an opinion of his Model T, little changed since its inception in 1908, whose embrace of function and utility left no room for emotional input. Behind the bonnet, Ford's sedans were wilfully square boxes with windows. Anxious not to sound critical of the austere style-free machine, and searching for an innocuous observation, the Italian said he noticed the large space between the front and rear seats. Ford was delighted. '"Where else would the farmers put their milk churns?" I was getting a lesson in functional bodywork.' After looking at some of Pinin's drawings Ford offered him a job on the spot. Pinin was flattered but declined, explaining that he preferred to be the boss of a handful of people than an employee in a factory and also, he was engaged to be married. Ford was persistent: 'Well, he said, get married and take your honeymoon wherever you want. If you accept then from now on you are on our books, including the journey there and back.'

Pinin Farina was being headhunted by the most successful automobile manufacturer on the planet. To start a new life in the land of opportunity as so many Italians had done, it was tempting. Could the austere Ford have accommodated Pinin's effervescent creative vision? Almost certainly not; as Pinin himself observed, 'America is the car's nursery, but the questions of shape and of line which make a car beautiful in its utility, found more suitable soil for invention in our part of the world.'

He took back with him some cans of Duco nitrocellulose, paint developed by DuPont at Ford's behest, which cut drying times from a week to just a few hours and could be sprayed rather than brushed. It would dramatically improve the Farinas' productivity. 'I had the circumspect attitude of the ancient explorers who brought unknown seeds from the Indies.' Another great American innovation he brought back was a set of shirts with pre-attached collars, which he said his mother approved of because they saved time in front of the mirror. Poignantly, when he arrived home, the dining-room table in the flat was covered in books and paper. Rosa, his wife, was teaching his parents to read.

For the rest of the decade, Pinin's work for Stabilimenti Farina sought to break new ground, but it was an uphill battle. Castagna, a Milan-based *carrozzeria* that dated back to the mid-nineteenth century, was one of the first to attempt a complete break with tradition. As early as 1913, for a commission from Milanese count Marco Ricotti, they created a dramatic teardrop-shaped body on one of Giuseppe Merosi's Alfas. This astonishing design, its silver fuselage inspired by airships of the day, was a total break with convention, decades ahead of its time. It boasted curved glass four decades before it appeared on production cars and oval porthole-shaped windows that even aeroplanes had yet to adopt. The streamlined shape was reported to have added 10 mph to the top speed, but it was a one-off; practicalities prevailed, particularly the challenges of managing the noise, heat and fumes of the engine which also occupied the single form. After his wife refused to travel in it because of the noise and fumes, Ricotti had the roof removed.

In the 1920s architects like Le Corbusier were pioneering a radical 'machine' aesthetic in housing design, eschewing adornment and celebrating functionalism. Impressed, Pinin Farina campaigned against decorative additions which 'only served to cover up the weakness of the design', and strove to break new ground, but progress was slow.

Bonnets began to get longer and taller; passengers sat lower down behind shallower windscreens and under lower roofs. As soon as cars began to move with any speed, they sprouted mudguards to deflect flying water and mud. Initially no more than a flat strip of metal, by the 1920s they were beginning to be given more sculpted shapes as designers, albeit tentatively, used them to explore new form. Pinin was straining at the leash, impatient for bigger changes. He objected to the sudden changes of angle between the radiator, bonnet and windscreen. His goal was to create 'a single unit right from the radiator, which I saw in my imagination as a mask melted onto the bonnet'. His vision would give a 'fluidity to bonnets, mudguards and running boards, matched by a rounding off of the sharp corners of the roof'. But any move in this direction met resistance. When he proposed a windscreen raked at an angle to reduce wind resistance as well as add to his evolving style, Milanese car dealer

Ernesto Minetti protested, 'Your proposal goes against all reason; ever since the world began windows have been straight.'

Another impediment to more streamlined shapes was limits imposed by a new form of body construction that came into vogue in the 1920s, known as the Weymann method. As cars travelled faster, traditional coachwork struggled to keep up. Wooden frames clothed in metal were heavy and at even low speeds over uneven surfaces were prone to developing squeaks as the frame's wooden mortise joints chafed and worked loose. In enclosed saloons and limousines, interior noise was another problem; speed turned passenger compartments into echo chambers. Charles Torres Weymann, French-Haitian former Great War aviator and inventor, found a solution to both problems.

He silenced the squeaks by fractionally separating the wooden spars with spring steel brackets, which eliminated the chafing of wooden joints. Instead of sheet metal for the body's outer shell, he stretched imitation leather fabric over the frame and padded it with wadding or horsehair which both insulated the interior from the elements and dampened the sound. Weymann's method was so successful that for a time it became the industry standard, licensed to coachbuilders throughout Europe and America. One of the first licensees in Italy was Carrozzeria Touring of Milan.

Carlo Felice Bianchi 'Cici' Anderloni could not have been more different from Pinin Farina. A law graduate, he joined the niche luxury car maker Isotta Fraschini in 1904, eventually rising to test driver. He found it a 'stern and high-principled environment'. Despite his lack of technical training, the experience of troubleshooting and liaising with suppliers as well as buyers was an invaluable grounding in the intricacies of producing viable, reliable products for demanding customers.

But during the 1920s Isotta began to struggle and acquired new owners. In the winter of 1925, aged forty-three, Anderloni teamed up with fellow lawyer-turned-banker Gaetano Ponzoni and took over Falco, a failing Milanese *carrozzeria* run by Vittorio Ascari, brother of Antonio. Like the Ceirano brothers with their creatively named Welleyes, Anderloni thought the English-sounding name Touring would add credibility for the very wealthy clientele he aimed to secure. Going up against established *carrozzerie*, in a difficult economic climate, was risky. Car makers and dealers had established connections with body suppliers. The best he could do to start out was to leverage his relationship with Isotta and build some bodies on spec to enter into shows and *concours d'élégance*. Boldly he went ahead. In its first year, Touring created eight bodies for top-of-the-line Isottas which all found customers, helped doubtless by Anderloni's use of money-no-object exotic materials, including damask, patterned velvet and crocodile and lizard skin. He also put his legal skills to good use, acquiring a licence for the Weymann system for the whole of Lombardy, with a clause in the contract that allowed him to license it to others in the area. Untroubled as yet by the limitations posed by the construction method, he was ahead of the pack when it came to offering his customers a quieter, more insulated ride.

But the design that really put Touring on the map was a striking open two-seater built on a straight-eight-cylinder Isotta chassis. To put a two-seater body on such a lengthy chassis was an act of shameless hedonism.

Ordered by wealthy Genovese Giuseppe Matteucci, who al-ready owned two Touring-bodied Isottas, it was intended as an eighteenth-birthday present for his daughter, Alma, and entered for the *concours d'élégances* at Genoa Nervi and Como Villa d'Este. Inspired by the tight-fitting bodywork of lean racing cars, which as a rule had each side of the cockpit cut low to leave room for the driv-er's elbows, the Flying Star's belt line made a swooping downward curve to form just such a cutaway. This striking shape was mirrored by three distinctive lateral motifs that ran along each side of the bonnet and into the doors. From there the body line ticked sharply upward again following the contour of the seat back and over the wheel arch before dropping right down to the rear bumper. These lines Anderloni likened to those of a shooting star, hence the name. Despite the size of the car, the result was a charming wasp-waisted look which heralded a move away from hard horizontals and verti-cals to more organic sculptural shapes. Finished in a bright cream enamel, it was a clean break from the dark-coloured angular square masses that had been the default shape of Touring's previous efforts.

Touring's precocious two-seater was itself something of a swan-song as the ripples of the Wall Street Crash reached Italy, decimating sales of top-of-the-range Isottas. As Anderloni's son wrote later, 'the Flying Star was for a gentleman like him, a way of marking the passing of a myth with a final gesture, akin to sitting on the terrace of the Villa d'Este and ordering a magnum of champagne with the last of one's fortune'. The Depression could have made Touring, with its reputation for expensive glamour, a casualty. In the event, it would set Anderloni and Touring on a bold and revolutionary new direction.

Gran Turismo

From 1930, a new category in the Mille Miglia called 'Turismo' allowed entry to enclosed saloon and coupé-bodied cars on production chassis. Touring seized the opportunity and built a number of bodies for Alfas to compete in this class, adapting the Weymann method to make the best use of weight saving. In 1932 a Touring-bodied Alfa came fourth, ahead of open sports two-seaters. A fast car with a roof was no longer a contradiction in terms, but as speeds got higher, wind resistance became more of an issue. By this time the Weymann method was falling out of favour. Wear and tear of the fabric outer skin emerged as a problem, but when it came to creating aerodynamic shapes the limitations imposed by having to stretch fabric ruled out shapes with compound curves. In America, Weymann construction had been rendered obsolete by pressed steel – panels stamped out in seconds by vast machines. This new method allowed designers to come up with much more sophisticated shapes with compound curves. But for Italy's *carrozzerie* this was never going to be an option. The tooling costs were prohibitive. The solution to shaping the next generation of cars would be found much closer to home, by tapping into a centuries-old Italian artisanal craft with little more than a hammer and the stump of a tree.

As far back as 1288, Milanese scholar Bonvesin da la Riva noted the number of forges in his city, 'that produce daily every kind of arms, like mail shirts, coats of plates, breastplates and splints, great helmets, basinets, caps, collars, gloves, greaves, cuisses and poleyens, spears, swords made from hardened and polished steel, gleaming like mirrors'. During the Renaissance, Milan became Europe's biggest supplier of armour, with off-the-peg stocks ready to equip an army for battle at short notice.

Milanese armour was revered for its winning combination: it was both hard yet light. The suit that Henry VIII wore at the Field of Cloth of Gold in 1520 was made in Milan. It was for show rather than battle since Henry's meeting with the French king was a peaceful occasion. Hereafter, armour for royalty and nobility became increasingly a statement of wealth, for posing rather than protection, not unlike the supercars of today.

In his *Le vite de' più eccellenti pittori, scultori, e architettori* (*Lives of the Most Excellent Painters, Sculptors, and Architects*), Renaissance biographer Giorgio Vasari included Milan's Filippo Negroli, 'chiseller of arms in iron with leaves and figures'. Negroli's clients included Philip II of Spain, the Holy Roman Emperor Charles V and Philip II of France. His was a family business, employing four of his younger brothers and revered for highly embellished helmets and breastplates with compound curves beaten out of single plates of steel. This combination of technical excellence and artistic flair seems to have survived long after the musket delivered a fatal blow to Milan's armourers.

Touring's first panel beater, Luciano Zappa, said that before he took them on Anderloni set every apprentice the '*balla*' test. He was handed two sheets of metal and a hammer, and shown a tree stump where he was told to make two hemispheres, which had to fit together perfectly along their common equator.

Embracing these time-honoured skills allowed designers to explore much more dramatic and extreme shapes, Pinin Farina sought inspiration in nature. 'Going to the mountains in winter I saw how the wind had sculpted the snow at the side of the road, carving out curved or sharp shapes. The wind even gave shape to the trees. I wanted to copy those lines.'

Touring first used the term 'aerodynamic' in their publicity material in 1931, but this was as yet no more than an aspiration. Pioneering German designers Wunibald Kamm, Paul Jaray and

Edmund Rumpler embraced aerodynamic principles and honed their shapes in wind tunnels. But the results were almost wilfully ugly. For Touring's Anderloni and Pinin Farina, style was all that mattered.

In June 1930 Pinin Farina took the plunge to go it alone. With the help of his wife's aunt, Olympia, and his mentor, Vincenzo Lancia, he bought a premises on Corso Trapani, which had a press shop attached to it. 'I was tired of waiting, of my prolonged youth. In our field, where personal initiative and temperament counted, it was hard to share people's success as well as their mistakes.' His first one-off based on a Lancia Dilambda was shown at the same Villa d'Este *concours* as Touring's Flying Star, but unique bespoke models were not to be his primary focus. Perhaps it was helped by coming from such humble origins, for he detected an appreciation of style that stretched beyond the wealthy.

When Fiat produced the modestly priced Balilla, Pinin Farina saw in it just such an opportunity to reach a new clientele. Although monarchs, heads of state and maharajahs were among his customers, by targeting the less well-off and offering bodies for humbler machines like the Balilla and supplying them to dealers in batches rather than bespoke one-offs, he put his new business on a sound commercial footing that also afforded him the means to explore his more radical ideas.

Pinin Farina's fame spread rapidly. In 1932, he was summoned to meet Mussolini in the garden of Il Duce's Villa Torlonia. Mussolini was dressed for riding: 'his steps as he walked were excitable, irregular.' Pinin was impressed by how much Mussolini knew about cars and engines and talked as if 'speed was all that mattered in the world'. He wanted a car that was both an official car and a sports car. As the meeting came to an end Mussolini suddenly asked if Pinin had joined the party. The designer felt he had to own up.

Pinin Farina was acutely conscious of his lack of education, but it doesn't seem to have got in the way of his learning. He took to heart the principles of Vitruvius, the first-century BCE Roman architect, of *firmitas, utilitas, venustas,* stability, utility and beauty. 'I do not want to talk about the car as art; there are already too many critics who do so, so it is better to keep one's feet on the ground.' He hated pretension. 'I was irritated by all those devices that looked like chromium ex-voto stuck on the car and I had learned from my work that what you take off counts more than what you add on. In fact as we know there are superfluous things everywhere.'

The Alfa Romeo 6C 2300B Pescara, which Pinin Farina presented at the 1936 Milan Motor Show, was his most dramatic design to date and broke a number of rules. Not only the radiator but the headlamps were contained behind curved mesh that followed the smoothed-out contours of the front end. The mudguards were ogival in shape – curves tapering to a point – and were mirrored in the tapering line of the tail. As well as no running boards or bumpers, there was a complete absence of adornment; the shape spoke for itself. The challenge he set himself was 'to avoid all precocity. The important thing has been to get rid of the sharp corners in order to let the wraparound lines dominate.'

The panel beater's craft offered limitless possibilities but large areas of curved metal, especially on coupé and saloon cars with a roof, presented problems of lightness and rigidity. At Touring, having led the way with his closed coupé Mille Miglia Alfas, Anderloni set about developing a new method of construction that allowed for dramatic shapes without adding weight. After several years experimenting with lighter alloy metals, he came up with a skeleton built from small-diameter tubing shaped to mimic the curves and contours of his ever-more streamlined shapes. The contact points between the tubular structure and the outer panelling were anchored by wire clips but insulated with felt or rubber pads, so none of the stresses of flexing of the frame were transmitted to the body. It was labour-intensive to make, requiring numerous welds to create the body frame, but was never intended for mass production.

Having trained as a lawyer, Anderloni had seen to it that all innovations developed in Touring's workshop such as reclining seats, flush door locks and handles and hood closure mechanisms were patented, so royalties could be earned to help the business. He called his new system, which he also patented, *Superleggera*. Needless to say, Ugo Zagato, having come up with something very similar, albeit for minimally clothed open-topped racers, was not pleased. 'Put them on the scales and you will find that the true Superleggera is mine.' But Touring's bodies achieved something truly groundbreaking. Anderloni's primary passion had always been style, now, with his *superleggera* construction, competition car bodies could be both light and stylish.

23

'O sole mio'

In the early 1930s, Alfa Romeo looked for all the world as if it was in an enviable position. Triumphant in Grands Prix, with multiple victories in the Targa Florio, the Mille Miglia and Le Mans, driven by the world's most famous racing driver, Alfas also frequently featured at *concours d'élégances*, clothed in the most exotic *carrozzerie*. The products of Portello appeared to radiate charisma and performance, but the business itself was close to collapse.

In 1933, Alfa managed to produce a paltry 408 cars. A newly appointed managing director, Corrado Orazi, pronounced the business unsalvageable and recommended it be shut down. Responsibility for the firm passed to yet another entity for distressed Italian enterprises, the Istituto per la Ricostruzione Industriale (IRI). In the aftermath of the Wall Street Crash, Alfa was by no means the only Italian business in trouble; the IRI, created by the Fascist government, was a means of propping up ailing businesses and would soon come to control almost half of Italy's share capital.

That September, Giovanni Agnelli made the IRI an offer, to take Portello off their hands and build trucks for Mussolini's rearmament programme. But Il Duce let it be known that was not an option. He was not about to give Agnelli yet more control over Italian industry and in any case he was a genuine enthusiast. On one occasion he had even turned up unannounced at the gates of Portello, driving his own Alfa – one of nine he would ultimately own. He was already on record declaring Alfa Romeo to be 'the maker of the best Italian product'. For such a symbol of national pride to be allowed to wither and die was unthinkable. The IRI got the message; Alfa Romeo was a passion project: somehow it had to be kept alive – but put on a viable business footing. In search of the right talent to undertake this unenviable task, they came up with Ugo Gobbato. Born in Treviso in 1888 into a farming family, as a teenager he worked for electrical generating firms while steadily acquiring qualifications from the local technical school. He then went to Zwickau in Germany, where at the age of twenty-one he got a degree in electrical engineering. After military service and time served in aircraft factories in 1919, he joined Fiat just as its sprawling operations were about to be concentrated under the newly completed Lingotto factory's test-track roof. There he excelled as a master of production engineering and logistics, organising the tooling and developing the processes whereby the plant would produce 300 cars a day. When Mussolini made his first visit to Fiat in 1923 Agnelli gave Gobbato the job of showing him round. Agnelli then sent him abroad to reorganise operations at Fiat's European outposts. Then a much more daunting task beckoned. Fiat won a tender to set up a ball-bearing factory in Moscow, as part of Soviet Russia's drive to industrialisation. Gobbato was put in charge and endured a miserable two-year struggle preparing the plant for production with a workforce who had no previous industrial experience. Two of his six children suffered from scurvy and malnutrition, so he sent the family home; by the time he joined them in the summer of 1933 he was so exhausted that he even considered giving up work altogether.

For the IRI, Gobbato could not have been a better candidate for the task of sorting out Alfa Romeo. Not only was he one of Italy's foremost production organisers, he had another quality vital for rescuing a company obsessed with its own glory. As his son Pier Ugo observed, 'always the head over the heart; never let yourself be carried away by sentiment'. Before he accepted, he insisted on an undertaking from the IRI to supply the investment he would need to turn the company round. They complied and, on 30 November 1933, the incumbent Orazi departed and Gobbato arrived at Portello.

One belt-tightening measure had already been taken. Earlier in the year, combing through Alfa's accounts in search of efficiencies, the IRI's accountants targeted the racing department. All competition activity was ordered to be put on hold and to head off any insubordination they ordered all Vittorio Jano's P3 Monopostos to be put under lock and key. For Enzo Ferrari the timing could not have been worse.

Since the mid-1920s the five Bologna-based Maserati brothers had been using their successful spark plug manufacturing business to bankroll their dream of building and selling racing cars, which they did in tiny numbers but with plenty of success. Among their innovations was the first use of hydraulic as opposed to mechanical brakes on a racing car. By 1933 their eight-cylinder three-litre machine was more than a match for Scuderia Ferrari's obsolete Alfas. They also secured the services of one of Italy's best-loved drivers, Giuseppe Campari. At that year's French Grand Prix at Montlhéry, after he took the flag for them, a victorious Campari wanted to thank the spectators but didn't know any French so the sometime opera singer treated them to a rendition of 'O sole mio' over the public address system. Nuvolari also jumped ship to Maserati and won the Belgian Grand Prix and two more races.

Stung by this humiliation, Ferrari sprang into action demanding that Alfa Romeo management release the six Tipo B *monoposti* to his team and set about luring back his drivers.

Campari had already decided that after nearly twenty years this would be his last season. He would retire after the Italian Grand Prix at Monza. His first race, the 1914 Targa Florio, had been for Alfa Romeo, and Ferrari convinced him it would be fitting for his last to be in one of their cars. It would be a fateful decision.

To attract a bigger crowd, the race organisers had added an extra event called the Monza GP, three short sprints using the venue's smaller but extremely fast banked circuit, the Pista di Velocità, which had been constructed within the Monza road course. In the second sprint, seven cars started, but at the end of the first lap only three were still on the track, Campari's Alfa was just ahead of driver Borzacchini's Maserati when it hit some oil. Campari went into a slide, smashed through the perimeter fence at the top of the banking and rolled down an embankment, killing him instantly. Borzacchini also lost control and left the track. He survived the impact but died later that day in hospital. Two other drivers, whose cars had over-turned in the melee, survived. It was Italian motor racing's blackest day – and it wasn't over yet. In the final heat, Polish driver Stanisław Czaykowski hit the same guard rail as Campari and was flung from his Bugatti, which then landed on top of him and burst into flames. That night Nuvolari, whose victory in the main race had been denied by a late puncture, joined the three widows and sat through the night with them and their husbands' coffins in the hospital chapel.

The tragedy sent shock waves through Italy's motor racing fraternity. But what was about to happen next would change the whole tenor of Grand Prix for the rest of the decade, as two Fascist nations went to war on the track.

24

Master Racers

Although Adolf Hitler, newly installed as Germany's Chancellor in January 1933, never learned to drive, he took a keen interest in the nation's motor industry. He saw it as the engine to power the nation out of its post-First World War malaise, to supercharge rearmament and be a showcase for the Third Reich's technological prowess.

In the period after the Great War, Germany's car output, although higher than Italy's, trailed Britain and France. Unlike Italy, Germany's Weimar government had welcomed foreign firms. In 1929, Detroit's General Motors bought 80 per cent of Opel and Ford built its own state-of-the-art plant in Cologne. Against this foreign competition, home-grown firms struggled to compete. Daimler and Benz, the founding fathers of the motor car, merged in 1926. And in 1932, four troubled Saxon car makers, Audi, DKW, Horch and Wanderer, pooled their resources under the umbrella name Auto Union. Despite the exigencies of the Depression, both harboured racing ambitions, which appealed to the incoming Chancellor.

Hitler had already agreed to back Daimler Benz's racing programme when the chairman of the newly formed Auto Union, Baron Klaus von Oertzen, made an appointment to see him in May 1933. Oertzen decided to bring along with him the 57-year-old car designer Ferdinand Porsche. Hitler did not like surprises, but after a frosty start he began to interrogate Porsche who then produced plans for his Auto Union Grand Prix machine. Porsche's dream racer was almost eccentrically high-tech, with a V16 engine and two superchargers, one for each bank of cylinders, all mounted behind the driver. Suitably impressed, Hitler was persuaded to fund both teams, each with an initial 250,000 Reichsmarks. As Porsche's secretary Ghislaine Kaes put it, 'Once Hitler had made his decision we were never short of money.'

For 1934, the Grand Prix regulations were heavily revised. The previous 'anything goes' Formula Libre rules, framed to encourage all comers during hard times, had favoured bigger, heavier machines. Fearing that both speeds and cars would become unmanageable, the governing body imposed a 750kg weight limit for entrants, minus the driver, tyres, fuel, oil and water. This, they believed, would also keep speeds from becoming excessive. It turned out to be a naïve hope. As it happened, 750kg was about the weight of the Alfa Romeos and Maseratis so neither firm needed to go back to the drawing board.

When he needed to, Enzo Ferrari knew how to turn on the charm and made sure to show his support for Ugo Gobbato's appointment as the new man in charge at Portello. His effusive welcome in the May 1934 edition of his newly launched in-house magazine *La Scuderia Ferrari* could have come straight from a Fascist playbook. 'With his arrival, the entire workforce realised that it had found a true leader ... May he march forward in the name of Fascist Italy, toward other conquests.' Ferrari's aim was to consolidate his role running Alfa's outsourced racing team and supplying technical and development expertise. But Gobbato had other priorities.

Itemising the factory's woes in a memo shortly after he joined, Gobbato pulled no punches, citing irrational layout, unnecessary material movement and non-existent cost accounting, low productivity and the supply of parts and materials that was at best erratic. And with the car market stagnant, the only opportunity was via Mussolini's buildup of Italy's armed forces. Gobbato framed Portello's recovery plan around securing contracts to supply vehicles and aero-engines for the military. From now on, cars would be a sideshow.

For Ferrari, this was a setback, but for Vittorio Jano it felt like a punishment. He had been passed over for the top job, which had wounded his pride. Consequently, he had not welcomed Gobbato's arrival or his plans, and further humiliation followed when in April 1934 Gobbato put himself in charge of the whole technical and engineering side of the business. Jano was moved sideways to develop a new radial aircraft engine, the AR D2. But after devoting himself to small water-cooled engines, his attempt at a big air-cooled unit failed to deliver.

Gobbato meanwhile had moved swiftly to build up output with bought-in designs, a military truck shared with Fiat called the Unificati and a licence to build British Bristol Jupiter aero-engines. Supplying Mussolini's armed forces was now Alfa Romeo's *raison d'être*. Output of cars which had risen to 700 in 1934 plummeted to just ten in 1936.

In spite of Alfa Romeo's change of priorities, Enzo Ferrari pressed on, fielding Jano's liberated Monopostos. In 1934 the Scuderia won thirteen of twenty-six races entered, with Achille Varzi taking five victories. But the Germans made their presence felt, Mercedes winning four and Auto Union three out of eight races they entered. Notice had been served.

At each race, the Mercedes-Benz and Auto Union convoys rolled into the paddock with formidable team support. Mercedes even had a supercharged truck ready to dash back to base for a last-minute repair or spare part. Beside the Silver Arrows as they collectively became known, low to the ground, independently sprung, boasting upwards of 400 bhp, Jano's red Alfas looked quaint and outdated and the Scuderia like a bunch of amateurish *garagisti*. None of this was lost on Italy's star drivers.

In August 1934, when Auto Union arrived at Monza for a pre-race practice, Ferdinand Porsche offered Varzi a test behind the wheel. A cool-headed precision driver, his temperament suited the Germans and their professionalism. But when an offer to join the team followed, he had one condition.

Too often he had found himself overshadowed by Nuvolari, who with wearisome regularity wound up the hero of the race even when he was not the winner. Varzi finally had the means to outshine his great rival – so long as Nuvolari didn't follow him to a German team.

Nuvolari also tested the Auto Union, but no offer followed. The letter from Auto Union's PR manager Richard Voelter, in their only common language of French, made no secret of why:

'*Quelques de nos autres conducteurs de véhicules que nous avons pris ene pour l'année 1935, on exprime de certaines doutes au sujet de votre engagement.*'

'Some of our other drivers that we took into consideration for the year 1935, expressed certain doubts about your commitment.'

There were other reasons. His extrovert theatrics behind the wheel unnerved them. And in any case, Nuvolari, twelve years older than Varzi, was surely past his prime. As it turned out, it was a choice Dr Porsche and the Auto Union team would bitterly come to regret.

With Varzi gone and Nuvolari decamped to Maserati, Enzo Ferrari had little choice but to look abroad for drivers. He signed two Frenchmen, Louis Chiron and René Dreyfus, for 1935. But at this point Mussolini intervened. Fearing that the loss of Varzi to the Germans would inspire others to follow, he offered an incentive to stay home, a 50,000 lire prize for the Italian Drivers' Championship.

Money was not a big motivator for Nuvolari, who lived a relatively humble life with Carolina and their two boys in Castel d'Ario. This modesty enhanced his appeal as an upholder of the best Italian values, one who was not swayed by the temptations, who had created a wholesome, homespun image all his own, with his trademark blue helmet, yellow shirt, blue trousers and yellow shoelaces. Gabriele D'Annunzio had been so impressed with Nuvolari's achievements that in 1932 he had invited him to visit his palazzo in Gardone Riviera and presented him with a small tortoise shell inscribed: 'To Tazio Nuvolari of good Mantuan blood, who, true to his race, has joined courage with poetry, the most desperate risk to the most obedient mechanical power, and lastly life unto death in the path of victory.' Nuvolari adopted the tortoise as his emblem ever after, always wearing one as a brooch in every race.

But Nuvolari was not living the dream. Now forty-three and grey-haired, humiliated at having missed out on a seat at the wheel of one of the all-conquering German teams, his move to Maserati had been a disappointment.

He and Ferrari had always had a difficult relationship. Both men were fiercely proud and single-minded, both still needed each other, but both were too proud to make an approach. So Jano was detailed to act as emissary, shuttling between Nuvolari's villa in Mantua and Ferrari's base in Modena to stitch together a deal. Nuvolari was not particularly enamoured of Mussolini, but when Ferrari and Jano pressed him to do his 'patriotic duty', sweetening the deal with all expenses paid and 50 per cent of total winnings, Nuvolari agreed to return to Scuderia Ferrari for 1935.

From the start of the season it was clear that Jano's ageing Alfas were hopelessly outclassed. Desperate measures were called for. Some of the year's lesser Grands Prix were still being run to the Formula Libre rules. Ferrari floated the idea of adapting one of the Scuderia's own Alfa chassis to take two of the eight-cylinder engines, one at the front and one at the back. Built off-site in Ferrari's Modena workshop, it neatly sidestepped any interference from Gobbato, and, if it failed, Alfa could distance itself from the project.

Ferrari built a pair of twin-engined cars, each weighing about half a ton more than the 750kg cars, producing nearly 550 bhp. One *bimotore* did enjoy one moment of glory when Nuvolari touched 208 mph on a closed section of the Florence–Viareggio autostrada, breaking the Germans' record of 199 mph for a flying mile, and briefly became the second fastest in the world to Malcolm Campbell's *Blue Bird*, which had just topped 300 mph. But the *bimotore* was an unwieldy brute, prone to shredding its tyres. Scuderia Ferrari ploughed on with the uncompetitive Alfa 8C. Against the German might, it would all be down to the driver.

By the time all the teams converged on the Nürburgring that July for the German Grand Prix, the Silver Arrows had already won all the season's other main races. Mercedes arrived with eight cars, three of them spares. Varzi was enjoying his season with Auto Union. The circuit, decked out with swastika flags, left no doubt that this was intended to be a showcase of Third Reich supremacy. The only question was which German team would win. Presiding over the event was long-time Hitler henchman Korpsführer Adolf Hühnlein. A speech honouring the German drivers' victory was already in his pocket when he prepared to drop the flag.

Grid positions were chosen by ballot and Nuvolari secured a place on the front row, but he made a bad start. In the early laps,

German drivers Rudi Caracciola and Bernd Rosemeyer duelled for the lead while Nuvolari languished around sixth, as it happened the same position as Varzi in his Auto Union, who was reported to be feeling unwell. By lap five the other three Alfas had already retired. Nuvolari was on his own. By lap seven he had moved up to third. The Germans were not showing any lack of form; Nuvolari was simply driving like a demon. To everyone's astonishment, on lap ten he squeezed into the lead. On lap twelve the first four drivers all chose to come in and refuel for the remaining ten laps. Nuvolari was stationary for an agonising two minutes and fifteen seconds, twice as long as his opponents, after the pressure pump that forced fuel into the tank failed and the Ferrari pit crew had to make do with cans. Back on the circuit, he was back down to sixth and surely out of contention.

But as so often happened when really pressed, Nuvolari threw what little remaining caution he had to the wind and drove at the very limit of his ability. One lap later, with a bravura display of his unique brand of driving, he was in second place, having passed Stuck, Caracciola, Rosemeyer and Fagioli in one lap. Wrote the *Motor Sport*'s reporter: 'Even now no one seriously thought that the Italian menace was a real one. At any moment we expected to hear the news that the AlfaRomeo had burst.' Manfred von Brauchitsch for Mercedes was in the lead, also driving brilliantly, bent on winning his home GP for the Reich. Over the next laps Nuvolari shaved seconds off the gap between them. As they went past the stands at the beginning of the last lap there were thirty-five seconds between them. 'Not even Nuvolari could hope to wipe out that lead, and the crowd cleared their throats to give von Brauchitsch his thoroughly deserved ovation.'

Nuvolari knew von Brauchitsch was famously hard on his tyres but with such a narrow gap between them he knew his team would not dare bring him in for a change. As the Italian bore down on the German, halfway round the last lap the Mercedes' left rear tyre, worn down to the canvas, exploded. For von Brauchitsch, the race was over.

Nuvolari's victory was met with almost universal dismay. Korpsführer Hühnlein, for one, would have to improvise a new speech and explain the outcome of the race to the Führer. The organisers, so sure of a German victory, had neither an Italian flag nor a recording of the Italian national anthem ready.

As it happened, as part of his armoury of good luck charms, Nuvolari had a disc of the 'Marcia reale' with him at the track. The anthem was played and Germans feted him at that evening's reception. By some margin the oldest driver in the race, with what had been thought of as the least competitive car, Nuvolari had stolen the German Grand Prix from the Third Reich's formidable racing arsenal.

Inevitably, the rest of the 1935 GP season was a walkover for the Germans, but Nuvolari did manage second place in the Italian GP and again at Brno in Czechoslovakia. Varzi had to be content with his two first places. The next season would be a struggle for both drivers, Nuvolari with his ageing Alfas, Varzi with his demons.

Racing Demons

Achille Varzi's absence from the 1936 German Grand Prix was enigmatically explained by *The Motor*'s Rodney Walkerley as his being 'neither unhappy with the team nor disappointed with the car, but simply in love'.

The sex lives of racing drivers in the 1930s went largely unreported, a distraction from the serious business of racing that in any case did not impinge on the drivers' performance. And the Fascist nations particularly had ideals about correct behaviour and not bringing the nation into disrepute, never mind the concerns of the papacy.

But Varzi, the supposedly cool, composed Italian hero, within weeks of joining Auto Union had dismayed his new employers by starting a passionate relationship with Ilse, wife of one of his fellow drivers, Paul Pietsch. Pietsch had left the team at the end of the 1935 season and the romance was an open secret.

Varzi, despite being in such a superior car, had not had an easy time of it. The mid-engined Auto Union was a handful and demanding to master. He had also suffered health issues, operations on his throat and an appendectomy that got in the way of his schedule. These setbacks disturbed his equilibrium; beneath the mask of sangfroid, Varzi's petulance was beginning to be glimpsed. In May the Tripoli Grand Prix had once again been engulfed by controversy, this time a result of increasing government interference. The race was largely a duel between the two Auto Union drivers Varzi and his German teammate, Hans Stuck. Stuck was leading in the closing laps when his pit signalled for him to slow. He followed orders, only to find himself being passed just before the finish line by another Auto Union. Varzi had also been given a signal – to speed up.

One by-product of the closer ties between Rome and Berlin was an unwritten agreement that, wherever possible, German and Italian drivers would take first place in their home races, and Tripoli was part of Italy's empire. The fiasco was exacerbated that evening when the colony's governor Italo Balbo proposed a toast to 'the real winner and raised his glass to Stuck'. Varzi, furious about the whole situation, stormed out. That night, to console him, Ilse offered him a shot of morphia, which she had been taking following an operation. As a dedicated professional, Varzi exhibited no obvious weakness for drugs, though he was a compulsive smoker, even known to light up during a race.

One week later, at Tunis, Varzi was in the lead when his Auto Union, travelling at top speed, was swept off the road by wind. Miraculously, he emerged from the wrecked car unscathed but badly shaken – it was the first crash of his career. Another dose of morphia from Ilse helped calm him. At the next race in Barcelona, after an argument about which car he would drive, he refused to race. Then, having campaigned for Auto Union to enter him in the non-championship Milan GP, he was beaten again by Nuvolari's ageing Alfa. After his failure to show up at the German GP, rumours were rife. Something was wrong. People close to him had noticed a change. Previously taciturn, he was now on occasion uncharacteristically talkative. His usually immaculate wardrobe became dishevelled and he frequently missed meetings. It didn't help that Bernd Rosemeyer, the newcomer to Auto Union who had replaced Ilse's husband Paul Pietsch, won both the German and Eifel GPs and was showing unmatched talent in the rain. Despite repeated denials, the truth of Varzi's predicament was revealed when the Auto Union team doctor made an unscheduled visit to Ilse's room and spotted a syringe. It spelled the end of Varzi's association with Auto Union. And it wasn't only the Germans who were upset. After Varzi crawled back to Milan, a furious Mussolini ordered that Ilse be denied entry into Italy.

Although both Ilse and Varzi did eventually kick the habit, the

Italian was gone from the front rank of motor racing and shunned by his countrymen and women. To be so publicly brought down by sex and drugs and while driving for Italy's increasingly formidable ally was a double national embarrassment. At least the nation could fall back on Nuvolari, the wild man of the track, but also the loyal husband and attentive parent who doted on his two sons. He was once more left bearing the torch for Italy.

But 1936 was hard going for Nuvolari, who won none of the major races in Europe, while at home his elder son Giorgio had fallen ill. But none of this undermined his commitment.

At Monaco, he fought a spectacular duel with Rudolf Caracciola's Mercedes in heavy rain, holding the lead against the much faster car until his brakes began to fade. In Tripoli he had another dramatic crash when a tyre burst and he was thrown out of his car. Plastered up and told to rest, he was back in the cockpit the next day and finished seventh. At the Eifel GP in thick fog he finished just behind Bernd Rosemeyer, won the Hungarian GP a week later in which all the Mercedes retired, and at the Milan GP the following weekend in Sempione Park, Nuvolari beat him by nine seconds. Ferrari believed the perfect balance for success was 50 per cent the driver and 50 per cent the car, but as he struggled with the ageing Italian machinery there was no question Nuvolari's input was more like 80 per cent.

Having rescued Alfa Romeo with government help, Gobbato felt obliged to fly the flag for Italy, but Mussolini was never going to come up with the sort of support handed out by the Third Reich to Mercedes and Auto Union. However, Nuvolari's heroics with the underfunded Italian team meant the Alfa boss had no option but to keep racing. Motor sport and national prestige were inextricably intwined. Withdrawal from the fray was politically unthinkable.

That October Nuvolari sailed to New York to compete in the revived Vanderbilt Cup race on Long Island. Before he left, at a ceremony in Siena honouring him as champion of Italy, Il Duce had warned him that he absolutely must win in America. Fascist Italy's image in Europe had been shaken by its imperial misadventures in Abyssinia and support for General Franco in Spain's civil war.

Nuvolari had made no conscious effort to show allegiance to

Mussolini; he didn't need to. He was now so famous in Europe that Il Duce was happy merely to bask in the glow which surrounded the 'Flying Mantuan'. All Nuvolari really cared about was winning races and his beloved family. A superstar in Europe, whether he liked it or not, Fascist Italy's prestige in America was now down to him.

On the other side of the Atlantic, motor racing had taken its own evolutionary path. High-banked oval 'speedbowl' circuits had become the norm, which demanded specialised machines built for speed rather than handling. But the Vanderbilt track at Roosevelt Field was laid out like a European-style circuit with plenty of twists and turns. Against the nimble visitors, the unwieldy American machines were outclassed. Europeans took the first six places. Despite starting from eighth on the grid and with only eleven of twelve cylinders working, Nuvolari delivered Il Duce a commanding win, eight minutes ahead of a Bugatti and two more Alfas. Happily for him, the Germans had stayed away.

The win came with $20,000, not that money meant that much to him. He passed up a further $50,000 for a three-minute radio interview, but accepted an invitation to drive a few demonstration laps of a dirt track that an Italian immigrant had built himself.

By the end of the year Nuvolari was Italian champion for the third time. But he could see that his victories were increasingly Pyrrhic, snatched from the all-conquering Germans when they were either absent or suffered a rare mishap. Nineteen thirty-seven would be his bleakest year.

The first casualty was Nuvolari's elder son. Giorgio, who had just turned nineteen, was seriously ill with pericarditis. Nuvolari had already booked his return passage to New York for the next Vanderbilt Cup. He was about to cancel but Giorgio gamely insisted he go, saying to his father, 'What would the team do without you?' So Nuvolari sailed.

His ship was halfway across the Atlantic when he was called to the telegraph room on the bridge to receive the news that his son had died. For a man who had cheated death most weekends of his working life the loss of his own son must have seemed unimaginably cruel. Determined to honour his son's wishes he went ahead and raced, but this year the Germans decided they had to compete, and dominated the race with Nuvolari having to settle for fifth place.

Back in Milan, Alfa Romeo was in more trouble. Ugo Gobbato had reluctantly accepted that his patriotic duty was on the racetrack as well as the battlefield and given Vittorio Jano the go-ahead to develop a brand new V12 engine to take on the Germans. But to Jano's frustration, most of his engineers had been diverted to military aero-engines. When the new engine finally emerged it was still no match for Mercedes and Auto Union, whose power and handling had leaped even further ahead.

Stung by the humiliation and anticipating the wrath of Il Duce, Gobbato abruptly sacked Jano. To everyone in the motor racing world this was a huge shock. Jano was an automotive hero, responsible for taking Alfa Romeo to the very top of motor racing, in Grand Prix and sports cars. Pinin Farina said of him, 'He lived life at 3,000 rpm at least ... he was at the top of the mountain during one of our most splendid periods in motor racing ... For ten years in Italy he was the man who sliced time from races, who collected prestigious records without taking the slightest notice of the commander's baton or corporate honours. His idea of happiness was speed.'

One witness to Jano's agony was his understudy, Gioacchino Colombo. In the absence of investment, 'the concern of the hierarchy only found expression in more or less authoritative messages, directives and appeals'. And because winning and fulfilling military contracts had become Alfa Romeo's priority, Jano was allowed 'very little of its resources, either in money or in men for the racing section'. And although Gobbato excelled at the organisation of production, compounding the problem, as Colombo saw it, was a 'great confusion of roles, too many people all wanting their own way'.

In January 1938, Auto Union's wunderkind, 28-year-old Bernd Rosemeyer, was killed during a speed record attempt on the Frankfurt to Darmstadt autobahn. This time Ferdinand Porsche had no misgivings about who to contact.

But Nuvolari, under pressure to do his patriotic duty, turned the German's offer down. In Modena Enzo Ferrari rushed into development a lower, slimmer version of Jano's Tipo C. In practice for the first race of the season in Sardinia, the new machine caught fire after the flexing chassis ruptured a fuel pipe, burning Nuvolari's legs. Furious and shaken, he decided that he had had enough, announced his retirement and set off on a month's holiday with his wife.

Porsche persisted and this time Nuvolari succumbed. At Monza for the 1938 Italian Grand Prix, in front of an adoring crowd who didn't seem to care whose car he was driving, Nuvolari in his Auto Union was victorious and finished the year with a memorable win in Britain at Donington Park. It's a measure of his prowess that at the age of forty-six the driver once judged too wild for them almost single-handedly transformed the fortunes of Auto Union that season. Other than Rosemeyer he was the only driver to master the fierce and unruly rear-engine car despite coming to it so late in his career. At last, Nuvolari had reason to look forward to the next season, but Europe was about to be engulfed in another war. Fittingly, perhaps, the driver who had done more than any other to make motor racing such a spectacle between the wars took the chequered flag at the last Grand Prix of the era, at Belgrade on 3 September 1939, just a few hours after Britain declared war on Germany.

For sheer bravado no other racing driver came close to Nuvolari. Frequently in inferior machinery, rarely in the best-financed team, he excelled regardless, despite several heavy crashes and multiple injuries, frequently racing against doctors' orders.

Nuvolari came to represent so much of Italy's unique blend of daring and style. It is astonishing that in a sport where fatalities were so frequent, the most outrageous driver of the age not only survived but would be back behind the wheel in 1945, driving against men half his age.

In Modena, Ferrari had kept clear of the crushing politics of Portello, but after Jano's departure, and Nuvolari's defection to Auto Union, Gobbato had to act. Mindful of Mussolini's fury at Alfa's dismal performance, he decided to take over Ferrari's operation and move it closer to home into a building adjoining Portello. So on 27 December 1937, after eight years, Scuderia Ferrari was dissolved. In one way it was a blow for Enzo Ferrari. During that time he had built up an exceptionally successful equipe, entering 225 races and taking 144 victories. But the payoff was handsome at over 1 million lire and a further 980,000 lire for the cars and spares. However, there were two caveats. He could not use the Ferrari name for a minimum of four years, and he was required to remain in charge of the racing programme in-house. Once again Ferrari was an Alfa Romeo employee which, in the current climate, was never going to work.

The two men were total opposites. Ferrari observed that Gobbato 'was no believer in improvisation or snap decisions. A great industrial organiser, he expected everything to be arranged in advance, with every last detail foreseen and worked out. He hated having to adapt himself to sudden changes, while for me the act of improvisation was almost part of my religion.' Gobbato's mistake, Ferrari believed, was to view a racing car as a product, no different from an ordinary car, the work of many departments, whereas Ferrari believed they could only come from 'a small auxiliary workshop ... with its own specialist staff so the ideas and designs of engineers might be rapidly translated into reality'.

Gobbato's replacement for Jano was a complete outsider. Wifredo Pelayo Ricart Medina was a Spanish engineer who Gobbato had befriended while setting up a Fiat outpost in Spain. Multilingual, with a passion for music, he was warm and diplomatic and technically gifted. Ferrari hated him on sight. 'When he shook hands it was like grasping the cold lifeless hand of a corpse.'

Gobbato, feeling the pressure from Mussolini, urged his new recruit to match the all-conquering German Silver Arrows. Ricart's first effort, the Tipo 162, was an almost wilfully complex V16 fitted with *five* superchargers. But it never raced and was soon succeeded by a restrained twelve-cylinder power plant with just two blowers. Like the groundbreaking Auto Union, its engine was mounted behind the driver, but test driver Consalvo Sanesi reported that sitting so far forward, almost between the front wheels, he could not anticipate the dramatic oversteer which could turn the car sideways in split seconds and pronounced it undrivable.

Ferrari was under no illusion that his relationship with Alfa was anything but doomed. In all arguments, Gobbato inevitably took Ricart's side. Matters soon came to a head and, when given his notice, Ferrari was sanguine. 'It seemed to me to be the logical solution to the problem.' It was actually a release, one that he would come to relish.

Detente

For much of the motor industry the 1930s was a turbulent decade. The fallout from the Wall Street Crash crushed sales worldwide, protectionist policies choked exports and forced producers back on their domestic markets. After Mussolini's Abyssinian campaign, sanctions imposed by the League of Nations was another weight on Italian producers. Fiat, alone, seemed to ride above these crises. In 1937 it made a record 66,000 vehicles, 68 per cent exports more than double that of French and American makes. From satellite plants it also produced a further 5,000 in Germany and 20,000 in France. But Fiat was only one part of Agnelli's sprawling empire. Mining, chemicals, aeronautics, railways, shipping, insurance, media and sport were pursued by thirty more of his companies. From this great height, Agnelli could look back on his achievements with some satisfaction, but as he entered his seventies he was about to face the most challenging decade of his life.

Susanna Agnelli's childhood memories of her grandfather are of an austere and formal character, an ageing former cavalry officer not given to frivolity nor entirely comfortable with the prodigious wealth that success had bestowed on him. Stony and remote, his visits made the whole household nervous. Susanna would watch him formally greet her father Edoardo, the son and heir to the Agnelli fortune, who was being groomed to take Giovanni's place at the head of the Fiat empire. Except for a brief smile at his daughter-in-law, Agnelli's expression remained stony as he took his place at the head of the table, a bowl of vegetables beside him. 'Every day at lunchtime he prepared his own salad and ate it slowly while he drank a glass of Punt E Mes vermouth and listened to songs on the radio.' After the meal he would take a nap. 'He would go to his room and lie on the bed, covering himself with his jacket in the military fashion, a habit he had learned when he was an officer in the cavalry. After a twenty-minute nap he would go back to Fiat.'

Her fun-loving father could not have been more different. Edoardo was born in Verona in 1892 while Giovanni was still a soldier and followed him into the cavalry before going on to study law. Tall, with a slight stoop and a relaxed personable manner, he fully enjoyed all the benefits his family fortune could provide. An enthusiastic socialite, keen gambler and passionate football fan, he was also a leading promoter of the then new sport of skiing. Although made vice-president of Fiat and regarded as the heir apparent, Edoardo was not closely involved in the core business. He was best known for his presidency of Juventus, the Turin football team the Agnellis bought in 1923. Under his control, it would be transformed into Italy's first professional club, going on to win five consecutive Serie A championships. He also became chairman of *La Stampa*, the Torinese newspaper also acquired by the Agnelli family, and led the development of Sestriere, Europe's first purpose-built ski resort.

In 1921, he married Virginia Bourbon del Monte, the Princess of San Faustino, an indication of how far the Agnelli family had risen in Italian society. Virginia's mother had started out as plain Jane Campbell, one of the generation of wealthy young Americans depicted in Henry James's novels, who had come to Italy in search of culture and marriage and found both, marrying Carlo Bourbon del Monte, Prince of San Faustino. The Palazzo Barberini, where Virginia grew up, had been commissioned by Pope Urban VIII in 1623. It became a running joke that when the Agnellis entertained the royal family, they joked about who should really be heir to the Italian throne, Prince Umberto or Edoardo, the heir to Fiat. Nevertheless, Susanna, 'Sunni' to the family, noted that status only went so far when they visited nobility in Rome, who considered them upstarts.

'The Roman children don't talk to us anyway. They don't

understand how we can live in Turin ... The girls are all called Donna Topazia or Dona Babu or Donna Francesca. We are called by our names.'

Fascism had little impact on Agnelli family life. Mussolini's visit to Turin in 1933 was the only time Susanna saw her father in a Fascist uniform. 'He looks at himself in the mirror and roars with laughter. For days afterward he endlessly describes the Turin ladies in their ridiculous uniform caps and soldier-like black suits, swooning at the idea of being on the same balcony with the Duce.' Her British nanny, Miss Parker, disapproved of the special uniform shops and pitied 'all the poor people who have to spend their money on this nonsense'.

When her mother gave birth to a seventh child she was rewarded with a pass entitling her to free rides on all tramways. '[She was] delighted with it even though she never has and never will ride on a tram.'

Susanna's charmed, carefree childhood came to an abrupt end in July 1935 when she was thirteen. The family were holidaying at their villa, Forte dei Marmi, on the Tuscan coast. On the morning of the 15th, Edoardo was due back in Turin. His father had his own seaplane, a Savoia-Marchetti, its Fiat engine attached above the wing. It was standing by to whisk Edoardo up to Genoa from where he could take the train. Before his departure, the pilot Arturo Ferrarin, a decorated air force veteran, took the children up for a spin. Wrote Susanna of their last lunch together, 'My father is gay and they are talking aeroplanes. "With a Fiat plane and Ferrarin as a pilot I am ready to fly anywhere," he says.'

A few hours after their departure the telephone rang. Susanna was with her grandmother when Princess Jane took the call. She saw her eyes widen as she swayed backward. 'Sunni, your father is dead.'

It was a freak accident. Ferrarin had landed the aircraft across the water from Genoa's harbour and was taxiing towards a mooring when it hit an obstacle, possibly a log, and started to capsize. Edoardo managed to extricate himself and climbed onto the wing only to be struck by the still-spinning propellor. He was killed instantly. Ferrarin survived unscathed.

Informed only that his son had been in an accident, Giovanni Agnelli drove to the Genovese hospital where Edoardo had been taken. Asking to see the patient, he was directed to the mortuary. 'He walked in and looked at his dead son, his only son, for ten minutes in silence then drove back to Turin.'

In the Agnelli palazzo on Turin's Corso Oporto mourners arrived in droves to file past Edoardo's open casket. Even the soon-to-be last king of Italy, Umberto II, came to pay his respects and attend a private Mass. For Agnelli, who had also lost a daughter in 1928, the death of his only surviving child, his son and heir, was a catastrophe. It also set in motion a crisis which nearly tore the family apart.

Curzio Malaparte was a controversial figure. War veteran, author and adventurer, his adopted name a play on 'Bonaparte', he had first crossed swords with Agnelli Snr when the proprietor fired him from the editorship of *La Stampa*.

He was also known for his striking matinee idol looks and outspoken views. An early supporter of Mussolini, he had fallen out with him after writing critically about Adolf Hitler. At the time he came back into the Agnelli orbit, he was under semi-house arrest along the coast from Forte dei Marmi, having recently been freed from prison, and was allowed to walk his dog on the beach where he was spotted by Susanna's grieving mother.

Malaparte's consoling attentions soon blossomed into something more complicated. As soon as Agnelli heard that the two were proposing to marry, he arranged for a court order to be served on Virginia, giving him custody of his seven grandchildren and banning Susanna from the family home. Furious, Virginia took Susanna and her siblings to the station and caught a train for Rome. But outside Genoa, in open country, it was brought to a halt. The police boarded, accused Virginia of abduction and took the children off the train.

What happened next gives a telling insight into the delicate detente that prevailed between Agnelli and Mussolini. Virginia continued to Rome and succeeded in getting an audience with Il Duce himself to plead for him to intervene. Her determination must have impressed Mussolini and, as Susanna observed, 'He liked her battling nature and liked acting like the magnanimous all-powerful giant.' He telephoned Agnelli, the court order was rescinded, Virginia went back home to her seven children. No more was said and no more was heard of Malaparte in the Agnelli household.

Agnelli's drastic action had been prompted by the crisis Edoardo's premature death posed for him. Seventy in 1936, an age when most of his contemporaries had retired, he was without an adult heir to the Fiat throne (Gianni, Susanna's brother, born in 1921, had some years to go before being ready to succeed his grandfather). At the first board meeting after Edoardo's death, Agnelli told the directors, 'I am here to continue what my son should have done.' He appointed his nephew, Giancarlo Camerana, as vice-president to maintain the family's board presence, but Agnelli Snr had always known that it would take more than another Agnelli to fill the void after his own demise.

Vittorio Valletta, seventeen years Agnelli's junior, was born in 1883 in Sampierdarena, now a suburb of Genoa. His father, a railway official, was not much of a role model, gambling away the family assets. After they moved to Turin, Valletta attended night school to train as an accountant, gaining a gold medal from the Turin chamber of commerce, then was accepted by the Scuola Superiore di Commercio where he also taught. He was only in his mid-twenties when Agnelli first approached him for his accounting skills during the protracted legal battle over Fiat's shares before the First World War. When they met again it was during a dispute over patents. Valletta, representing the other party, refused to be intimidated. The tenacity with which he defended the interests of the small business against the mighty Fiat impressed Agnelli who then hired him to overhaul Fiat's accounts. By this time Valletta was dividing his time between business and teaching both professionals and workers seeking adult education and had become known as *il professore*.

But Agnelli was not simply looking for an accountant. Once he was installed at Lingotto in 1921, Valletta's role soon widened into a complete reorganisation of the company's methods and processes along the more scientific lines pioneered in America by Henry Ford and Frederick Taylor. It wasn't until 1928, when Agnelli promoted him to general manager, that he gave up academic teaching to devote himself full-time to Fiat. His influence is evident from the company's production figures, which rose from 96,882 between

1911 and 1920 to 309,660 in the 1920s. Enzo Ferrari describes him as 'Chaplinesque' in appearance, but with 'an unusual talent for choosing the best brains and putting at their command an almost perfect organisation'. In Valletta, Agnelli had identified the same mix of talents which he too possessed.

With Valletta's help, Agnelli had secured his family's future with the formation in 1927 of the Istituto Finanziario Industriale (IFI), a holding company for his considerable portfolio of companies. From here on, Agnelli had begun to delegate control to the multi-talented Valletta, finally crowning him CEO in 1939.

His tenure got off to an inauspicious start when one of his first duties was to preside over Mussolini's visit to open Fiat's new Mirafiori plant on the outskirts of Turin that May. Il Duce enjoyed nothing like the universal adoration heaped on Hitler by the German people. Twenty thousand police and militia members were drafted in to clear the streets of troublemakers and more biddable people from the countryside were bussed in to line the streets and lead the applause as his motorcade passed. And at Mirafiori, Herculean efforts went into scouring abusive graffiti from the factory facilities and steps were taken against mass absenteeism on the day of the visit. Il Duce, in a petulant mood, flounced off the specially constructed stage after the workforce greeted his rhetorical flourishes with universal stony silence. Later that day, he was heard to utter '*Torino, porca città* [damn city]', but later that day order was restored after a charade conducted by both parties, in which Agnelli spoke of how Il Duce's presence had been honoured by 50,000 Fiat workers and Mussolini in turn communicated his satisfaction with the scale of the turnout. As Valletta's biographer observed, 'Agnelli expressed feelings he didn't feel, while Mussolini's response was totally at odds with reality.'

27

The Shadow of War

Dante Giacosa was in his drawing office at Lingotto when he heard the news. 'On June 10th 1940, we received a peremptory order: all office workers were to stop work and line up, ready to proceed to the public square and the courtyards of the Fascist district headquarters. I had to join the columns of gloomy anxious fearful men. When the booming belligerent voice of the Duce came fiercely over the loudspeakers, announcing the declaration of war, my heart missed a beat and the crowd was shaken by perturbation. "We'll have the French bombers over our houses tonight," I said. They came the night after.'

Many had underestimated the consequences of Mussolini's rule, including Enzo Ferrari, who ruefully admits to having expected it to 'all blow over or something of the kind'. When he expressed this to a customer who had turned against Mussolini, and was having to sell his prized Alfa, the reply was prophetic. 'Fascism is too strong; it has nothing to fear from anyone and everything to fear from itself.' When war was declared it came as a shock to many – especially those with some insight into how unprepared Italy was to fight a war, one conducted by its far superior ally, Germany. The Pact of Steel, signed in May 1939 by Hitler and Mussolini, committed Italy to following Germany into any war it wished to wage. Il Duce's son-in-law and foreign secretary, Galeazzo Ciano, had accepted empty assurances from Berlin that no war was imminent, but as soon as the pact was signed Hitler ordered preparations for the invasion of

Poland. Ciano's desperate pleas for a delay of two or three years were rebuffed.

No one in Italy escaped the shadow of war. Susanna Agnelli's charmed life came to an abrupt end when she volunteered to become a nurse and saw its consequences first-hand. 'We spend the day looking after the wounded soldiers, listening to their tales of how they had been sent walking into the snow without socks in their leaking cardboard boots, of how they had been massacred while they hardly knew what was happening to them.' She then got posted onto a hospital ship that was sent to the desert war in Africa and then to Naples. Her antidote to confronting times dealing with wounded Italians and POWs was skiing in St Moritz with what was left of Italy's aristocracy.

As with the previous war, Italy's vehicle manufacturers benefited from military contracts to supply trucks and other equipment. Since his arrival at Alfa Romeo in 1933, Ugo Gobbato had rebuilt the business around fulfilling Mussolini's rearmament programme and transformed Portello into a powerhouse of aero-engine production. The workforce, under 1,000 in 1933, by 1943 had grown to 9,300. Gobbato's transformation was such a success that in 1938 the IRI commissioned him to create an entirely new Alfa aero-engine factory to be built at a brand-new plant in Pomigliano d'Arco, near Naples, far from the northern industrial heartland. With his experience setting up factories in Russia and Spain, Gobbato was the ideal man for the job. He created a state-of-the-art plant, one of the most modern in Europe, with 600 houses for employees, each with a small garden. By 1942 it was churning out engines of a design licensed from Germany's Daimler Benz.

Still far and away the biggest supplier to the war effort was Fiat, whose workforce had swollen to 43,000 by 1942. As Turin inevitably became a priority for Allied night bombing, Giacosa witnessed black-shirted gunners on rooftops swinging outdated machine guns up at unseen aircraft, the shells falling back to earth. 'It was a marvellous sight and tragicomic at the same time.'

As the bombing intensified, life in the city was transformed. At Lingotto air raid shelters were improvised in the basement of the office block where the canteen had been. But after a massive air strike on the plant on the night of 21 August 1942, Giacosa's drawing office was moved to a less identifiable location, the ground floor of the Duca degli Abruzzi school half a mile away, which happened to have an air raid shelter under the playground.

By summer 1943, Turin had suffered nearly thirty bombing raids. Gas was turned off to prevent explosions and the city was blacked out every night. People moved about on bicycles with phosphorescent brooches which glowed in the dark. Over four hundred factories had been hit, fifty churches were in ruins. On just one night, 13 July, 702 tonnes of bombs were dropped. With nothing like enough air raid shelters, many sought shelter at night in the hills around the city. Giacosa moved his family to a house in the Albese hills.

In Milan, Alfa Romeo's Portello plant received the same treatment. After one particularly heavy raid in 1942, Alfa boss Ugo Gobbato struggled to keep assembly going, dispersing as much activity as possible to locations outside the city. Chief engineer Wifredo Ricart, who had elected to remain at Alfa rather than return to his home in neutral Spain, evacuated his development team to Lake Orta north of the city near Lake Maggiore and directed his team's focus back onto cars for peacetime. He gamely stayed on to the end of his contract in March 1945, when 195 of his team signed a farewell message.

Like other small metalworking businesses, Enzo Ferrari's workshop in Modena was a beneficiary of war. With the proceeds of his payoff from Alfa Romeo he set up a new company called Auto Avio Costruzioni to supply the auto and aero industries, initially engines for air force trainer aircraft. Critically important to the war effort was the manufacture of ball bearings, a vital component. To produce them, Ferrari obtained specialised machine tools from the German supplier Jung. Then, on discovering that German patents didn't apply in Italy, the enterprising Ferrari hit on the idea of creating the ball-bearing-making machines himself and selling those as well.

Two years into the war, with Allied bombers targeting industrial centres, railways and main roads, the government ordered industry to disperse. Ferrari's premises on Viale Trento e Trieste were close to Modena's railway yards, another target for attack, so he started the search for a location further from harm's way. He settled on Maranello, a small town about ten miles to the south, where he already owned a plot of land. He acquired more properties on either side of the main street from a local millowner and set up his new 40,000 square foot workshop. He kept his home in Modena, cycling to and fro when petrol was unobtainable, using country paths.

He fitted out his workshop with new lathes and began making grinding machines for ball bearings, shamelessly copying the German Jung machines for which he had no licence, each one bearing the inscription *Scuderia Ferrari*.

By early 1943, Turin's citizens, never entirely behind Mussolini or his war, were growing increasingly angry over shortages of food and fuel as well as long hours and frozen wages. On 5 March, a strike broke out at Fiat's Mirafiori plant. Leo Lanfranco, a communist activist who had served five years in a penal colony and was now working as a Fiat labourer, led a walkout of what was initially only a few dozen workers. But the unrest spread rapidly to other plants, to the railways and to Milan.

Rather than striking, which was overtly confrontational, some preferred *sciopero bianco* – work-to-rule – which was harder to punish. Soaring inflation and food shortages had a galvanising effect.

28

Resistance

Mussolini lamented to his cabinet on 17 April 1943 that the crisis had 'suddenly taken us back twenty years'. A protest in Rome on Easter Sunday caused the Pope to cancel his benediction while students distributed leaflets proclaiming 'long live the northern workers'. Although 850 workers were arrested, Mussolini's faltering administration decided to give in to some of the demands in the interests of maintaining the war effort. Workers got a rise in wages, but it was now plain to see that Il Duce's grip on Italy was slipping.

From the start, Agnelli and Valletta had been on maximum alert, trying to anticipate the course of the war. It was clear to them that Mussolini had grossly overestimated the nation's capabilities; what was less well known was that similar wishful thinking was rife in Nazi Germany. Fiat had a spy at the heart of the German war machine – Carlo Schmidt, one of their executives who was serving as economic attaché in Italy's embassy in Berlin, advised Valletta of 'huge illusions surrounding the overpowering invincibility of our ally'.

On 8 September, as soon as Italy surrendered to the advancing Allies who had landed in the south, Agnelli dispatched Schmidt to Rome to make contact with the Allied command to seek a means of collaboration. For the purposes of sweetening any deal, he was handed 20 million lire. But as soon as word reached Berlin, the Germans swiftly secured the northern half of the country and instead of the comparatively arm's-length autonomy Agnelli had enjoyed under Mussolini, the Germans applied a tight grip. For the occupying Germans, Turin was a strategic prize. The *Militarkommandantur* occupied a palazzo in the city centre and took control, aided by a remnant of Italian Fascist diehards.

From Fiat the Germans ordered trucks, tanks and aero-engines made to their own designs. Giacosa couldn't help admiring the high-altitude, supercharged Daimler Benz inverted V12 with fuel injection and water cooling being prepared for production in a cordoned-off section of the Mirafiori plant. But Fiat and other factories in Turin were never entirely absorbed into the Nazi war machine. If little love had been lost between the Torinese and Mussolini, attitudes to the Germans, against whom many remembered fighting horrific campaigns in the Alps just a few decades before, were downright hostile.

An incident just days after Mussolini's downfall served notice on what the next phase of the war would be like. On Saturday 11 September, German troops descended on the barracks of the Nizza Cavalleria regiment, a mounted division stationed in Turin, ordered them to hand over their weapons and mount their horses and prepare for transportation. While this was happening, women looters raided the barracks' stores on Corso Regina Margherita for food, blankets and boots, carrying off their plunder in wheelbarrows and prams. When the Germans discovered what was happening, seventeen of the women were shot.

The cavalry were ordered to ride towards the railway yards to be shipped north, but at the Corso Sommeiller, a tram temporarily halted half of the procession. Another crowd of women shouted at them to dismount and escape. A volley of stones caused the horses to panic. In the melee that ensued, cavalry troops melted into the side streets as the stampeding horses ran amok. The Germans opened fire and the streets were littered with carcasses, which were also spirited away to help feed Turin's starving people.

Despite the increasingly repressive presence in the city and its environs, resistance spread and strengthened with every passing month. Valletta found himself playing a double game of keeping their new masters at bay with product while secretly passing money, vehicles and fuel to the increasingly well-organised and effective local partisans. Agnelli's and Valletta's priorities were to preserve their factories and prevent their workforce from being carried off to work in German plants. Paolo Ragazzi, one of Fiat's senior managers, remembered meetings between his two bosses and representatives of the Wehrmacht, and recalled Valletta saying afterwards: 'We could have been good Germans, Americans or fascists, anything to save Fiat.'

The firm was expected to produce 180 engines a month, but for the first months only managed eighteen. Of 1,500 engines planned, fewer than a third were completed. By 1945 there were only ten trucks a day – and most of them disappeared. Meanwhile, according to his biographer, Agnelli donated 55 million lire to the resistance and kept 3,000 partisans on the payroll. The Fascist authorities in Turin were alert to Fiat's position. 'The executives of this company are definitely working for the enemy ... and the entire block of subversives, saboteurs and obstructionists. Rather than based in the mountains, the rebel problem is here in the city – and this is where Fiat is.'

Giacosa, pleased to find himself released from the aero-engine department back to the comparatively 'serene and systematic activity' of designing cars, got used to regular dashes to an underground shelter as bombs fell, 'sometimes very close to us, blowing doors and windows off their hinges, shattering panes of glass and sending our papers flying off the drawing boards, a bewildering muddle of blueprints among the dust and splintered glass'.

After his drawing office evacuated to a nearby school, he was not unduly surprised when it was raided by Fascist police in search of some young draughtsmen who had joined the resistance.

'Boxes that were supposed to be filled with sand to absorb blasts from explosives were actually filled with weapons that the young draughtsmen belonging to the SAP [partisan action squads] active in the city had hidden in readiness for an uprising. In the classrooms behind the teachers' desks, which had been turned into tables for the directors, there were air vents covered with grating fitted to the wall a few inches from the floor.

'When the uprising eventually broke out, engineer Bona was

courteously requested by Massano, one of his draughtsmen, to move away from the blackboard for a moment. Under his astonished gaze the young Massano deftly removed the grating and in next to no time had extracted pistols, grenades, and rifles from the air vent.'

In February 1944 came the first strike in occupied Europe when an estimated one million stopped work across northern Italy. Fiat workers demanded a doubling of wages. Hitler demanded that a fifth of the strikers be arrested and deported. By the time it was called off, 1,100 of them had been sent to Mauthausen concentration camp. As a placatory gesture, a 30 per cent wage increase was offered, along with more food and salt rations, but by November Fiat was short of raw materials and going broke. Output was constantly interrupted by protests about food shortages and rising absenteeism. Winter temperatures plunged to minus twenty. When women staged a raid on Fiat's coal stores, overwhelmed guards stood by as they carted off all they could in wheelbarrows.

In Maranello, Ferrari was at some distance from the action but after the collapse of Mussolini's administration the Germans had taken charge of all war production. In September 1944, a delegation of German officials arrived to inspect the facility. By this time Ferrari had also allowed local partisans to stash funds and documents on his premises and was also contributing funds. On seeing the copied ball-bearing machines the Germans announced they would be confiscating them – but nothing happened; the Germans' days in control of northern Italy were numbered.

Retribution

Around the same time in Turin, Giacosa, ever the optimist and with an eye to the peacetime that surely could not be far away, late in 1944 began drafting a manifesto for the future. 'As a result of the technological progress achieved by the auto industry during the war, and the improvement in fuels and lubricants, the automobiles that will emerge after the war will be marked by an appreciable saving in weight, lower manufacturing costs, better materials and notably superior quality. So it is necessary to begin designing post-war models right now, freeing ourselves from the restrictions of outworn schemes and traditional production systems.'

Despite fear and uncertainty work went on 'serenely as there were no schedules and deadlines to be kept ... it was pleasant to let one's mind wander off onto the most disparate projects ... an excellent exercise that helped transform our younger draughtsmen into proficient designers'.

In anticipation of the war's end, he threw himself into the development of a pair of prototype cars, but both were destroyed in another raid, which left him dejected, and after his digs were bombed he wound up living in a former psychiatric hospital that Fiat had taken over as a boarding house for workers evacuated from the city. Almost as a hobby, from here he began to experiment with a battery-driven scooter and an electric version of the Topolino, installing generators to recharge the battery overnight at the hospital and use on his commute into Turin.

In the last months of the war, Giacosa's bosses faced competing forces. The Germans, doggedly hanging on to their presence in the north of the country, pressed Fiat's bosses to keep producing, while the increasingly powerful and effective partisans harried them for more support. As one female partisan noted, 'the closer the Allies advanced, the deeper the factory owners dug into their pockets'.

It was not the Allied armies advancing northwards who liberated Turin. Towards the end of April 1945, tricolour flags began to appear above factories. A grand resistance coalition of communists, socialists, liberals and monarchists had temporarily parked their differences and united against their common enemy. On 26 April, to stop the Germans destroying them as they retreated, Fiat workers occupied the factories while partisans encircled the remaining enemy forces for a final standoff. The Germans threatened to blow up the railway station unless they were guaranteed safe passage out of the city, but the partisans were in no mood to negotiate. After a threat to shoot 250 prisoners held hostage, a retreat was agreed. And on the night of the 27th, the Germans and Italian Fascist collaborators departed. To the dismay of the Allied forces, with their low opinion of Italians' fighting capability, by the time they arrived in Turin not only had all the Germans fled, the shops were open and the trams were running again.

On 18 April, Mussolini arrived in Milan, from where, with the help of the city's Cardinal Alfredo Schuster as an intermediary, he hoped to negotiate terms with the Allies and partisans. But having failed to broker a deal, on the 27th he left the city heading north, with a retreating German anti-aircraft unit. En route he was joined by his mistress, Clara Petacci, and her brother. The pair were travelling in the 1939 Carrozzeria Touring Alfa Romeo 6C Sport Berlinetta Mussolini had given her as a birthday present, the brother posing as a Spanish diplomat. The roads were jammed with fleeing Germans as partisans set up roadblocks to check for escaping Italian collaborators. To disguise himself, Mussolini donned a German great coat and helmet and travelled in the cab of a Wehrmacht truck, to no avail. Despite the disguise, his appearance was unmistakable to partisans who detained and then assassinated him and Petacci. Their corpses were loaded onto a lorry and driven back to Milan, where they were strung up by their feet outside a petrol station.

Lorenzo Delleani's painting captures the moment in July 1899 when Fiat's founding fathers gather to sign the company into existence. Giovanni Agnelli is third from the left.

Appassionato di auto. Celebrated composer Giacomo Puccini was among the first of Italy's car enthusiasts, seen here with one of his fourteen machines.

Felice Nazzaro passes through the hilltop village of Petralia Sottana, en route to victory in Sicily's 1907 Targa Florio.

Fiat's Lingotto factory, designed by Giacomo Matté-Trucco, boasted a rooftop test track. Opened in 1923, it was Europe's biggest car plant.

Giovanni Agnelli, right, with Henry Ford, on one of several fact-finding missions the Fiat boss undertook to Detroit.

Giovanni Parodi, second from the left, leader of the September 1920 Fiat workers' factory occupation, seated at company boss Agnelli's desk.

Works driver Enzo Ferrari came second in the 1920 Targa Florio, his first race for Alfa Romeo.

Il Duce Benito Mussolini at the wheel of an Alfa Romeo raced by Tazio Nuvolari, third from right. In 1933 the Italian ruler intervened to save Alfa from closure.

Perfect pitch: Company founder Vincenzo Lancia had a gift for diagnosing a mechanical fault just by listening to the sound of an engine.

Rival Italian track stars, Achille Varzi (left) and Tazio Nuvolari (right). Varzi's stellar inter-war racing career almost crashed due to drug addiction. Nuvolari always raced wearing a tortoise brooch, bestowed on him by poet and war hero Gabriele d'Annunzio with the words, 'To the fastest man, the slowest animal.'

The French Grand Prix at Montlhéry, 1934. Italy's Alfa Romeo looks antiquated beside the low-slung, rear-engined Auto Union from Germany.

Nuvolari, after joining the Auto Union team in 1938, is presented to Adolf Hitler.

Superleggera – the ultra-lightweight body frame pioneered by Carrozzeria Touring in 1937.

Gianni Lancia, centre, with Francesco De Virgilio, left, and Vittorio Jano, right, with their groundbreaking creation – the Lancia Aurelia of 1950.

Art of the Car: Battista Pininfarina readies his Cisitalia coupe for exhibition at New York's Museum of Modern Art in 1951.

The car that fell to Earth: Unveiled at the 1955 Turin motor show, Giovanni Savonuzzi's Ghia Gilda, designed for Chrysler, was the inspiration for the tail fins that sprouted on American cars of the late 1950s.

LAT Images / Stringer

Britain's King George VI meets the all-conquering Alfa Romeo team at the very first Formula One Grand Prix at Silverstone, 1950.

Masters of the track: Juan Manuel Fangio and Alberto Ascari (l-r) at the 1950 Modena Grand Prix. They swept the board for Alfa Romeo and Ferrari in the early 1950s.

The Monaco Grand Prix, 1955: Alberto Ascari's Lancia D50 is sandwiched by the two Mercedes of Fangio and Moss. Ascari's race ende in the harbour. Four days later he was killed at Monza and soon after, the Lancia team were taken over by Ferrari.

British racing red: Peter Collins (l) and Mike Hawthorn (r) celebrate their first and second places in the 1958 British Grand Prix. In search of victories, these passionate patriots had no option but to drive for Italy's Ferrari.

Alberto Ascari winning the 1954 Mille Miglia. He covered the 1,000 miles from Brescia to Rome and back in 11 hours, 26 minutes. In 1957, the road race was banned after nine spectators died, five of them children.

Gianni Agnelli in his 1966 Ferrari 365 P Berlinetta, built specially for him with a central driving position.

Fiat's Nuova Cinquecento, designed by Dante Giacosa, became the preeminent symbol of the economic miracle that transformed post-war Italian society.

Just twenty-four years old, Giorgetto Giugiaro at work in the Bertone studios clothing a Ferrari 250GT in 1962.

The insurgent: in the 1960s tractor-make Ferruccio Lamborghini took on Ferrari with a series of spectacular supercars.

The 1966 Alfa Romeo Duetto, Battista Pininfarina's last design, shared its cinematic debut with Dustin Hoffman in *The Graduate*.

Ford's GT40 and Ferrari's 330 duelling at 200mph. Piqued after Enzo Ferrari spurned his proposed buyout, Henry Ford got his own back at Le Mans in 1966, taking the first three places.

Petacci's Alfa fared better. Seized by a US Army major, Charles Pettit, who had it shipped back home to his family farm in upstate New York, he drove it until it broke down. Stored in a barn then sold off, its identity was eventually confirmed by Franz Spögler, who used to chauffeur Mussolini and Petacci and treated it to a ground-up restoration.

During the Wehrmacht's occupation of Milan, Alfa's German-speaking boss Ugo Gobbato had bought time for his workers by joining a consortium with other Milanese firms to produce parts for German Junkers aero-engines in the Costozza caves, near Vincenza, controlled by the German air ministry. When there were no more aircraft engines to be built, like Giacosa at Fiat, he began to plan a post-war car programme. But as the German surrender neared, his co-operation with the Nazi war machine became a problem. Retribution was swift, as vengeful Italians took back control of their homeland. People's courts were convened to try suspected collaborators. On 27 April 1945 Gobbato was brought before a tribunal, accused of criminal collaboration with the German occupation. He was acquitted, but the following day, as he walked home from Portello, a blue Lancia came alongside and he was shot dead.

In Turin, Agnelli and Valletta hoped that their overtures to the victorious Allies and their tacit support for the resistance would vindicate them. In France, an ailing 67-year-old Louis Renault had expected to regain control of his business after the liberation of Paris in 1944. Like Agnelli he had faced the choice of supplying the Nazis or having his plant shipped to Germany. But unlike the Italians, Renault had failed to lend support to the Resistance or make over-tures to the Free French. That September, Charles de Gaulle's new government had Renault arrested on charges of collaboration and he died in a nursing home a month later while awaiting trial. Rather than the business being passed back to his heirs, the company was nationalised in January 1945. In Italy, on 18 March, the Comitato di Liberazione Nazionale (CLN) ruled that Agnelli's and Valletta's properties be confiscated, on account of them having benefited financially during the occupation. A few weeks later they called for a general strike and informed Valletta they were taking over the company. With the blessing of the Americans who were now in control, four 'commissars' were appointed.

Valletta went on the run. Arriving at the home of a colleague whose child answered the door, he was mistaken for a beggar. A week later, a Croce di Malta ambulance from Turin arrived at a nursing home near Monte dei Cappuccini and dropped off an apparently elderly man; but instead of being admitted he was put into a car and driven to Alfiano Natta and the house of the mother of Paolo Ragazzi, Valletta's right-hand man, who was also a member of the resistance in Monferrato with the *nom de guerre* Lino Rovere. With help from America's OSS, the precursor of the CIA, he organised clandestine radio stations inside the Fiat factories and oversaw the preparation of an effective emergency plan for distributing food and fuel to the liberated population of Turin.

In hiding, Valletta appealed his case with letters from the British and American special forces representatives, and even a telegram from the Gestapo ordering his arrest in October 1943 at the time of the German takeover. His twenty-three-page statement itemised the funds given by the Agnelli family to the partisans and the donations of food and clothing for workers' families.

During those months, the future of Fiat was hotly debated within the CLN. Paolo Ragazzi recalled a conversation between two Fiat workers on a tram: '"We should hang Agnelli," said the first worker. "Listen," snapped the second, "If it weren't for Agnelli you would still be milking cows in the fields."' Fiat, all agreed, was at the heart of Turin's prosperity, the biggest employer by far in the city. But while resurgent communists regarded it – along with all other means of production – as a candidate for nationalisation, sceptics further to the right asked where investment vital to its reconstruction would be found since the state itself was effectively bankrupt. Rumours of a foreign takeover also focused minds at the thought of General Motors snapping it up as war reparation. This brought patriotic Italians across the political spectrum to a consensus that Fiat's survival was dependent on strong independent leadership, but the four-man committee appointed by the Allied authorities, chaired by a local physics professor, were out of their depth.

By the time hearings to decide Valletta's fate took place, the Allied command in Turin had already concluded that Valletta's return was essential if Fiat was to get back on its feet. All charges were dropped and Valletta was reinstated.

No such rehabilitation came in time for Giovanni Agnelli. Seventy-nine in August, having outlived both his children, his assets seized, the future of his giant corporation in the balance, he confided in a close friend, 'For forty years I have been assailed by the demon of work, I have never done anything else in my life. Now that I have reached the end of my day, I wonder if it wasn't a mistake.'

Agnelli died on 16 December 1945, just days before he was cleared of collaboration. Press coverage of his passing was modest, his funeral confined to a handful of mourners, the procession pausing briefly at the gates of the half-destroyed Lingotto factory where red flags were flying again, en route to his birthplace, at Villar Perosa.

By the end of 1945, the two men who had done more than anyone to shape the fortunes of Italy in the first half of the twentieth century were gone. Whether Agnelli or Mussolini made the bigger impact on Italy is a matter of debate. But Agnelli's legacy was secure. For now, Fiat's future was in the hands of Valletta, a talented technocrat, soon to be joined by an internationally notorious playboy.

Wild Spirit

G ianni Agnelli: 'When I arrived in Turin, I was greeted by a sea of red flags. I felt a certain amount of joy, but also a certain amount of fear ... everything needed to be rebuilt.' Italy in the spring of 1945 was a land scarred by bomb damage, much of it reduced to a battlefield on which the Allies had fought a protracted and devastating campaign.

Of Italy's population of 44.4 million, 291,000 servicemen and 153,000 civilians were dead. In Milan 70 per cent of all homes were either damaged or destroyed. Forty per cent of the bridges – 13,000 – and railways were damaged or destroyed. A third of the road network had been rendered unusable. A third of Italy's wealth had been lost; during the period of the war inflation had shot up twentyfold. By the time it ended, 20 per cent of jobs had disappeared through businesses lost. Italy was on its knees.

For those whose task it was to rebuild the Italian auto industry, there was some small comfort that others in the rest of Europe faced similar challenges. Who would finance the rebuilding of shattered factories? Where would they find the raw materials, the rubber and the fuel, as well as the steel? And if production actually resumed, who would have the money to buy their products? These existential questions were about to be faced in France and Germany – Britain, too, where no cars at all had been made since 1940.

From France's Peugeot plants, thousands of machines had been shipped off to Germany, Auto Union's factories, mostly in what was soon to become East Germany, were subsumed by the Soviet industrial operation. What was left of Daimler Benz got by repairing old and damaged vehicles. Amid the flattened remains of Hitler's vast showpiece factory built to produce Ferdinand Porsche's 'people's car' British Army engineers combed the rubble for enough parts to assemble a few Volkswagens.

In Italy, the nationalistic bravado of Mussolini's fascism which had supercharged so much of Italy's enterprise in the 1930s had been erased, leaving behind a bitter taste of destitution. Before the war, Roberto Rossellini enjoyed a charmed life as a successful film-maker, making Fascist propaganda at the Cinecittà film studios outside Rome. But the experience of war set him on a radically different path. *Roma città aperta (Rome, Open City)* would be a brutally naturalistic portrait of the city under Nazi rule. Starting production in January 1945, when Italy was not yet fully liberated, he used stock discarded by US Army Signal Corps film units and electricity 'borrowed' from the generators of the Allied armies.

The title was ironic; after Mussolini's capitulation in 1943, King Victor Emmanuel had declared the city 'open', only for it to be rapidly overrun by the Wehrmacht. Hundreds of homeless people were still camped among the sixteen sound stages at Cinecittà. Rossellini put them to work as extras. Future film-maker Federico Fellini was one of the scriptwriters, who detected among them a remarkable spirit, 'drawing hope from the very hopelessness of their situation. There were ruins, scenes of disaster and loss, yet everywhere a wild spirit of reconstruction.'

Roma città aperta opened that September to a mixed reception. Italians had little appetite for being reminded of what they had just come through. But the following February, when it opened in America, it caused a sensation, was voted Best Foreign Film by the New York Film Critics Circle and was the first Italian film to earn an Oscar nomination for Best Original Screenplay.

American audiences, far removed from the European war zone, were impressed by the defiance and courage of ordinary Italians. The style of the film also seemed fresh and new, different from anything they had associated with the country before. It was as if an entirely new aesthetic was about to emerge from the ruins of Mussolini's folly.

Italy had strong ties with America. Four million Italians had emigrated there since the late 1800s. The two nations had a tenuous affinity since the continent had been 'discovered' by one Italian, Christopher Columbus, and named after another, Amerigo Vespucci. Mainstream cultural heroes of the 1940s included Frank Sinatra, the baseball player Joe DiMaggio and New York mayor Fiorello La Guardia, who all wore their Italian descent as a badge of pride. Those four million immigrants included the parents of Amadeo Giannini, who had settled in the San Francisco Bay Area. In 1904, as a young trader, he noticed that established banks did not give loans to immigrants so he formed the Bank of Italy. It was so successful that in the 1920s he took over another bank in Los Angeles and renamed it Bank of America. Having made it in America, he was only too ready to give something back to his parents' homeland. Early in 1946 he toured Italy and in Turin met Fiat's Vittorio Valletta.

In August 1946, as part of Italy's delegation to the Paris Peace Treaty negotiations, Valletta flew into the French capital in a battered Savoia-Marchetti. Italy had been bankrupted by the war. But on the American side of the table was a representative of Giannini's Bank of America with a message for the Fiat boss. 'Allow me to tell you' – Giannini wrote to Valletta – 'that we will always be ready to come to the aid of you and your company at any time ... My personal opinion is that Italy will be among the first countries to recover and I expect that many deals can be done between Italy and this country.' Two years before Marshall Aid began to flow, Valletta came away from Paris with Fiat's first line of credit. Thanks to America, Fiat and Italy would have a future. Later, according to his sister Susanna, Gianni Agnelli would say, 'Without the Americans we wouldn't exist.'

31

The Homecoming

Luigi Chinetti was something of an outlier in the world of Italian motor sport. The son of a gunsmith from a small town north of Milan, he was apprenticed to his father's workshop and qualified as a mechanic by the age of fourteen. In 1917, now sixteen, he started at Alfa Romeo, where he first met Ferrari. Chinetti was a capable mechanic, but his other skills were driving and selling. He was also impatient and ambitious. In 1930, claiming to be no fan of Mussolini, he moved to Paris where he sold Alfas and won the Le Mans 24 Hours twice at the wheel of Jano's 8Cs. Then, in 1940, as part of a team competing in the Indianapolis 500, he set sail for America and, with the fall of France, decided to stay on.

Adjusting to life in America posed no problem for Chinetti. He gained US citizenship and worked at Rolls-Royce's New York agents, Inskip, whose Manhattan premises became a mecca for wealthy American enthusiasts of European cars. He also befriended Hollywood Cadillac distributor Tommy Lee, selling him several exotic French-built Talbot-Lagos. At the end of hostilities he journeyed back to Europe, first to Paris, where he found his premises and assets gone. So he hired a Citroën and made the pilgrimage back to his homeland.

Having seen out the war in the comfort of Manhattan, the sight of Milan in ruins came as a profound shock. He travelled on to Modena. He had heard a rumour that Ferrari was intending to build a V12 racing car, but what he saw when he arrived on Christmas Eve

1946 did not give him much confidence. Ferrari, he thought, looked aged beyond his forty-eight years in his unheated, dimly lit office in the Viale Trento e Trieste. Its dusty display of trophies, testament to glories past, struck Chinetti as reminiscent of a mausoleum.

But Chinetti had a hunch that he wanted to share with his old comrade from their Alfa days. The American market was one that European manufacturers had barely touched. The driving conditions were too different and there was no demand there for small cars. The term 'sports car' was almost unknown. Auto racing in America was the preserve not of the rich, as in Europe, but a predominantly blue-collar crowd who followed stock car and Indianapolis-style 'speed bowl' events. But the Americans that Chinetti had met through his time at Inskip were different – wealthy, cosmopolitan heirs to fortunes who, with the war out of the way, were keen to spend money and have fun. In 1944, a group of them had founded the Sports Car Club of America with a view to putting on a road circuit event along the lines of a European race. A leading light was Briggs Cunningham, whose family fortune came from railroads, meat packing and Procter & Gamble. Chinetti was convinced that Cunningham and his like were just the right clientele for the sort of cars Ferrari wanted to build, where no one would be fazed by the fuel consumption of a V12 – Europeans were still coping with petrol rationing. Chinetti told Ferrari that he would commit to selling five cars, and if Ferrari made twenty more he would sell those as well.

Ferrari listened but made no response; he had a lot on his mind. His workshops had been bombed twice by the Allies, and there was no certainty that with peace would come demand for the machine tools that had become his sole revenue stream. He also had fresh responsibilities. In May 1945 a second son, Piero, was born in secret to his mistress, Lina Lardi. Ferrari's commute from Modena to Maranello now included a detour to Castelvetro, where he had installed Lina in a secluded farmhouse. And his first, legitimate son, Dino, now thirteen, was beginning to show the symptoms of the undiagnosed muscular dystrophy to which he would succumb a decade later.

Despite these pressures and the uncertainty of what the post-war era held, Ferrari decided to go for broke, abandon for good the toolmaking business that had got him through the war and put everything into building his very own car. It was as if everything he had done before was an apprenticeship for what he now intended. In December 1946, when his machine had yet to turn a wheel, he had held a news conference in Modena and boldly announced his plan to build his own car and go racing. Franco Cortese, who acted as both test driver and salesman of his machine tools, was aghast at the decision which, he recalled, came in for heavy criticism. '"He's a nut-case. It will eat his money and finish him," was the prevailing view.'

After parting ways with Alfa Romeo and winding up Scuderia Ferrari, he had been commissioned to build a car based on Fiat parts for a truncated 1940 Mille Miglia. It had not been a success, but five years of war had made him impatient to try again. The logical thing to do would have been to use 'off the shelf' parts once again, but Ferrari wasn't having any of that; this would be 100 per cent his own car. All he needed was a designer, and he knew who to call.

32

Crossing the River Po

A decade before, at the 1936 Italian Grand Prix, as they watched a swastika-clad Auto Union take yet another victory, Enzo Ferrari had told Alfa Romeo's chief engineer Vittorio Jano that he should build a car for the smaller 1.5-litre 'voiturette' class of races, 'where there will be no Germans.' But Jano replied that he was already too busy. So Ferrari proposed he oversee the construction himself in Modena: 'You send me your best man, I will supply the Lambrusco and Zampone' (the latter stuffed pig's trotter, a Modenese delicacy).

Jano's best man, the one he called his 'right arm', was Gioachino Colombo. Born in Legnano, a small town outside Milan, he had started his draughtsman's training at the startlingly young age of fourteen before winning a scholarship sponsored by Alfa founder Nicola Romeo. Arriving at Portello in 1924, he had worked at Vittorio Jano's elbow from the P2 onwards. He was a mere twenty-five when he was put in charge of the drawing office, a great responsibility for one so young, overseeing the technical drawing for all road and racing cars. But after ten years, what he called his 'long apprenticeship' was starting to pall.

Jano, knowing Colombo would relish the opportunity, agreed to let him go to Scuderia Ferrari. It would also help to know that one of his closest lieutenants would be steering the outsourced project. For Colombo, the move was a liberation. There he was paired with Luigi Bazzi, another Alfa veteran, who had masterminded the dramatic twin-engined 16C *bimotore*.

Colombo arrived in Modena bristling with ideas he was keen to try out. He had in mind a layout similar to Ferdinand Porsche's all-conquering Auto Union with the engine behind the driver, but Ferrari vetoed it, uttering the famous line that would come back to haunt him two decades later: 'It has always been the ox that pulls the cart.' But back then, Ferrari wasn't being conservative so much as realistic. He had neither the resources nor the time to develop anything radically new. Nevertheless, Colombo's design broke new ground. Low-slung, with hydraulic brakes and independent suspension, it oozed modernity of a kind that Jano had latterly struggled to find. The Alfetta 158, the numerals denoting its 1.5-litre capacity and eight cylinders, was an innovative supercharged straight-eight design with dual cylinder blocks in light alloy, with twin overhead camshafts driven by a cascade of gears. To even out weight distribution, the gearbox was mounted directly onto the rear axle. Within a matter of months, the first machine was completed, and at Livorno in 1938 the Alfetta won its first voiturette race. There were a few more victories before the war intervened.

Could Ferrari prise Colombo away from Portello a second time? He had got through the war working on Alfa's diesel engines for military trucks, but by the summer of 1945 he was at home. He explained it as 'a temporary suspension, caused by political misunderstandings'. The Portello works liberation committee were investigating allegations of Fascist sympathies. But at the time what preoccupied him rather more was 'the sense of uselessness inside me which I'd already been feeling for some time'. Now forty-two, he feared his best years as a car designer were behind him, so the call from Ferrari was heaven-sent, 'something which could obliterate for me in one stroke those five years of war, bombardments, and sufferings, and all the upsets of evacuation'.

But just to get to a meeting with Ferrari posed challenges. In July 1945, petrol was only available on the black market, and all the bridges over the River Po still lay in ruins, so to make the 100-mile journey to Modena, Colombo had to queue for seven hours in the boiling sun for a barge to make the crossing.

After a tortuous drive along cratered roads, he met Ferrari at the old Scuderia premises in Modena. Colombo had enough experience of the man to know that he would not want anything too clever, that he believed that more than 50 per cent of success on the racing circuit was down to raw power. But when Colombo ventured to suggest he should build not a six or an eight cylinder, but a V12, Ferrari beamed, 'My dear Colombo, you read my thoughts.'

Like so many landmark moments in Italy's automotive story, the birth of a legend was preceded by a good meal. On the August public holiday, *ferragosto*, after a long lunch at his sister's house, Colombo sat down under a shady tree in her garden and started to sketch out the cylinder head of the first Ferrari V12. In the weeks that followed, back in his flat in Milan, on a drawing board borrowed from his cousin who worked for Carrozzeria Touring, he drafted the details of all the engine components – the technical drawings from which the first assemblies would be made. At Alfa, there were always components to be handed on or adapted to the next design, but not at Ferrari. Colombo was starting with a clean sheet.

Colombo called in Angelo Nasi, who had also worked on the Alfetta. He was delighted to be offered the task of designing a five-speed gearbox. By the time Colombo submitted his drawings to Ferrari, he had mapped out the entire car in such detail that he even included a helmeted driver grasping the steering wheel.

Colombo couldn't believe his luck. *Persona non grata* at Portello, which in any case was still in a state of ruin, he had miraculously managed to find a way back into motor racing. But in November 1945, just as he was handing over his drawings for the new Ferrari, he received a summons from Alfa Romeo – but not to answer charges about his erstwhile Fascist associations.

A Kind of Affliction

At the end of the war Portello was a factory in a state of near dereliction; two thirds of the plant had been destroyed. To get by, the firm was making window frames and wood-burning stoves which were in high demand as Milan had yet to be reconnected to a gas supply.

The assassination of Ugo Gobbato and chief engineer Ricart's return home to Spain had left a leadership vacuum at Alfa Romeo. Born in 1910 and not yet forty, Orazio Satta Puliga, known to all as Satta, was a different generation from the old guard. Hired by Ricart from the same Turin technical school as Dante Giacosa, Satta had arrived at Portello in 1937 with a degree in aeronautical engineering and expected to work on aircraft engines. He was in time to witness first-hand the tensions and upheavals that had dogged Alfa's last pre-war years under Gobbato.

Unlike his predecessors, Satta was no autocrat. Slim-built and unassuming, he was famous for never raising his voice or losing his temper. Consalvo Sanesi, Alfa Romeo's forthright pre-war test driver, thought him 'too soft, too nice'. But his manner belied a quiet self-confidence and a big brain that found room for four languages as well as engineering expertise. Tenacious and determined, he was very effective at getting his way without drawing attention to it.

With a ruined factory and all aero-engine activity outlawed by the Allies, Alfa was obliged to concentrate on automotive products. The first post-war cars were rehashes of 1930s models, but Satta saw little chance of a market for their sort of upmarket, largely hand-built machines. He and the newly appointed Alfa boss Pasquale Gallo agreed that a radical rethink was necessary. He started to lay down plans for a modest but thoroughly modern four-door saloon, which would have a wide enough appeal to give the company a chance of growing out of what was essentially a craft-based business. But developing it would take time.

Meanwhile, test driver Consalvo Sanesi found himself with time on his hands. Now thirty-four, since the age of eighteen he had worked for Alfa variously as a riding mechanic, test driver and occasional competitor. Now he was given a new assignment – behind the wheel of a truck in search of hidden treasure. During the war, fearful that one or other occupying force might confiscate them, Alfa's engineers dismantled and hid their precious racing machines away in various locations around Lombardy. 'It took more than a month to find them all,' Sanesi recalled. And when he did, 'they were so covered in grease it was difficult to grab hold of them!' Some were under a fake wood pile on a pig farm, others at a former textile mill in Melzo, 15km from Milan, at a farmhouse in the Abbiate region owned by the family of racing driver Achille Castoldi, and in the basement of a cheese factory.

Sanesi found the remains of Ricart's complicated Grand Prix machine, which he had dismissed as undrivable, but he also discovered three examples of the Colombo-designed 1.5 litre 158 Alfetta which had brought Alfa success in voiturette races before the war. Beyond getting the cars back to Portello, there was no plan for what to do with them until a rumour reached them from Paris that would put these pre-war machines in a whole new light.

Meeting for the first time since the war, motor sport's governing body, the Fédération Internationale de l'Automobile, was about to set out the rules for the first Grand Prix season. To keep the field as open as possible, they agreed there would be two engine sizes: 4.5 litres or 1.5 litres for those with superchargers. Since it would be a good while before anyone was in a position to build new racing motors, they reasoned that this inclusive formula would open it up to more machines and ensure a decent field.

Pasquale Gallo had served Alfa before. In 1926, after Nicola

Romeo had been ousted, it was Gallo who was brought in to replace him, but his tenure came to an abrupt end two years later when he was arrested for helping smuggle the anti-Fascist politician Cipriano Facchinetti out of the country in an Alfa prototype. Twenty years on, Facchinetti was now in the post-war cabinet and in a prime position to help Gallo and Alfa secure much needed financial aid.

For Gallo and Satta, preoccupied with the rebuilding of their shattered company, a return to motor racing should have come a very long way down their to-do list. More than once before the war, Alfa's competition activities had had to be scratched due to a financial crisis. But for all his pragmatism, Satta had to admit he had also fallen under the marque's spell. 'Alfa Romeo is not merely a make of automobile; it is truly something more than a conventionally built car. There are many automotive makes, among which Alfa Romeo stands apart. It is a kind of affliction, an enthusiasm for a means of transport. What it resists is definition. Its elements are like those of the human spirit which cannot be explained in logical terms. They are sensations, passions, things that have much more to do with a man's heart than with his brain.'

So, when presented with Sanesi's exhumations, 1.5-litre voiturettes now eligible for Grand Prix competition, the question for Satta and Gallo was not 'how could we go racing?' so much as 'how could we *not*?' And there was another question: who would be the best person to prepare the cars for their return?

In November 1945, as Colombo handed over his drawings to Ferrari, the message from his erstwhile employers came as a total surprise. Evidently any lingering concern about his political affiliations appeared to have been forgotten. He was needed back immediately; Alfa was about to go racing again.

Two Households in Fair Modena

The irony of this was not lost on Ferrari. He was about to lose Colombo, his key designer, to revive a car which the two of them had created and which Ferrari would have to compete against. And there was another problem: he was about to face more competition even closer to home – in fact, right across the street.

Since the late 1920s, the machines of Officine Alfieri Maserati S.p.A. had been an enduring presence on Italy's racing circuits. Brothers Alfieri, Bindo, Carlo, Ettore and Ernesto had worked for Fiat, Isotta Fraschini and other firms before joining forces to make spark plugs in their hometown of Bologna. Mario, yet another brother, an artist, designed the Maserati trident emblem. After Alfieri died in 1932 the other brothers carried on building racing cars, sometimes with great success. They were all talented engineers but none of them were businessmen.

Adolfo Orsi, born in 1888, was the eldest of eight. As a child, he helped his impoverished father collect scrap, which he continued after his father's death when he was fifteen. Determined to lift his family out of poverty, he made enough to purchase a forge and developed it into a thriving iron and steel plant. He also took over Modena's bus service and even the local football team. In 1937, attracted more by the lucrative spark plug business than the racing cars, he added the Bologna-based Maserati to his empire and moved the business closer to Modena, right opposite the original Ferrari premises.

Its presence had not troubled Ferrari until the end of the war when Orsi's son Omer, now managing director of Maserati, decided to resurrect the racing car business. Before the war, like Alfa Romeo, Maserati had produced a voiturette-sized racing car, the four-cylinder 4CL which was ripe for revival. To Ferrari's further irritation, Orsi hired another Scuderia Ferrari alumnus, Alberto Massimino.

On his recall to Alfa Romeo, Colombo did not leave Ferrari entirely in the lurch. He proposed another underemployed Alfa Romeo engineer, Giuseppe Busso, who jumped at the opportunity. But he struggled with Colombo's plans, which he found insufficiently focused. 'I had to be ruthless in order to pull the 125 through its childhood illnesses, which were neither few nor insignificant.' He and Luigi Bazzi had to struggle with poorly machined parts from suppliers and the scarcity of sufficiently high-grade materials in a country still recovering from the war.

Impatient to move forward, Ferrari hired in more expertise. Aurelio Lampredi, an aircraft engineer, was only twenty-seven when he joined Ferrari. Four years younger than Busso, he soon discovered that the two of them had diametrically opposite approaches to their work. As Lampredi explained it, 'To me the number-one priority was reliability. I came from the aeronautical industry where it was a matter of paramount importance. Here there was a tendency to improvise.'

This tension echoed the conflict that had divided Ferrari and Ricart at Alfa Romeo. Ferrari valued improvisation, but he also respected Lampredi's methodical approach and the fine-detailed mathematical precision of his drawings. Yet Ferrari, who liked to think of himself as 'an agitator of men', believed that creative tension between colleagues was a positive force, especially with the calming presence of Bazzi, the engine builder with whom he had worked since they first met at Portello in 1923.

When the Ferrari V12 burst into life in September 1946, little more than a year after Colombo sat down at his drawing board, the results were underwhelming. According to Lampredi, 'it gave 60 to 65 horsepower ... and revved up to 5,600, not even 6,000'. After six months he told Ferrari he was leaving; Isotta Fraschini were developing a new car. Ferrari agreed to let him go on the condition that if he called him back he would come. Remarkably for someone so young, and a relative newcomer to the business, Lampredi made several conditions for his return, the foremost being total independence from Busso and 'unlimited powers within the scope of my own work. A possible improvement of my salary was also mentioned.' Astonishingly, Ferrari agreed. The precocious Lampredi evidently knew his market value.

Seven months later Ferrari did call him back, telling him that 'there had been a number of developments within the company and that the conditions I had set before leaving could now be complied with'. Lampredi agreed, only after they had 'discussed my assignment down to the smallest details'. Busso was gone, headed back to Alfa Romeo to work on the engine for Satta's new family car, while Colombo returned to Ferrari as a part-time consultant.

Initially, Lampredi was delighted with the arrangement. Colombo more than made up for Lampredi's lack of racing engine experience and the two men bonded. Frequently after work they finished the evening in the local trattoria, talking about engines until late into the night. But it did not last. Lampredi soon despaired of Colombo's appetite for trial and error. 'If something doesn't work, he used to say, you just throw it away and make another one. My idea was that each plan should be carefully assessed before implementing it. I was firmly against plunging into things headlong, with the risk of losing time, money and credibility.'

On 12 March 1947, in his customary double-breasted suit, Enzo Ferrari squeezed behind the wheel of the first car to bear his name. Unlike him, the car was barely dressed, the engine was completely exposed and the dashboard sprouted a mass of wires. In those days, a racing car could be tried out on the public roads if the word 'Prova' (test) was painted on its tail along with two letters to indicate the town or city it came from, in this case MO for Modena. He didn't go far from Maranello, just up the Abetone road towards Modena before turning back at the village of Formigine. There were just six weeks to go until its first race, with Franco Cortese at the wheel.

Cortese found the Ferrari V12 a very different kind of beast from anything he'd driven before. 'If you were used to normal fours and sixes, this twelve was like an electric motor. It revved so easily, you always had to be on your guard. You had to drive it with your head and with your eye on the tachometer.' Cortese took part in ten provincial races and won six of them. Despite the clash of engineering egos during its development, Ferrari's new car worked. The bar was low – the rest of the field was all made up of pre-war machines – and the Ferraris were both fast and reliable.

Raymond Sommer came from a wealthy Parisian textile dynasty. In the early 1930s, he had co-driven both of the Le Mans-winning Alfa Romeos with Chinetti and Nuvolari and at forty-one was itching to get back behind the wheel. Entered for the Turin Grand Prix on 12 October, Sommer drove the cycle-winged Ferrari to a convincing victory against strong opposition, which included the revived Maserati. It was an emotional moment for Ferrari. The circuit was laid out in the Parco del Valentino where in 1918, jobless, cold and rejected by Fiat, he lay down and wept. 'I went and sat on that same bench. The tears I shed that day were of a very different kind.'

Return of the Champions

Tazio Nuvolari was a sick man. The emphysema he believed was caused by exhaust fumes was more likely to have been the result of his heavy smoking. Having already lost his first son, Giorgio, before the war, in 1946 his second, Alberto, died of kidney disease at just eighteen. Now, at fifty-five, an age when most other drivers had hung up their helmets, Nuvolari spent the winter in a sanitorium near Lake Como being nursed by nuns and emerged ready to race. Nobody would have judged him fit enough, but as he explained to British reporter Rodney Walkerley, 'I continue to race because what else is there for me to do? Besides, it makes me forget.'

In the first post-war Mille Miglia in 1947, at the wheel of an open-topped 1100cc Fiat-engined roadster, he showed that age, illness and grief had not dented his dedication. By the time he reached Rome, he was up in the lead, pursued by Clemente Biondetti in a supercharged 2.9-litre Alfa with more than twice the power. On the Apennine passes of Futa and Raticosa, Nuvolari increased his lead but during a huge downpour on a fast autostrada stretch between Turin and Brescia, Biondetti, in the comfort of his closed Touring coupé-bodied Alfa, caught him up. Nuvolari came to a stop with magneto failure brought on by the rain, but his mechanic Carena managed to fix it in time for them to come home second. As Biondetti observed magnanimously, 'I didn't win the race: I merely came first.'

Nuvolari visited Ferrari in Modena and told him he was ready to drive for him again – for the right price. Ferrari agreed on 145,000 lire for a two-race deal. Immediately he won an event at Forlì, before moving on to the Circuito di Parma where he had agreed to judge the Miss Parma contest the night before. On pole for the start, his engine failed and he was left behind, whereupon the crowd were treated to a vintage Nuvolari performance as he fought his way past fourteen cars in eighteen laps, leading Cortese home to a one–two Ferrari win. Mobbed by the ecstatic crowd, he freed himself by summoning the newly anointed Miss Parma and treating her to a lap of honour.

Not to be outshone by his lifelong rival, Achille Varzi made an even more unlikely return to the track. Having been written off as a hopeless drug addict, in 1941 he married Norma Colombo, the woman he had spurned for Ilse Pietsch six years before, and with her help overcame his addiction.

The 1946 Turin Grand Prix was the first race to be held according to the new FIA regulations. Alfa Romeo were back with their revived 158 Alfettas and Varzi, now forty-two and fit, led the team to victory. He followed up with three second places and another win the following year. But in July 1948, practising for the Swiss Grand Prix at Bern, he lost control in the rain, clipped a kerb and overturned. He was killed instantly. Alfa Romeo promptly announced their withdrawal, but Norma insisted they race. She was in no doubt it was what her husband would have wanted. Alfas came home first and second.

Unlike his two rivals, Ferrari had only one thing to focus on. His sole interest was motor racing. He had no shareholders to satisfy, no other businesses vying for his attention. Nothing would distract him. Single-minded and driven, Ferrari had his own unique method of man management, as Romolo Tavoni would discover when he was taken on as Ferrari's secretary.

The son of a local farmer, Tavoni had been a clerk for Maserati, a job he loved because he got to meet racing drivers, but during a violent dispute between Orsi and militant foundry workers he was sacked. He found work in a bank where Ferrari happened to be a customer. When Ferrari let it be known he was looking for a secretary, the manager offered to let him try out Tavoni. 'I did not want to work for him. I'd heard that he had a new secretary every two or three months and worked from eight in the morning until ten at night.'

Ferrari summoned him to an interview and asked where he had worked before. 'I told him I had worked as a bookkeeper for Maserati, hoping that he would say, "Go away!", because in Modena if you worked for Maserati you never worked for Ferrari. But he said, "Fine."' On his first day Tavoni didn't get home until after eleven.

Ferrari identified qualities in Tavoni that he liked: total obedience and discretion. Soon he was delivering money to Ferrari's wife, and to Lina Lardi, Ferrari's mistress, the mother of his secret son Piero. After two months Tavoni summoned up the courage to tell Ferrari he wanted to go back to the bank. 'He was astounded. "Why? Ferrari is not as good as the bank?" I told him that I was tired of staying until ten at night. At the bank I started at nine, at eleven took a cappuccino, at twelve had lunch and at six it was time to go home. "Are you stupid?", said Mr Ferrari. "Maybe you get a job in a bar or a restaurant? At Ferrari this is work. If you'd like to stay you can, otherwise I will see to it that there is no place for you at the bank."' Tavoni stayed.

After three months he got a 5,000 lire raise but after another two months Ferrari cut his pay by 7,500, telling him, '"I'm not satisfied so you will get less money." . . . Ferrari owned the factory but the way he saw it he also owned the men who worked there. Ferrari could be very kind and friendly but he was like a bomb waiting to go off and he would suddenly explode.' And it wasn't just with newcomers. Luigi Bazzi had been with him since the start of Scuderia Ferrari and was responsible for building the engines. Tavoni witnessed Bazzi's protest when Ferrari complained about a job that was running late.

'"Mr Ferrari, I have been working twelve hours every day." To which Ferrari shouted, "But there are twenty-four hours in every day." On other occasions he was complimentary – and then would complain again. Ferrari was *simpatico e terrible – terrible e simpatico*.'

The quest for a viable Grand Prix contender was costing Ferrari more than he had bargained for in time and money. In Italy's first post-war Grand Prix at Monza in 1948, Alfa Romeo took the first four places while the two Ferraris both retired.

He needed big high-profile races to attract attention so he focused on sports car events where outright top speed and acceleration were less critical. Before his return to Alfa Romeo, Giuseppe Busso enlarged Colombo's V12 to two litres and Ferrari put it into what became known as the 166, a sports car that he could also sell to the sort of wealthy private 'gentleman racers' who had been his Scuderia clientele before the war – and who Luigi Chinetti claimed were also to be found in America.

French-Russian Prince Igor Troubetzkoy was a penniless playboy but a capable athlete who had just made an expedient marriage. Barbara Hutton, granddaughter of F. W. Woolworth, the department store magnate, was one of the world's wealthiest women. At the end of 1947, she bought him a two-litre 166 and with Count Bruno Sterzi, who bought another, he formed the Scuderia Inter racing team. Troubetzkoy had every intention of trying his hand at racing. In May 1948 he paired up with the vastly experienced Clemente Biondetti to enter the first post-war Targa Florio, and gave Ferrari its first high-profile win. The gruelling race, rerouted to avoid the war-damaged roads, showed that Ferrari, in sports car form at least, had the necessary stamina as well as the performance to win.

Emboldened, Ferrari entered two cars in the upcoming Mille Miglia. A few days before the event he got a call from Nuvolari. The team he was due to race with wasn't ready. He didn't have to try too hard to persuade Ferrari to bump one of his drivers and let him have a car. Once again, despite his age and health, Nuvolari shamed the naysayers, fighting his way past two Alfas, a Maserati and the other Ferrari. Leading at Ravenna, he had already lost the engine cover and a mudguard when he left the road in the Abruzzi mountains. On the Raticosa pass his seat came loose, so he threw it out and sat instead on the sack of oranges he had brought along for refreshment. At Rome, where he stopped for fuel and tyres, a radio reporter thrust a microphone in his face but Nuvolari showed no response. By Bologna he had opened a formidable twenty-nine-second lead over Biondetti in the second Ferrari and with the mountains behind him all he had was a straight, fast run back to Brescia. But with less than 200 miles to go, his rear brakes stopped working, then a pothole smashed the rear suspension. He struggled on until he approached the next checkpoint at Villa Ospizio, where Ferrari was spectating, and came to a sliding stop. He was out of the race. Ferrari told him not to be downhearted: 'We will do it again next year', to which the driver replied, 'at our age days like this don't come along too often'.

Nuvolari asked for somewhere he could lie down, and a village priest gave him a bed. Biondetti won for Ferrari, but, as was so often the case with Nuvolari, there was no question who was the hero of the race.

But it wasn't Nuvolari's last Ferrari drive. In Mantua, his home-town, he led the field in a fifty-lap race in memory of his two sons, the Coppa Alberto e Giorgio. But Biondetti overtook him and after seven laps, convulsed by a coughing fit, Nuvolari retired. After his last event in 1950, he disappeared from public view, remaining at home among the cherished model cars of his dead sons, poring over photo albums of his past glories.

'Bury me in my uniform' was the instruction he gave his wife. He died in the last place anyone expected him to, not at the wheel of a racing car like so many of his contemporaries and successors, but in his bed, age sixty, succumbing to the emphysema from which he had suffered for years. He was buried in the family vault beside his sons, in his trademark blue trousers, yellow shirt with embroidered tortoise, and leather helmet.

The Little Boat

uccess in both the Targa Florio and the Mille Miglia, two long, punishing road races, proved that the new V12 Ferrari 166 sports car was both competitive and durable, but it lacked charisma. Like many racing cars, the workmanlike bodies of the first Ferraris had been little more than functional afterthoughts. From his Scuderia days fielding Alfa sports cars, Ferrari was familiar with Touring's lightweight *superleggera* construction and in March 1948 asked Felice Bianchi Anderloni to prepare two designs, an open two-seater and a four-seater coupé, in time for that September's Turin Salone dell'Automobile. But in May, Anderloni died, leaving his 32-year-old son Carlo in charge. On the face of it this seemed a huge blow for both Touring and Ferrari. As well as triumphing with his patented *superleggera* construction method, Felice Anderloni seemed to have an intuitive understanding of what customers wanted from the shape of a car. But Ferrari needn't have been concerned as Touring had a secret weapon.

Like Pinin Farina, Federico Formenti came to car design with no training or education. At fourteen, Mimo, as he was known to all, started work in a Milan machine shop sweeping floors and washing down the machinery. But he possessed a natural gift for drawing three-dimensional forms and making models of them. Observing this, his brother-in-law, a technical draughtsman at Touring, introduced Formenti to Felice Anderloni who was sufficiently impressed to take him on as an assistant to his chief stylist, Giuseppe Belli.

When Belli left Touring in 1948, Formenti took over. Although well taught by Belli and an admirer of the swooping lines of his pre-war Alfas, Forment's Ferrari owed nothing to the past.

Unlike the entrepreneurially minded Pinin Farina, Mimo Formenti was happy to stay in the background, at his drawing board in the Touring factory in Via Ludovico di Breme in Milan, wielding a Caran d'Ache Technograph pencil and shrouded in cigarette smoke, where he attracted nothing like the attention or credit of his more flamboyant peers. With Anderloni's son Carlo in charge of the business he was left to get on with the project. The one-tenth scale model they showed Ferrari was approved at first sight. The ultra-modern design was smooth and clean-lined. Any hint of separate wings was gone. Instead of going straight down to the chassis, the sides of the body curved under and hugged the big wire wheels, giving the shape a muscular composure. A thin 'belt line' rib ran from the front-wheel arch along the sides all the way to the rear, tapering to the back which featured just the licence plate holder and a pair of lights. At the front an 'egg crate' design for the grille would become a standard feature of Ferraris ever after. It was wilfully simple and became a template for all sports cars of the 1950s.

The Turin Motor Show in 1948, the first since the war, was a showcase for pent-up talent and creativity. 'It was like a giant compressed spring,' recalled Filippo Sapino, then still a boy but a future designer who was aware of what was happening. With Italy's populace now starting to look forward rather than back, that 'spring' was released. The Ferrari caused a sensation. When journalist Giovanni Canestrini saw it, finished in a gleaming, faintly metallic vermilion, he exclaimed that it reminded him of a *barchetta*, a little boat. The name stuck. Luigi Chinetti, back again from New York, was thrilled by what he saw. Even though it was barely finished, lacking an exhaust system and with an engine borrowed from a previous race car, he snapped it up for the wealthy West Coast enthusiast and dealer Tommy Lee. A few months later he sold a second 166 to his other top client, Procter & Gamble heir and amateur racer Briggs Cunningham.

Chinetti was now determined to give Ferrari the profile it would need to make its mark in America. But winning the Mille Miglia and the Targa Florio did not mean much across the Atlantic. The only European race that resonated over there was Le Mans. Badly damaged by the war after the Luftwaffe used it as an air base, the roads and grandstands of the track were not repaired until the spring of 1949. Even then a section of the infield remained off limits as it had yet to be cleared of land mines.

A change in the regulations favoured Ferrari, who by then had only produced a handful of cars. Since its start in 1923, Les Vingt-Quatre Heures du Mans had been exclusively for production cars, but fearing a field full of warmed-over pre-war machinery, the organisers opened it up to one-off sports prototypes 'as an exceptional measure to contribute towards a faster revival of automobile manufacture'.

But when Chinetti took his proposal to Ferrari he hesitated, worried that the demands of twenty-four hours on a road circuit, which included the two-mile-long flat-out Mulsanne Straight, were so punishing it might not survive the night. Still, undaunted, Chinetti bought two machines and entered them privately, one for himself and his co-driver Lord Selsdon, the other for a French crew.

As it turned out the organisers, the Automobile Club de l'Ouest, were swamped with more than a hundred prospective entrants, which they whittled down to a still substantial forty-nine. The field was dominated by French cars from Delage, Delahaye and Talbot-Lago, big, exotic machines with their roots deep in the 1930s, while a solitary pre-war Bentley recalled the British streak of victories in the twenties. Another team which took advantage of the new prototype rules was Aston Martin, recently revived by David Brown, embarking on what would be a ten-year campaign to win the great race.

Initially it looked like the Ferraris, the only Italian cars entered, would be no match for the pair of Delahayes that led after the start, both of which eventually overheated and expired early in the night. After a second privateer's Ferrari crashed, Chinetti was on his own, battling Talbot-Lagos and Delages, but by midnight he had taken a slim lead. Having driven from the start, Chinetti let Selsdon take over at 4.30 a.m., but an hour later he was back behind the wheel, where he stayed to the finish almost twelve hours later. Despite a slipping clutch, one lost gear and an oil leak, he managed to keep the lead and fend off the French cars. Ferrari won at an average speed of 82.28 mph without even changing a tyre. Three weeks away from his forty-eighth birthday, Chinetti, who had won twice before for Alfa Romeo, would also become Le Mans' oldest victor.

37

Spare Room in the Palazzo

While Italy's cars and drivers stamped their authority on the post-war racing scene with dizzying speed, the nation's mainstream motor industry was taking its time. Fiat's Vittorio Valletta sought investment to rebuild and modernise Fiat's badly damaged factories, his hopes for a rapid return to production dogged by the scarcity of parts and raw materials. Alfa Romeo president Pasquale Gallo's contacts with the post-war government had helped secure support for the state-owned business, but as yet it had no product suitable for the market, while Lancia struggled on with its pre-war models. All three companies were in danger of being left behind by the rest of the world.

While the war in Europe effectively froze all car design and development, Detroit had powered ahead. Pressed steel bodies had become the norm on American cars, which altered dramatically their shape as well as their construction. Previously separate parts, bonnet, wings and roof, were absorbed into an all-enveloping single 'shell', the panels stamped into shape by vast hydraulic presses. The American cars of the 1940s made everything in Europe look obsolete. Italy's car makers had a lot of catching up to do.

What Italy had no shortage of was talent. Like Alfa Romeo's Gioachino Colombo and Giuseppe Busso, Fiat's Dante Giacosa, creator of the Topolino, was just as impatient to get back to making cars. In October 1944, when the war was still raging and Fiat's drawing offices shut down, he had secretly agreed to design a racing car for

Piero Dusio, textile industrialist, former Juventus midfielder-turned-club president and amateur racing driver. An added attraction for Giacosa of moonlighting for Dusio was the use of his Turin palazzo which the family had vacated. Except for a caretaker and a servant, it lay empty and although there was some bomb damage, Giacosa thought it 'extremely beautiful ... Dusio offered me a pleasant bedroom on the top floor with a bathroom and two other rooms for my drawing boards. A palace no less, even though the heating was provided by a cast-iron stove that burnt wood.'

One casualty of the war was Giacosa's initial design for the body shape, which he had done as a 1:5 model carved in plasticine. 'I had just finished it ... when the German police raided the house – during my absence – in search of Dusio, who was accused of some crime or other. They hunted high and low for him, naturally in vain as he was hardly ever there. But when I came back I found that my model had been squashed flat by the fist of some fulminating German.'

Inspired by the frames of the Beltrame bicycle made by one of Dusio's businesses, he came up with a groundbreaking chassis made entirely from tubular steel. '*Ngegne! Che curage ... quel telaio in tubi!*' was his friend and racing car engineer Alberto Massimino's reaction in Piedmontese dialect when he saw it: 'Engineer, what a nerve you've got: that chassis is made of tubes!'

Dusio organised its manufacture in his bicycle works and named the new venture Cisitalia, a compression of Consorzio Industriale Sportiva Italia, and by September 1946 seven cars were ready to race in Turin's Parco del Valentino. The cream of Europe's racing drivers, including Nuvolari, desperate to get back behind the wheel, queued up to drive the little cars, powered by tuned-up production Fiat engines. With just three French Gordinis as competition, Cisitalia swept the board, with Dusio himself the winner. However, Giacosa's joy was tempered by the fate of Nuvolari. Because of the surrounding tubular frame, the cockpit was a tight fit so Giacosa came up with an ingenious solution. The steering wheel was mounted on a locking hinge so that it could be lifted up to ease access. But after a few corners Nuvolari's steering wheel came off in his hands, so he tossed it away and attempted to drive on using the spurs on the steering column to which the wheel had been fixed.

Spurred on by this success, Dusio forged ahead with plans for a two-seater. But Giacosa's time at Cisitalia came to an end when he was summoned back to Fiat. Before he left he drew up the chassis for the two-seater. All it needed was a body.

Merchants in the Temple

Like Giacosa, Battista Pinin Farina had not allowed the war to dampen his boundless optimism. And like almost every other small metalworking business his had kept afloat by turning out parts for the war effort, in his case aircraft fuselage parts and, as the war wore on, the more mundane necessities of life. He possessed a rebellious energy not unlike film-maker Roberto Rossellini's, impatient to make his mark on the post-war world, to make a noise, no matter what.

But would the time-honoured customs and practices of the *carrozzerie* survive in the post-war world? The style-conscious Gianni Agnelli thought so. 'A client of Pinin's could watch the preparation of their car they had ordered step by step, week after week, something like watching the construction of a house in which you are going to live. More than a coachbuilder's shop it was an atelier, a jeweller's with an artistic genius overseeing it all.'

In 1946 Pinin Farina prepared two new designs on pre-war chassis, an Alfa Sport 2500 which boasted innovative ideas like simple buttons rather than handles to open the doors and a Lancia Aprilia cabriolet with a hood that folded right down into the bodywork. Both cars were startlingly smooth, unadorned shapes. Hearing that Paris was mounting its first post-war Salon d'Auto, he confided in his 20-year-old son Sergio, an engineering student at Turin Polytechnic, his hope that they would exhibit. But Sergio discovered that the organisers had banned both Italy and Germany from exhibiting. His father would not be put off. Along with two friends, they set off in the two cars for Paris. At the border, the customs officers sounded doubtful: 'Pininfarina is going to set up shop in the European markets which are still closed.'

But as they made their way through France, stopping in town squares along the way, Pinin Farina was pleased with the reception they received. When they reached the outskirts of Paris, they cleaned the cars and proceeded to the Grand Palais where the show was taking place. Sure enough, they were not allowed in but 'With the help of two obliging *flics* we found space for the two cars opposite the entrance to the exhibition, so people coming in and out of the Grand Palais stopped to look at them.' Soon 'hundreds of onlookers' were examining the Alfa and the Lancia. When word got round, the officials came to look and then the exhibitors, many of whom were old acquaintances.

'*Ce diable de Farina*,' they exclaimed, '*a ouvert son salon personnel*.' Then they escorted him into the show, 'and took me round the stands as if I was an important person'. The next day, Pinin Farina's cars were on the front pages of all the Paris newspapers. '*Antisalon du carrossier Turinois Pininfarina*', father and son, and their cars photographed in front of the Opera, under the Arc de Triomphe and at Les Invalides. 'For me the war ended that day.'

But any sense of triumph was short-lived. The day before Christmas Eve, Pinin was woken at 3 a.m. with a phone call. It was his works caretaker: their factory was on fire. From his upstairs window he could see the orange glow coming from the direction of Corso Trapani. It was so big that the firemen were at a loss to know where to start. 'Master models, prototypes and plant which had cost me money, sacrifice and patience were all going up in flames.' Despite the heat of the fire, the water being pumped by the fire engines began to freeze in the cold night air. There were explosions in the roof of ammunition hidden there by the resistance. As well as all his materials, trophies from *concours* events, photographs, drawings and models were all lost. Pinin estimated the damage at 50 million lire. 'They were things which represented my history – if I had a right to a history – and in half an hour all that was left was a floor of thick, muddy ash.' Having got through the war almost unscathed, Pinin's factory was gone.

His insurance covered no more than one sixth of his loss. All the available concrete was being used for reconstructing the city, so Farina and his staff built a temporary wooden canopy. Two months later the business was almost back to normal. 'But I left some smoke stains on the façade – to remember.'

European coachbuilders were struggling after the war. Extravagance was out of fashion, as were big cars needing bespoke bodywork. Pressed steel brought mass production to car bodies and the separate chassis was beginning to disappear with the development of monocoque or 'unibody' construction. Paris ceased to be the capital of automotive couture as French taxes heavily penalised expensive cars while traditional British coachbuilders, some of them centuries old, became irrelevant in a country increasingly enamoured of all things American.

The cars that Pinin Farina had shown off in Paris were designs he had done on spec and sold on afterwards to private individuals. What he needed was a commission from a car manufacturer to design a body and then make it in numbers to create a revenue stream. Cisitalia looked like a good opportunity. Piero Dusio had ambitions to join the ranks of Italy's car makers so Pinin and his team set to work on a template.

The car would be tiny, much smaller than anything he was used to working on, but for him that was part of the challenge, to make something special in spite of its size. 'I knew that the old shapes were out. Decorations on shirt fronts were deemed ridiculous so cars had to have pure smooth essential lines too. We could no longer use the same old symbols which looked like a bunch of sanitary fittings ... If a designer pursues the cosmetics of a vehicle too far then he forgets the function ... I did not just care about the newness of the details; I was interested in the renewal of the architecture of the whole unit.'

On Pinin Farina's Cisitalia, the bonnet sat lower than the tops of the wings, the opposite of current American fashion. 'I had reached the point in my profession where what counts is neither the technical knowledge nor the pure form, what counts is being able to put them together without any effort or at least making this effort obvious.' The result was an astonishingly simple, organic shape devoid of eye-catching features or precociousness. Only a few were made; Cisitalia was doomed by Dusio's own ambition, over-extending himself on an advanced racing car project, after which he decided to move to Argentina and make a fresh start. And Pinin Farina's little coupé might have disappeared into automotive history had not its striking purity caught the attention of two of New York's most influential art commentators.

In 1951, Arthur Drexler had just joined the city's Museum of Modern Art as curator of architecture and design. One of his first acts was to mount an exhibition entitled 'Eight Automobiles'. The intention was to explore how cars had evolved into 'hollow rolling sculptures', and recognise automotive styling as a craft worthy of intellectual contemplation, criticism and broader discussion. Among the cars chosen were imposing Mercedes and Bentleys from a bygone age, but from the vast array of post-war designs Drexler singled out Pinin Farina's little Cisitalia as the most modern expression of this development.

Reaching deep into the lexicon of design criticism to explain his reasoning, he noted how, 'The Cisitalia's body is slipped over its chassis like a dust jacket over a book ... To maintain the sculptural unity of the entire shape its surfaces are never joined with sharp edges, but are instead wrapped around and blunted. The door is minimized to prevent it from contradicting the appearance of a taut metal skin. ... Thus both ends of the car gain an extraordinary tension, as though its metal skin did not quite fit over the framework and had to be stretched into place. This accounts, in part, for that quality of animation which makes the Cisitalia seem larger than it is.'

On seeing his car on show in such a hallowed space, 'I felt like I was walking through a dream,' Pinin Farina recalled, noting how it made him reflect on his life, going back to the poverty of his childhood and his apprenticeship. The Cisitalia would become the first car to join MOMA's permanent collection, but even in the face of such recognition, Pinin Farina didn't let the accolade go to his head. 'I still saw myself as an outsider in that ambience. I could not free myself from certain complexes to do with my profession: I knew that the intellectuals of Europe would have considered us to be merchants in the temple.'

Viva Italiana

In mid-twentieth-century America, Paris was regarded as the style capital of the world. Of Italy's products, Gucci bags and Ferragamo shoes had found an exclusive clientele among the fortunate few, but the French put them in the shade with their exclusive exotic fashions. Before the war, Florentine entrepreneur Giovanni Battista Giorgini had tried selling Italian ceramics and glassware to American department stores and developed a sense of what suited American tastes. In 1945, back in Florence, the Allied authorities put him in charge of the Allied Forces Gift Shop, selling Italian-made goods which found a ready market among British and American troops. Emboldened by his success, he created a travelling exhibition, 'Made In Italy', which toured American museums and galleries showcasing Italian craft. But his breakthrough came in fashion. Through his contact with American store buyers he discovered that what appealed to them was not the haute couture of the Paris catwalk but something much more attainable and mainstream.

In February 1951, right after Paris Fashion Week, he organised what he billed as the 'First Italian High Fashion Show' at his family villa in Florence and invited six buyers. There was no catwalk: it was more of an intimate house party. One of the designers on show was Emilio Pucci.

An accidental fashionista and accomplished skier, Pucci had managed to wangle a scholarship to Reed College in Portland, Oregon. In exchange for tuition he would coach their ski team. He also revamped the team's uniform, dispensing with their bulky winter clothes in favour of specially made form-fitting garments in stretch fabrics. When department stores picked up on it, he turned his attention to beachwear – stylish, fun and relaxed. 'Fashion,' he explained, 'is the essence of modern life. It is movement. We must capture it and give it freedom. It is the vision of tomorrow realised today.' Pucci's dictum could have applied just as well to Pinin Farina's Cisitalia.

Giorgini's shows were a hit. 'Italian Styles Gain Approval of US Buyers' ran a headline in the fashion bible *Women's Wear Daily*. The next show before Paris Fashion Week attracted 150 buyers. 'Everyone seems interested in Italy,' Bettina Ballard, fashion editor of *Vogue*, told Giorgini.

Rossellini's *Roma città aperta,* along with Vittorio De Sica's 1948 classic *Bicycle Thieves (Ladri di biciclette),* had an impact on Hollywood, as did the idea of using Italy as a location. The whole of Cinecittà and thousands of Romans were mobilised for *Quo Vadis* in 1951, but the 1953 sparkling romantic comedy *Roman Holiday* had a far greater cultural impact, juxtaposing the timeless beauty of Rome with the modern energy of its stars. Audrey Hepburn as a bored European princess escapes her suffocating, entitled world to discover simple, everyday pleasures, darting around the Italian capital with reporter Gregory Peck not by car, but astride a brand-new device that would come to be a symbol of post-war Italy's reinvention, a triumph of ingenuity over adversity.

Corradino D'Ascanio had graduated from the same Turin Polytechnic as Giacosa. In the 1930s he became a celebrated helicopter designer, pioneering the ultra-sophisticated engineering behind the first viable helicopters. But after the war, the restrictions imposed on Italy included a ban on all aircraft construction. D'Ascanio was no stranger to hardship; after the previous war, to feed his family he had designed ovens and even a war memorial.

Asked to rethink cheap two-wheeled transport appropriate for a country struggling to get mobile again, D'Ascanio, who hated motorcycles and had never ridden one, came up with a wilfully simple domesticated alternative. All the controls were confined to the handlebars. Its engine was totally enclosed, protecting the riders from the oily mechanical parts and fixed right next to the hub of the rear wheel, dispensing with chain drive; the frame was fabricated out of sheet metal and included a splash guard that shielded the riders' legs from road dirt. And the space between the steering column and the seat meant it could be mounted without having to swing a leg over the saddle, a particular plus for women in skirts. The small-diameter wheels were easy to change as there were no forks and there was even room for a spare.

When its eventual manufacturer, Enrico Piaggio, who had built trains and aircraft before the war, saw the design, he noted the slim metal footrest that connected the steering column to the bulbous engine and is reputed to have exclaimed, '*Sembra una vespa!*' ('It looks like a wasp!'). The production run of 2,000 sold out in its first year and 10,000 were sold in the second.

Piaggio's marketing exhorted customers 'to take up the opportunities that come your way, to not give up your desires; to enjoy your freedom and fill it to the brim; to race, on a Vespa of course, to reach the goals which your heart gives you – even if others want to stop you from reaching them'.

Not only did the Vespa create a revolution in domesticated two-wheeled transport, the ingenuity of its design, simple yet clever and appealing, laid down a template for the direction much of post-war Italian design would take. Simple, resourceful, accessible, enjoyable and entirely modern, it owed nothing to the past or heritage. Its starring role in *Roman Holiday* endorsed the Vespa as an item that was functional yet also stylish and chic. It would be easy to make too much of this fortuitous product placement. The scooter never took off in America, but the film featuring two of Hollywood's biggest stars of the era astride D'Ascanio's cunning creation carried a message for Italian designers that what was chic could also be made affordable; style could be democratised.

El Chueco

Like the United States, South America in the nineteenth century was a destination for Italians fleeing poverty in search of a better life. One such émigré family, farm labourers from the Abruzzi mountains, settled in the town of Balcarce, a potato-farming centre 220 miles south of Buenos Aires. Born in June 1911, Juan Manuel was the fourth of six Fangio children.

Argentina was a motor-racing backwater. Ford and Chevrolet cars and trucks were virtually the only vehicles. As a boy, Juan aspired to be a footballer and showed promise as a midfielder, his particular stance earning him the nickname 'El Chueco', 'the bow-legged one'. At thirteen he dropped out of school to work in the local garage. Parts were scarce and so was money, so he soon learned how to apply ingenuity to prolonging the life of tired machinery. 'You had to be a bit of a blacksmith as well as a mechanic,' he recalled. He learned to drive delivering customers' cars. On the untarmacked mountain roads that turned to fine, choking dust in the heat and rivers of soup-like mud in the rain, Fangio perfected the art of car control with the throttle and gears to tame wild slides – all at an impressionable age.

Capable and enterprising, he set up his own workshop and petrol station in Balcarce when he was still in his twenties and in 1936 took part in his first competition in a borrowed Ford taxi, removing the body before the race and replacing it afterwards.

South America had its own brand of motor racing in the 1930s, two-week-long dashes across plains and over mountain passes, which were brutal tests of driver and machine. In the 1939 Gran Premio Argentino de Carretera covering 4,600 miles, he came seventh. Two hundred and forty citizens of Balcarce stumped up to help Fangio buy a car for the race. He wanted a V8 Ford but, unable to find one, settled for a six-cylinder Chevrolet. His aptitude for ingenuity came into its own when dealing with a shortage of oil in the sump, which he cunningly overcame by adding water on which the oil would float, raising its level to meet the moving parts. Having come seventh in that race, he claimed first a year later in a marathon to publicise the Pan-American Highway. The route went from Buenos Aires up to Bolivia, Lima in Peru and back, a round trip of 10,000km. Stamina was everything – for car and driver. 'We kept ourselves going by eating cloves of garlic and chewing coca leaves.' On one occasion, in blazing heat, he took apart a back axle and changed a half-shaft; another time, parched with thirst, he drank water from horses' hoof-prints.

Shrewd in business, he built a haulage company around his public fame and by the end of the war was thriving with a busy trade in US Army war surplus trucks. And Fangio might well have remained no more than a local hero but for the election in 1946 of General Juan Perón. Of Spanish-Sardinian heritage, Perón had trained in mountain warfare in Italy and studied in Turin where he developed a strong affection for all things Italian. Building commercial ties with Europe, he believed, would be an antidote to the overbearing influence of the United States.

In January 1949, while Europe was in the grip of winter, Argentina hosted a Formula Libre racing series called Temporada, offering big inducements to tempt Europe's top drivers and teams to cross the Atlantic. For local drivers, the Argentine Auto Club purchased a pair of Maserati 4CLTs. Tested against such Italian luminaries as Alberto Ascari and Nino Farina, they hoped they might keep up. Fangio went one better than that. In the fourth event at Mar del Plata he came first, ahead of Ascari in another Maserati, with more power. The track was only 35 miles from Fangio's hometown and of the 300,000 crowd an estimated 30,000 had made the journey from Balcarce for that Sunday's race. Observed Fangio: 'The only person in church was the priest.'

Perón, thrilled by the showing of his countrymen, seized what he saw as an opportunity to promote Argentina in Europe and sponsored a four-car team to compete in the nation's blue and yellow colours. Slightly reluctant to leave his now thriving garage business, Fangio accepted an invitation to join the team thinking that maybe he could give it a year and try to get 'one win'.

At their first meeting in San Remo, Fangio immediately excelled – in the garage first. When his Maserati engine lost oil pressure he got to work, found the failed con-rod bearing, polished out the scoring on the rod journal and fitted a new bearing before going to bed at 1 a.m. The next day he led the race from start to finish.

Enzo Ferrari first saw Fangio in action testing at Modena's Autodromo and was immediately impressed. 'He was perhaps the only driver who came out of the bends without shaving the bales of straw on the outer verge. This Argentinian, I told myself, knows his job: he comes out of the bends like a cannonball, keeping right in the middle of the track.'

British motor sport reporter Rodney Walkerley was another admirer who observed Fangio 'driving as fast as possible from start to finish of the race, sliding all his corners and giving very little quarter – in fact motor racing all the time.' Gregor Grant in *Autosport* remarked on Fangio's lack of personal conceit and how he was 'completely free from the petty jealousies that invariably go with continual striving for recognition'. He scored a hat-trick in the first three races he entered in Europe. En route to victory at Pau in the South of France he stopped for oil and when the mechanic couldn't restart the engine, Fangio leaped out, pushed him aside and cranked it himself. The band didn't have the music for the Argentine anthem so instead they played a Brazilian march. He achieved his fourth win in a row in Marseilles.

When he flew home, he was a national hero, greeted personally by General Perón at the presidential palace. The next year, 1950, he was back in Europe for the first ever Formula One season, though not yet with a drive. At San Remo, Alfa Romeo's Giuseppe 'Nino' Farina, recovering from a crash, was unable to race. Fangio convinced them to let him have a go up against Ascari and Villoresi's Ferraris. Despite a bad start he worked his way up to the front and won. Alfa immediately offered him a contract. '"First we have to agree what money you want." I just signed it and told them to fill in the noughts ... They were the greatest Grand Prix team in the world and they were giving me the chance to drive their fantastic car. I felt like a singer suddenly invited to perform at La Scala di Milano or the Metropolitan in New York.'

41

Taking on the Victors

As ever at Alfa Romeo, a sudden fit of fiscal prudence tempered the competitive urge. Despite the success of its 158 Alfettas in 1948, they elected to sit out the next Grand Prix season, but a whip-round by a passionate Alfa Romeo dealer network raised 200 million lire and the team was back with a vengeance for 1950.

New recruit Juan Manuel Fangio regarded himself at thirty-nine as middle-aged, but, as it turned out, alongside Giuseppe 'Nino' Farina, forty-four, and Luigi Fagioli, fifty-two, he was the 'baby' of the team comprising men who had made their mark in motor racing in the 1930s. After the five-year-long interruption of the war, they were impatient to make up for lost time. Together they came to be known as Alfa's 'Three Fs', with Farina the self-appointed team leader.

Nino was born in 1906, the day his father Giovanni and uncle Pinin opened their first workshop in Turin, Stabilimenti Farina. But his upbringing was in stark contrast to their humble beginnings. Initially, his career path looked more like that of an Agnelli. He studied law to doctorate level, distinguished himself in the cavalry and off duty excelled on the ski slopes. But he had been driving since the age of nine when he was given a twin-cylinder Temperino. Competing against his father in his first race in 1925, he crashed and broke his collarbone. He did not race again until 1933 when he immediately demonstrated his potential driving for Alfa Romeo, but the war stopped his progress. In 1946 he was hired back to Alfa. Of him Fangio said, 'He drove like a madman. We used to say that he was protected by the Madonna, but even the holy Madonna's patience has a limit and he should have considered that she could not be at his disposal all the time.' Ferrari described him as 'a man whose courage was so great that it bordered on the impossible . . . He was like a thoroughbred at the gate who would sprint away from the pack; he was also capable of madness as he neared the finish line. So he had memberships of the hospital wards.'

Luigi Fagioli was one of the oldest of the pre-war old guard. Vastly experienced, having driven his first Grand Prix in 1926, he served in both the dominant German Silver Arrows teams of the 1930s, his enthusiasm and aggression showing no signs of decline.

There was a certain poignancy about the choice of venue for the opening of the first ever Grand Prix drivers' world championship. Just five years before, RAF Silverstone had been a wartime air base, training bomber crews for missions that would have included raids on Turin and Milan. A large complement of the 150,000-strong crowd had only recently been demobbed from military service fighting the Axis powers in Europe. Among the competitors was Tony Rolt, who just five years before had helped to build the glider in which he hoped to escape from Colditz. Many of the ex-servicemen who had faced Mussolini's army in North Africa had joked about its inferior arms. As it happened, Fiat's clever SPA air-cooled truck won the respect of British Army Royal Engineers struggling to fix water-cooled British vehicles boiling over in the desert heat.

For the victorious British, hosting the first ever Formula One race was a major coup. Never before had a British motor race been lavished with so much attention. Even the royal family turned out in force for what would be the only appearance ever of a reigning British monarch at a Grand Prix. For some of the Italians venturing onto British soil for the first time, the last encounter they had had with the British was in uniform. But any trepidation was dispelled when all the drivers were invited to have their hands shaken by the royals, in an appropriate show of magnanimity. For team manager Gianbattista Guidotti, who had been with Alfa since the early 1920s and rode as mechanic with Nuvolari for his legendary 1930

Mille Miglia duel with Achille Varzi, to be presented to the king of England counted as a career high. And as a courtesy, perhaps, to their hosts, Alfa Romeo had offered a drive to the then leading British driver Reg Parnell.

After the serial humiliation delivered by the German teams in the 1930s, Alfa were leaving nothing to chance. They arrived at the Northamptonshire circuit in force with two spare cars, two dozen mechanics and a mobile workshop with its own generator.

As it turned out, the race was a walkover. Three of the four Alfas that filled the front row of the grid cruised to victory, with Farina the winner, who also bagged the fastest lap. Only Fangio's car suffered a rare mechanical failure, which put Parnell on the podium. Alfa Romeo went on to win all six of that year's European Grands Prix with only fellow Italians Maserati offering any real challenge. The team from Portello were operating at another level from the rest of the field with the only true competitors coming from within the team itself.

At Monaco, Fangio and Farina shared the front of the grid with another Argentinian hopeful, José Froilán González, in a privately entered Maserati, but a crash on lap one wiped him out along with Farina and Fagioli, gifting Fangio an easy victory. The Swiss Grand Prix gave Farina his second victory, but Fangio won in Belgium and France, which put him ahead of Farina. The scene was set for a showdown in the final race at Monza, but Fangio's retirement and Farina's victory clinched the Italian the first drivers' world championship by just three points.

An Italian in an Italian car was the world's first champion. Coming a mere five years after the end of the war, it was a stunning achievement. Farina now claimed the crown that he had long thought was his. But Fangio, with his calm, measured style, that suggested he was not going as fast as he always was, had served notice that he would be a formidable opponent.

42

The Tender Touch

S uch was Alfa Romeo's domination of Formula One that Aurelio Lampredi, struggling to show the V12 Ferrari as a worthy competitor, began to have serious doubts about their whole strategy in the 1.5-litre supercharged category.

Aside from Maserati and Alfa Romeo, Ferrari's only other competitors on the Grand Prix grid were French – albeit with an Italian soul. Before settling in France in the 1930s, Venetian-born Antonio Franco Lago had already led a colourful life. A major in the Italian Air Force in the First World War, he was studying engineering at Milan Polytechnic when he became a founder member of the Fascist Party. But he soon fell out with Mussolini and turned into an outspoken critic, which put a price on his head. For protection he kept a grenade in his pocket, which he deployed in 1919 when a pair of armed Fascist youth cornered him in a trattoria. He fled first to America then London where he sold Isotta Fraschinis before settling in Paris in 1934, taking charge of what had been the company founded by Alexandre Darracq, the builder of Alfa's Portello plant. Now known as Automobiles Talbot, it was near bankrupt. To revive interest Lago audaciously presented a trio of Talbot-Lago badged T150s at a *concours d'élégance* in the Bois de Boulogne, painted in the colours of the French flag and driven by three French female racing drivers in matching outfits. He also commissioned a Grand Prix racer with which Talbot-Lago valiantly fought its own losing battle against the might of Germany's Silver Arrows. Happily for Lago, when the rules were being drawn up for post-war Grands Prix, the FIA permitted unsupercharged machines up to 4.5 litres to compete alongside super-charged 1.5-litre cars like the Alfa. Although in pure speed Lago's cars were no match for the Italians, his drivers often found themselves on the podium for reaching second or third. Lampredi realised that the French cars could go the whole distance without refuelling. On closer inspection he discovered that the French cars were managing nine miles to the gallon against the Alfas' prodigiously thirsty 1.5 mpg. Perhaps a new *un*supercharged Ferrari would give the Alfas a run for their money. He pressed the Commendatore to let him have a chance to prove himself and create his own new engine from scratch. Ferrari, despite all the time and investment that had gone into Colombo's engine, agreed to give him a chance. Lampredi came up with a bigger engine block, which adhered to Colombo's general principle of a V12 with single camshafts, but he added his own touches. Strength and simplicity were his watchwords; he used steel cylinders, bolted direct to the cylinder heads, which avoided the need for problematic head gaskets and added a heftier crankshaft, more akin to one found on an aero-engine. Capacity was also gradually increased to 4100cc.

Development progressed while Ferrari convalesced from an illness at the Viserba resort on the Adriatic. He sent Lampredi a postcard featuring a woman sunbathing with the caption 'The sun's tender touch' printed across the front. Ferrari's message on the back of the card was 'Hoping the 4100 will be a tender touch to Alfa Romeo'.

When Bazzi, Ferrari's long-serving engine builder, gave the new V12 a bench test he thought there had to be a fault. The power it was recording was too high. He took the test equipment apart, reassembled it and tried again. The results gave the same astonishing reading: 335 bhp at 7,000rpm. Lampredi drove down to the Maranello post office and sent Ferrari a telegram: 'Tender touch to Alfa Romeo is possible.' Three hours later, Ferrari was back at Modena, his recovery complete.

But the power was too much for the Ferrari chassis. Lampredi had no experience of chassis engineering, but Bazzi came up with an old-fashioned solution: 50kg of lead added to the inside of the chassis members. Lampredi also designed a new rear suspension, gearbox and stronger twin-piston brakes. They called the new car the 375.

43

Shadow of the Father

Alberto Ascari, along with his best friend and mentor Luigi 'Gigi' Villoresi, had joined Ferrari in 1949. Like Farina, the Ascari name was from another Italian automotive dynasty and very well known to Ferrari. Alberto's father Antonio had been the star driver who took Alfa Romeo to its first championship back in 1924. Alberto was just six at the time of Antonio's death, but even before that moment, as a little boy he was set on following in his father's tracks. 'I only obey one passion, racing', he said, 'I wouldn't know how to live without it.'

In 1940, Ascari married his childhood sweetheart, Mietta. When Italy entered the war, he and Villoresi established a lucrative transport business supplying fuel to army depots in North Africa, and had a lucky escape when a ship carrying their trucks was sunk in Tripoli harbour. As their business supported the Italian war effort, it exempted them from being called up.

When Ascari signed up with Ferrari, he and Lampredi became great friends. As it happened, the engineer was born on the same date – 16 June 1917 – as Mietta. 'We certainly enjoyed some fabulous birthday dinners on that day!' Lampredi recalled.

With Lampredi's big new unsupercharged engine, 1951 would be make or break for Enzo Ferrari. The championship might still be beyond his grasp, but he desperately needed some wins to prove himself. Alfa responded with an upgraded machine. Designated the 159 and overseen by Colombo, now back full-time at Portello, it produced an astonishing 400 bhp, at least 30 bhp more than the Ferrari. True to form, Alfa won the first three Grands Prix of the season.

Alongside Ascari and Villoresi, Ferrari had contracted the promising Argentinian Froilán González. Eleven years younger than Fangio, he was his polar opposite. As Ferrari observed, 'Whereas Fangio could be counted on to keep going as regularly as clockwork, González alternated bursts of furious speed with spells in which he seemed to be taking his time. When he was in the lead he would inexplicably slacken his speed and let himself be overtaken; when he was in pursuit, he ate up his adversaries.'

Nor did he particularly look the part. Heavy-set, he found the Ferrari cockpit a tight fit. For the British Grand Prix at Silverstone, Lampredi had added twin spark plugs – two for each cylinder for Ascari and Villerosi. González, as de facto number three driver, was given an older car with single spark plugs. But in the race, while his teammates struggled with their newer twin-spark machines, González came into his own, qualifying first, one second ahead of Fangio's Alfa.

In the race, Fangio had to make two fuel stops, taking on 90 gallons at each stop. Not only did the visits to the pit cost time, the sheer weight of a full tank slowed the car as well. González did need to stop, but only once, by which time Ascari had already retired. Assuming that Ascari as team leader would be taking over, González started to climb out of the cockpit, but Ascari was having none of it; this was González's race to win, which he duly did, coming home to the chequered flag more than a minute ahead of Fangio. At last, Ferrari had comprehensively beaten Alfa Romeo. Such a high-profile victory over the team which weaned him and given him his start in racing prompted another operatic moment for Enzo Ferrari: 'I cried for joy. But my tears of enthusiasm were mixed with those of sorrow because I thought today I have killed my mother.'

But was it a fluke? Could the new Ferrari be relied on to keep delivering? At the German Grand Prix, Ascari repeated the success, beating Fangio by over half a minute.

At Monza, Alfa responded with a further uprated car, now known as the 159M. The M was for *maggiorata* for the output had been boosted to 450 bhp, fifty more than the Ferrari. Fangio smashed all lap records with it at an astonishing 124.53 mph. The circuit was hot and crammed with spectators rooting for either the Milanese marque, Alfa Romeo or the Milanese driver, Ascari. It was a race full of drama. Fangio got away first but by lap twelve he and Ascari were duelling for the lead. On lap thirteen the tread on one of Fangio's tyres unwrapped itself and the tyre exploded as he limped to the pits. Half a minute later, he was away again. When Ascari came in to refuel on lap thirty-four, Lampredi was in the pits. The crew were using an air pressure system to speed the refuelling process. But the pressure was too much and split between the flexible section and the nozzle's metal tube inserted in the tank. 'While the steel tubing remained sticking out of the tank, the flexible tube began to flail around in the air, spraying fuel all over us, including some officials and a couple of carabinieri. Then it whacked a mechanic in the stomach, knocking him to the ground.'

Ascari, seeing this and knowing precious seconds were being wasted, roared off with the fuel lid open and the steel pipe sticking out of it, steering with one arm as he tried to free the pipe from the lid directly behind his seat. He pitted a second time but was still ahead when Fangio retired with piston failure. After all the drama, only one Alfa made it to the finish line while Ascari and González cruised home with a 1–2 for Ferrari.

Pasquale Gallo, president of Alfa Romeo, was at the trackside and asked to be introduced to the designer of the triumphant Ferrari. Lampredi was escorted to the Alfa pit. 'The first thing Gallo said was "But you can't be Lampredi, you're too young." To which I replied, "Sir, was it my fault that I was born so late?" then Gallo smiled and said, "Today, you, young Sir, have indeed killed the supercharged racing car."'

Ferrari, it seemed, had found his dream team: Lampredi's engineering talent with Ascari's gifts behind the wheel. Ascari was no engineer, but he was good at communicating any problems he detected. Following his win at Monza, the driver gave his engineer a photograph with the dedication 'I am Ascari inasmuch as you are Lampredi, but you are Lampredi inasmuch as I am Ascari'.

There was now a possibility that the world title was within their reach. When they went into the final race at Barcelona that October, Fangio had twenty-eight points from five races to Ascari's twenty-four from four events. Ascari set a storming lap record but a decision to use smaller diameter wheels and tyres cost Ferrari their chance of victory. Alfa once more came out on top.

Fangio's progress to the championship in 1951 can best be described as majestic. He drove faultlessly, enjoyed his wins and was philosophical about his retirements, which were rare. From the start he showed a maturity that made some of his rivals look like petulant prima donnas. Only Ascari, who Fangio said it was a 'great honour' to race against, showed a similar balance of grace, precision and aggression. For Alfa Romeo's exceptional Alfetta, still a winner fourteen years after its creation, it was the end of the road, but for Fangio, it was just the beginning.

Then, Gallo took the decision to close Alfa's racing operation and quit while they were ahead. The FIA's biggest fear was a weak field. Fewer teams meant fewer spectators, and less revenue. But who would compete with Ferrari? Their decision would send Lampredi back to the drawing board – again.

New Jacket, Frayed Trousers

In the first years after the war, motor racing in Europe was crowded with Italian cars and Italian drivers. Alfa Romeo, Ferrari and Maserati were locked in a battle for supremacy as drivers and engineers swapped between them in search of ever better, faster results. And into this crowded field ventured a fourth marque, Lancia.

Surprisingly perhaps, having made his name as a star driver for Fiat in the first decade of the century, Vincenzo Lancia, after he founded his own company in 1908, chose to stay away from motor racing. While Alfa Romeo's devotion to competition stretched the company's resources, family-owned Lancia made steady progress in the inter-war years. Having set a high technological bar with his revolutionary chassis-less Lambda in 1922, Lancia followed it with a succession of advanced designs, culminating in the 1937 Aprilia. For a four-door family sedan it was packed with innovative features such as all-round independent suspension and a teardrop-shaped, stressed skin body, which like the Lambda dispensed with the traditional chassis frame. Despite its modest 1350cc engine it could reach 80 mph.

Lancia's company remained very much a tightly run family business with Vincenzo as both the business and technical lead with a loyal team of engineers. In 1928, the journal *American Machinist* devoted eight pages to Lancia's factory, calling its unique blend of craft-based series production 'inventive industrialisation'.

'No complicated system of executives or management. Mr Lancia deals directly with the shop superintendents and holds each responsible for the results obtained by his department.' In contrast to the dramas at Alfa Romeo, Lancia built around him a gifted team whom he encouraged to think imaginatively.

Forty-one when he married secretary Adele Miglietti, together they produced three children. Gianni, the only boy, was just fifteen when his father died suddenly of a heart attack in 1937, leaving Adele in sole charge of the business. Having already worked inside the company, she was primed for the role, which she managed with some support from Vincenzo's cousin Arturo, who had set up a Lancia factory in France.

One particularly canny move of hers would have a dramatic effect on the future of the business. That October, Alfa Romeo's boss, Ugo Gobbato, had sacked Vittorio Jano, the gifted engineer behind so many of their groundbreaking cars. Four months later, Jano was back in his hometown of Turin, starting work for Lancia. From the outside it looked like a perfect move, but Jano, already wearied by the internal politics of Alfa Romeo, was not exactly welcomed by the tight circle of engineers Vincenzo Lancia had gathered around him and was put in charge of testing. Also joining the company, fresh from his studies at Turin Polytechnic, was Francesco De Virgilio in 1939, a 27-year-old engineer and mathematician from the south. Together, they would prove to be a formidable combination.

De Virgilio was born in 1911 in Calabria, deep in the south of Italy. Although his parents were comparatively well off, at the time of his birth, along with hundreds of others, they were living in an army barracks. In 1908 an earthquake, the most destructive ever to have hit Europe, flattened the cities of Messina and Reggio Calabria, causing more than 80,000 deaths. Not until Francesco was six did the family move into a new apartment of their own in Messina. From an early age, he took an interest in his father's work as a civil engineer and built his own boat – and a crane to lower it to the street. His mother suggested a career in forestry, but he opted to do engineering, first in Messina, then Rome and eventually Turin where he studied under Dante Giacosa's boss at Fiat, Antonio Fessia. Despite being a long way from home in the very different north, De Virgilio, affable and also a good guitar player, made friends easily and composed a song about student life which he sang on national radio.

Having come top in his class at Turin Polytechnic, he joined Lancia in 1939 on 800 lire a month. He soon discovered what a close-knit family business Lancia was. In 1941, shortly after some work solving a problem on the Aprilia's suspension, he was invited to Gianni Lancia's seventeenth birthday party at the family residence across the street from the factory. Adele Lancia seemed to know all about De Virgilio, noting approvingly, 'I've been told that finally the Aprilia suspension works well.'

He was put in charge of a small department, the Office of Special Studies, Calculations and Patents. Innovative company that it was, Lancia had already acquired several patents. Since the Lambda of the early 1920s, Lancia had adopted compact, narrow-angle V-formation engines. De Virgilio was asked to evaluate a prototype V6 that had been developed by the design team. Like other Lancia engines, the V was at the narrowest possible angle for maximum compactness. But no V6 had ever made it into production; the odd number of cylinders in each bank caused vibrations and a noise that did not occur in V4s and V8s. De Virgilio soon concluded that this V6 in its present form was unacceptable, but it inspired him to experiment with different combinations of the angle of the V formation and different camshafts. Having found what he thought was the optimum combination, he presented his findings to his bosses, but being new to the company and not yet thirty, expected them to be treated merely as a theoretical exercise. He then got involved with the development of a rear-engined V8 design. A coupé with three-abreast seating and the steering wheel in the centre, it was backed by Gianni, studying for his engineering degree in Pisa but already starting to exert some influence on the family business. Privately, De Virgilio regarded it as 'a useless exercise that deserved to die'.

But after a management reshuffle in 1943 elevated Jano to technical director, one of his first moves was to inform De Virgilio that the V8 was being dropped, telling him, 'Signora Lancia has decided that we turn our attention to the V6 because you have found out how to balance it.'

Adele's idea was that the new engine should go into the existing Lancia Aprilia, still a relatively new design. But the cylinder blocks of De Virgilio's V6 were angled at sixty degrees, too wide to fit in the Aprilia's engine bay. He tried a slimmer forty-five-degree version but it suffered the old V6 problems of noise and vibration: 'It was like putting on a new jacket with frayed trousers.'

By now, De Virgilio had become part of the family. In 1947 he married Adele's niece Rita. One consequence of this was that when Enzo Ferrari approached him with a tempting job at Maranello, he felt obliged to turn it down. When Arturo Lancia died, the role of general manager was taken over by Gianni Lancia, who had not yet graduated. One of his first decisions was for them to design an entirely new car around De Virgilio's sixty-degree V6.

Gianni's presence at the company was very welcome. Not only was he the son and heir, who would ensure family continuity, he was very much in his father's mould, both in character and appearance. Despite his relative youth, he was a big, heavy-set man reminiscent of Orson Welles, and a capable engineer who shared his father's passion for innovation.

But for such a young man there were some very grown-up issues facing the business, particularly the need to improve productivity. Along with his mother and two sisters, the family controlled 80 per cent of the company. Of the 5,500 workers, a majority had worked at Lancia for over twenty years. Company loyalty was strong, and the unmodernised factory was heavily dependent on skilled craftsmen. 'Imaginative industrialisation' came at a price.

Like Fiat and Alfa Romeo, Lancia had a lucrative sideline in commercial vehicles but after the war this was disrupted by a flood of ex-army trucks onto the market. The government, not entirely unsympathetic to Lancia's predicament, placed orders for a fleet of trucks and twenty-five buses for Rome, but, without the state support Alfa Romeo enjoyed, or the lucrative loans Fiat had secured, Lancia's plants remained unmodernised. All the attention was on product development. And with Gianni's ambition, Jano's experience and De Virgilio's technical focus, what emerged was truly groundbreaking.

At the May 1950 Salone dell'Automobile in Turin's Palazzo

Esposizioni, Lancia unveiled its first all-new post-war car, the Aurelia sedan. Under Adele Lancia's direction, it was displayed on a revolving stand covered in real grass. Beside it, also on show was a 'cutaway' example showing off all the mechanical parts. The 1750cc V6 engine was a world first. Built to De Virgilio's specifications, it had light alloy cylinder heads and a single central camshaft driving the valves. The gearbox mounted on the rear axle to give more even weight distribution was pure Jano, a feature of his Grand Prix Alfa Romeos, and all the wheels were independently sprung. The neat four-door saloon was a smooth, unadorned shape designed in-house by Amedeo Piatti, which echoed Pinin Farina's groundbreaking Cisitalia. Beside Fiat's rather chunky 1400 and Alfa Romeo's understated 1900, the Aurelia was undoubtedly the star of Italy's first post-war saloons. Britain's *Autocar* magazine called it 'one of the most interesting cars to have evolved in post-war Europe'.

It was a sweet moment. The new Aurelia proved that Gianni could deliver the same alchemy of refinement and innovation as his father. But this was just a beginning. What followed would raise Lancia's game to dizzy and ultimately insupportable heights.

World-class Couturier

Alfa Romeo's retirement and BRM's V16's failure to be competitive – only managing fifth and seventh at Silverstone in 1951, its only race that year – posed a problem for the FIA: who would race against Ferrari? The decision was taken to run the Grand Prix to Formula Two regulations with two-litre unsupercharged engines. Poised as they had been for a winning season with the big V12, this was a blow for Ferrari. Colombo's V12 had already been enlarged to two litres as the 166 Sports car engine, but its weight and complexity compromised it as a Grand Prix contender. British Formula Two teams had made headway adapting four-cylinder engines which were light and offered torque and weight characteristics that suited the twisty street circuits that predominated in European racing.

After a discussion with Lampredi one Sunday morning in June, Ferrari concluded he had no option but to commission another entirely new engine. Lampredi cancelled his plans and by evening had drafted the basics of what would become one of Ferrari's most successful engines. The four-cylinder 500, as it became known, was the first engine Lampredi designed from scratch. Deceptively simple, it retained features of Colombo's V12 like the double-walled crankcase and screwed-in cylinder liners, but tellingly, compared to the two-litre 166 engine which weighed 440lb, the similarly sized 500 tipped the scales at just 348lb. Plus it was strikingly reliable. Ferrari's bold decision to send Lampredi back to the drawing board had paid off handsomely. In Ascari's hands the Tipo 500 dominated the 1952 and '53 seasons, bringing him and Ferrari two successive world championships. Lampredi's car was completely unbeatable but, as the designer observed, 'Engines either run well or they break down. The only characteristic of a good racing engine is that it never breaks down. It never stops. This has always been my principle, but without Alberto that principle might never have been publicly affirmed.'

After Spa in 1953, Ascari had won nine championship races in a row. He also broke all records by setting the fastest lap in six races in succession. Enzo Ferrari had achieved his overwhelming ambition – triumph at the highest level of world motor sport. The Ferrari name, little known before outside the Grand Prix cognoscenti, was now world famous. But fame alone did not make money, most teams like Alfa and Mercedes went racing to promote sales. Ferrari now needed to focus on his road cars.

Pinin Farina and Enzo Ferrari first met in August 1921 when they were both on the threshold of their careers. Both were competing in the Aosta–Grand St Bernard race, which Farina won in an Itala. His first impression of Ferrari was 'a tall young man, with dark hair who wasted no words ... who looked beyond the person he was addressing, yet very alert'. Family pressure put a stop to Pinin Farina's motor racing, but he remained an enthusiast and noted how, while so few racing teams lasted more than a few years, Scuderia Ferrari was an exception. 'He has always managed to survive, and what is more, emerge.'

Three decades later, they were each leaders in their respective fields, and proud of it, which made their second meeting more complicated to arrange. Early in 1951, Ferrari sent an intermediary to invite Pinin Farina to visit him in Modena. Farina demurred, indicating that he would prefer Ferrari to visit his factory in Turin so he could show off his body-making facilities. Ferrari's intermediary responded that his boss didn't travel. In the end, as Farina put it, both of them had to 'dismount'. That September, they met on neutral ground at a restaurant appropriately named the Cavallino San Marziano in Tortona, equidistant between Turin and Modena.

Pinin Farina's observations on the human psyche are as acute as his perceptions about automotive form. He found Ferrari, 'As tightly closed as a walnut, disdaining the bonds the world proffered.' But Farina with his boundless geniality managed to prise him open, with their 'common language of the machine shop and the background music made by engines on a test bench'.

As Ferrari observed, they were a perfect fit. 'One of us was looking for a famous and beautiful woman to dress and the other was looking for a world-class couturier to dress her.' Sergio Scaglietti, who had a workshop in Modena and had graduated from mending damaged racing cars to building entire bodies for Ferrari, found himself in the middle of the two. Despite being nearly a foot shorter than Ferrari, Pinin was no pushover. 'He was pretty gruff. Even with Ferrari he was anything but pliable. Both of them had pretty similar characters: they went straight to the point.' The consensus was that the partnership would never work, that it would be like putting two prima donnas in the same opera or two priests in the same parish. But just one month later, at the Paris Motor Show, the first Pinin Farina Ferrari, a 212 Inter Cabriolet, was shown. It was such a success that seventeen more were made. The Ferrari's spectacular power inspired Pinin Farina to come up with more thrilling shapes, like the 375 America, with faired-in headlamps and dynamic air scoops on its flanks. The sheer jaw-dropping drama of the car fitted the bill for his new-found clientele.

Roberto Rossellini had come a long way from the war-torn streets of *Roma città aperta*. Flushed with success from three more gritty films about the war, he had acquired Hollywood backing for his next feature and embarked on an affair with the Swedish star Ingrid Bergman. As both Rossellini and Bergman were still married, their affair caused a scandal in Italy, but Ferrari wasn't put off by that. He invited them to Maranello and was delighted to be photographed with them when he took them to lunch, basking in their celebrity.

Rossellini decided to enter the 1953 Mille Miglia; Bergman was waiting for him at the checkpoint in Rome. When he pulled in, she flung herself on the bonnet, refusing to move until he agreed to withdraw from the event. He then bought her one of the first Pinin Farina-bodied Ferraris, a 375 MM Aerodynamica, finished in a shade of pale gold that was for ever after available on the Ferrari colour chart as Grigio Ingrid. But Bergman had few illusions about who the car was really for. 'I sat in it for a moment and I put my fingers on the wheel in the sign of the cross like we do on the forehead of the children when they go to bed. I am sure Roberto does not know the effect it has on me when he roars off in one of these monsters.'

They divorced in 1957, but Rossellini remained faithful to Ferrari.

Chasing Ferrari

For a time, Gianni Lancia followed his father's rule about keeping his company out of motor sports. But having Vittorio Jano, one of the nation's greatest racing car engineers, designing cars for him, it is not surprising that they were imbued with qualities that made them naturally competitive. The Sestriere rally, held in February 1951, was a tough winter test through the hills around Turin in which good driving and roadholding counted for more than outright speed and power. A privately entered Aurelia sedan with racing stars Alberto Ascari and Gigi Villoresi at the wheel won outright. Egged on by Gianni Lancia, Jano and De Virgilio pressed ahead with giving the Aurelia more power and bodywork to match. On the beach under an umbrella, De Virgilio sketched out a new valve layout to improve the flow of gases through the engine and increase power. When he calculated the results, which added 15 bhp, 'I cannot tell you enough of the enthusiasm of Gianni Lancia.'

'Someone had suggested a coupé for gentlemen drivers, and this resulted in the B20. Exactly who said this, I don't know. Gianni had been urged by friends to do something for the gentleman drivers, and so a coupé was born.' This is how, according to De Virgilio, one of the most celebrated post-war Italian cars came to be. The B20 was unusually roomy for a coupé, with three-abreast seating in the front and two seats in the rear. Although designed in-house, construction of the bodies was outsourced to Pininfarina where they were built up from numerous separate sheets hammered out to a form and welded together. Although it was not his own design, Pinin Farina was pleased that it bore all the hallmarks of his influence. 'The B20 had a rather peaceful line but it unsheathed its claws in competition.' Convinced from the outset that it would be a success, when he got the order for 200, he told Jano he should build 1,000. But Jano was sceptical. In the end they built 8,000.

Four B20s were entered in the Mille Miglia, each painted a different colour. Technically they were 'owned' by the drivers, who were each required to sign letters confirming that the cars would be returned to Lancia after the race. De Virgilio was at Brescia to witness the finish.

In the rain-soaked event, Giovanni Bracco's black coupé came home second to Gigi Villoresi's 4.1-litre V12 Ferrari, with more than twice the power. Writing in *Auto Italiana*, Giovanni Lurani observed that, although Ferrari was the winner, this race was 'the Mille Miglia of the Aurelia'. Unlike the rest of the field, the Aurelia seemed to thrive in bad weather. 'Before a race we always prayed for rain,' recalled Gino Valenzano. 'Then we could run away from anybody ... The Aurelia was always lacking in power but it compensated with handling qualities. It was a miraculous car.'

Lurani, a seasoned driver as well as a journalist, had booked a place for himself in that summer's Le Mans and was so impressed by the Lancia's performance that he asked if Bracco would partner him in his car. Lancia's pretence of non-involvement in competition was slipping away as Gianni insisted that the car be repainted Italian racing red for such a high-profile race, in which it proceeded to win its class. For a virtually standard car to succeed in two of Europe's most demanding long-distance races was astonishing. That year, Aurelias won eighteen events. After such a successful debut, Lancia, inundated with orders for the Aurelia, could do no wrong. Gianni Lancia, with his mother's blessing, now embarked on a spending spree, commissioning the architect Nino Rosani to design a new headquarters for the firm in Turin's Borgo San Paolo district. With its sixteen floors, it soon became known as Il Grattacielo Lancia (Lancia's skyscraper).

The Aurelia was rapidly followed by another equally successful Jano design, the smaller V4 Appia sedan. For Jano, thirty years on from his debut and now in his early sixties, it was an extraordinary continuation of form, his troubled last few years at Alfa Romeo long forgotten. For Gianni Lancia, having Italy's most gifted race engineers on his payroll was an opportunity not to be missed. Logic dictated that he should break with Lancia tradition and have his own competition department.

Over the winter of 1951–2, Jano supervised the construction of the first racing Aurelia GTs. Although they looked almost identical to the standard car, their lightweight, all-aluminium bodies were subtly streamlined and lowered. With additional carburettors and new cylinder heads the engines now produced 106 bhp.

But the 1952 Mille Miglia was crowded with serious competition. As well as Ferrari, Lancia was up against a revived Mercedes-Benz team and Alfa Romeo with Fangio at the wheel. Giovanni Bracco, who had starred the previous year with his second place for Lancia, warned De Virgilio, 'Before I stop racing I want to win the Mille Miglia at least once, so I am going to race in a Ferrari.'

In the two-litre class, eleven of the first fifteen were Aurelia GTs and thirteen of the first twenty in the touring class were Lancia sedans. Bracco was in a Ferrari 250S, with a three-litre version of Colombo's V12 uprated by Lampredi. An old-school racer, Bracco covered the 1,000 miles chain-smoking Nazionali cigarettes and sipping cognac and snatched victory just four minutes ahead of a Mercedes. Not long after this, Gianni Lancia informed his friends that he was going to have to make sports cars. 'I want to win races; I don't want to be number two.'

In 1952 the Targa Florio was run over eight laps of a shortened 72km circuit full of tight turns and abrupt changes in altitude from sea level to 600 metres. Once again, Bracco was entered in the Ferrari that he hoped would bring him a victory and led until his gearbox failed on the second lap, putting him out of contention. Lancia's Felice Bonetto fought his way up from fourth place and set about chasing down Franco Cortese, who was hoping to repeat his previous year's victory in a British Frazer Nash. But on the last 73km lap Cortese crashed and disappeared off the road, unbeknown to Bonetto, who was driving flat out thinking he would chase him down. He was on the long straight coast road that led up to the finish line when his Aurelia ran out of petrol. He managed to beg a cupful and staggered on to within 50 metres of the line when he stopped again. There was a slight incline to the finish and it was viciously hot. Exhausted after seven hours' driving, Bonetto began to push the car while Vincenzo Florio, almost seventy and still presiding over the event he had created nearly half a century before, shooed away spectators offering to help.

Bonetto managed to get across the line before the runners-up, both of which were Lancias. For Gianni Lancia, this was a particularly powerful moment since exactly forty-five years before his father had competed in the same race – and come second.

But having tasted victory, Gianni wanted more. To take on the mighty Ferrari, he recognised that he would need entirely new cars, designed exclusively for racing and Jano, his *éminence grise*, was gently egging him on. De Virgilio recalled Jano pointing out that for the Mille Miglia they had to have staff positioned along the route, all the way from Brescia to Rome, whereas at a racing circuit a team could manage with just four in the pits. If Gianni Lancia had any doubts about ploughing more of his company's finances into racing, he could rely on Jano to dispel them. According to Lancia driver Gino Valenzano, the chief engineer even made the somewhat contentious claim that single-seater racing cars were cheaper to develop than sports cars and gained more publicity. When De Virgilio queried this, Gianni responded simply: 'I want to defeat Ferrari.'

The Most Dangerous Road Race on Earth

In the late 1940s the Mexican government was looking for a way to celebrate the completion of their section of the north–south Pan-American Highway. The result was the Carrera Panamericana, a five-day, 3,300km (2,100-mile) race, not unlike the treacherous town-to-town European races in which Gianni's father had raced for Fiat at the turn of the century. The combination of fast, open roads and tight, mountainous sections held in a mix of suffocating tropical heat, high altitudes and bitter cold soon earned it a fearsome reputation. The first, in 1950, limited to five-seater production cars, mostly attracted local teams in big American sedans, but the following year the rules were relaxed and Ferrari stunned the world by coming home first and second. The huge publicity it brought them caught the attention of Gianni Lancia.

To fulfil his ambition and take on Ferrari, Lancia realised he would need the right machinery, and with Vittorio Jano on the payroll, now in his sixties but raring to return to front-line competition, he believed he had the means. The result was the D20 series of racing sports cars. Its engine bore a passing resemblance to De Virgilio's sixty-degree V6 but with three litres and twin overhead camshafts on each cylinder bank, and dual ignition fed by three double-barrel carburettors. The chassis, a space-frame assembly of tubes, was clothed in an elegant berlinetta coupé body styled by Pinin Farina.

Ready for the 1953 Mille Miglia, the new machine showed instant promise, finishing third and eighth. In Sicily, Umberto Maglioli drove the D20 to its first victory, in the Palermo–Monte Pellegrino time trial, and four days later delivered an outright win in the Targa Florio. After drivers complained that the cockpit was hot and prone to misting up, Jano simply did away with the roof so the berlinettas became spiders.

Gianni Lancia seemed to be fulfilling his dream: he was giving Ferrari serious competition. The last big event of that season was the Carrera Panamericana, now a fixture in the newly launched World Sports Car Championship. Lancia entered five cars, D24s for Fangio, Bonetto and Piero Taruffi, and two D23s for Giovanni Bracco and the 23-year-old Eugenio Castellotti, who had distinguished himself at Ferrari before being signed by the Turin team. The Lancia team travelled in style with five cars, a specially built transporter and twenty mechanics. To follow the race, Gianni leased his own aeroplane. They left the port of Le Havre on 17 October and arrived in New York six days later, from where they travelled nearly 3,800km to Mexico City on Lancia's specially commissioned transporter. They were up against seven Ferraris.

As well as the Ferraris, Lancia's drivers could not help racing each other. A furious battle developed between Taruffi and Bonetto in their D24s, both wanting to add the Carrera to their name. Bonetto won the first stage from Tuxtla Gutiérrez to Oaxaca, Taruffi won the second to Puebla, but after the third stage Bonetto was back in the lead. Just before the village of Silao, the two cars touched when Bonetto braked harder than Taruffi had anticipated. Taruffi went off the road and bent a steering arm.

During practice, Bonetto had painted brake signal markings on trees and posts but on the approach to Silao he must have overlooked them. He hit a deep trench at high speed which threw the car into the air and smashed it into a wall.

Taruffi knew nothing of this. He found a nearby petrol station, borrowed a welding torch and fixed the steering arm. The job was done in twenty minutes and he roared off in search of Bonetto. Passing through Silao he glimpsed the battered Lancia surrounded by crowds but pressed on. Only when he had finished the stage did he learn that Bonetto had been killed along with seven spectators. The organisers opted to continue and Gianni Lancia, following the race in his chartered aircraft, ordered the drivers to carry on, but each had to take one of the mechanics as passenger to discourage his surviving drivers from racing each other.

Maglioli, in the only Ferrari still in contention, was saved by a mixture of luck and skill. After a bearing broke at over 150 mph he lost a wheel and only just managed to keep the Ferrari on the road, rolling to a stop on the brake drum.

On day four there were two more stages, to León and then on to Durango, with a thirty-minute break. Just forty-one seconds split the leading Fangio and Taruffi, and for 200km they pushed each other to the limit at speeds of up to 155 mph. Maglioli took over the 375MM of Mario Ricci, who hadn't felt at all comfortable in his race car, and gave chase to the Lancias, driving so fast that the Mexican press nicknamed him 'el Italiano loco', 'the Mad Italian'. But it wasn't quite enough.

Fangio and Taruffi in the remaining two D24s and Castellotti's D23 were able to drive to the finish more or less in formation, accompanied by mechanics. The trio crossed the line with Fangio the victor, his average speed over the whole distance an astonishing 105 mph. For the comparatively young team, and the youthful Gianni Lancia, it was a tremendous achievement. Enzo Ferrari had been put on notice, but Lancia was just one of the problems he was about to face.

Contract Terminated

After such a magnificent run of success, Ferrari's domination of Grand Prix turned out to be short-lived; the return of Mercedes-Benz was about to upend the status quo. The presence of a big manufacturer with all the resources of technical expertise and money was an unwelcome reminder of what had happened to Scuderia Ferrari in the 1930s. And Mercedes had signed Fangio. To add to Ferrari's woes, his long-time on-and-off engine designer Gioachino Colombo had crossed the road to Maserati, to oversee the creation of their all-time star machine, the 250F.

Maserati sold racing cars to privateer drivers and teams, which went some way to cover the prodigious development costs and, long before Ferrari got its own foundry, Maserati were doing all their own castings and machining and pattern making.

Lampredi was not helped by Ferrari's disinclination to invest in more engineering. Nevertheless, for 1954 he designed a completely new chassis with the team's first space frame, ball-joint front suspension, side-mounted fuel tanks and a new transaxle. Known as the Squalo (Shark), its unpredictable handling did not endear it to drivers and it was no match for Colombo's peerless new Maserati 250F.

The Commendatore's solution was to bring in more engineers. Valerio Colotti and Alberto Massimino reworked the Squalo's suspension and chassis. Although Lampredi's 1955 121 LM sports car was more powerful than any other sports racer of that year by some 60 bhp, his other efforts no longer matched his past glories. After producing an extraordinary thirty-eight engines for Ferrari, by July 1955 his time at Maranello was over. 'One Monday morning, on returning to work . . . I was summoned to Ferrari's office. We sat and talked for some time and by 2:00 p.m. I was a free man once more.'

But not for long. The next day, he was in Turin at Mirafiori, discussing his future with Fiat supremo Vittorio Valletta. Dante Giacosa, who needed help improving Fiat's main family car engine, welcomed him with open arms. 'He skilfully produced a sophisticated and naturally more expensive design for a new combustion chamber which was very close to the hemispherical ones used for racing engines. The new chamber was excellent.' For the next twenty years, Fiat engines boasted Lampredi's imprint.

Ferrari's other challenge was his relationship with Ascari, his star driver. Despite their joint success, the two men never had much of a rapport and Ferrari was parsimonious with his compliments. Ascari could only remember one occasion when he was thanked for his victory. As one of the most successful drivers of all time, he was also expecting to be better paid. Any winnings he was obliged to share with Ferrari. On average his share was approximately 500,000 lire whereas a racing cyclist could expect 4 million lire and footballers even more. According to his wife, 'Even press agents organising races for the drivers earned more than Alberto did. He was not paid in relation to the risks he took.'

Ferrari assumed Ascari would be driving for him again and, towards the end of 1953, he summoned him and Villoresi to Modena. Ferrari saw Ascari alone in his office and pushed a contract in front of him to sign there and then. But Ascari declined. Instead, he put it in his pocket, told Ferrari he would think about it and left the office. Ascari, Villoresi discovered, had other plans. 'While Alberto drove he reached inside his pocket and pulled out two pieces of paper and said "Read this". The first was a contract from Gianni Lancia for Alberto to race for the new Lancia GP team in 1954, which he had already signed. The other was an identical contract signed by Gianni Lancia with my name on it and Alberto said, "Sign it". I couldn't believe it; Alberto had just had a long discussion with Ferrari about a contract for 1954 knowing that he had already signed with Lancia.'

Although it was the first Grand Prix car to be built under Jano's direction in twenty years, the D50 bristled with innovations. He divined that there was only so much power to be extracted from an unsupercharged 2.5-litre engine so the competitive advantage needed to be derived from making the car as small and as light as possible. He opted for a four-cam V8 with a wide ninety-degree V configuration to lower the engine's height, which, along with the rear transaxle, was bolted directly to a tubular frame so that it formed part of the structure, which needed exceptionally precise machining of the mounting faces. The engine itself was angled eight degrees off centre so the drive shaft could pass beside rather than under the driver, so that he could sit 15cm lower. Another cunning feature was the position of the fuel tanks in a pair of aerodynamic panniers attached to each side of the car between the front and rear wheels. Tested with a one-tenth model in a wind tunnel at Turin Polytechnic, it was discovered that the panniers also improved aerodynamics by filling the space between the wheels and suppressing wind turbulence. Short, squat and light, the design produced a lower polar moment of inertia than the D50's competition, giving drivers a cornering advantage, but it needed careful handling. Drivers found a high level of adhesion on fast corners but right at the limit; if either front or rear tyres lost adhesion, there was no warning and it was hard to recover from a spin.

These innovations enabled the car to be much shorter than the competition, but they took precious time to get right, causing the D50's racing debut to be delayed well into the season. When September approached the pressure was on to make an appearance at the Italian Grand Prix at Monza. But while Mercedes, Ferrari and Maserati were all lapping at under two minutes, the best the Lancia could manage was two minutes and eight seconds. However, with key last-minute changes the car began to meet expectations. A switch to coiled valve springs and the replacement of Weber carburettors with Solex units improved the engine's breathing as well as better cooling for the oil and brakes. By the end of September, Ascari's Monza lap times were down to a very competitive one minute fifty-six seconds, and Lancia announced they would debut at the Spanish Grand Prix on 24 October. Formula One had never been so competitive.

Rockets on Wheels

The new Lancias set the pace in Spain, described by British magazine *The Motor* as 'rockets on wheels'. By the end of the first day's practice Ascari's Lancia was fastest, ahead of Fangio's Mercedes, Mike Hawthorn's Ferrari and Harry Schell's Maserati. On race day, the Maserati managed to take the lead on the first lap but was soon crushed by Ascari, who left the pack behind by lapping two seconds faster than any other car. By lap nine, when he pulled into the pits with oil leaking into his clutch, he was twenty seconds ahead. Hawthorn's Ferrari won the race, but Lancia had made their mark.

In 1955, Gianni Lancia aimed to make his entry into Formula One in style, by chartering a KLM Douglas DC6 to transport the entire Lancia team to Buenos Aires, the first time a Grand Prix team had flown to a race. Maserati, not to be outdone, arrived with no fewer than seven 250Fs, designed by Gioachino Colombo of Alfetta and Ferrari fame. While Ascari struggled with the skittish handling of the Lancia, Mercedes had trouble finding the best gear ratios for the track. But by the end of practice there were four different marques on the front row, the three Italians and Mercedes. A crowd of a quarter of a million turned up to watch and by four o'clock the temperature had reached a searing thirty-five degrees. By lap two conditions were taking their toll and four cars were out in a mini pile-up. Ascari was in the lead by lap fifteen but none of the Lancias finished. The intense heat played such havoc with the cars and their drivers that few useful lessons could be learned. Local hero Fangio came home first for Mercedes.

There was a four-month interval before the next European Grand Prix at Monaco but three non-championship events before that, a useful opportunity for Lancia to hone its improved D50A. The first was at their home circuit in Turin. Thrillingly, Ascari was almost an entire lap ahead of the pack when he took the flag and the crowd were ecstatic to see their home team win. Pau was something of a throwback, a Grand Prix still held on public roads that had not changed for twenty years. Ascari produced another virtuoso performance putting forty seconds between him and the rest until, with twenty laps to go, he pitted with a fractured rear brake pipe. The only thing for it was to hammer the pipe shut so Ascari only had use of his front brakes. Having lost two laps, he dropped to fifth place. The race was Maserati's, but Lancia bounced back in Naples where Ascari won from pole. British journalist Denis Jenkinson observed the difference in behaviour between the Maseratis and the Lancias. While the Maserati's rear wheels were inclined to break away sooner where surfaces were smooth or slippery, the Lancias stayed firmly on the line – up to a point when 'the whole car slid boldly across the road a matter of two or three feet, with all four tyres apparently at the same angle of slip'. Jenkinson concluded that the reason why Lancia was taking so long to find its form was in part because 'the drivers had to learn how to drive them'.

Thrilled by this progress, Gianni Lancia led his team to the next championship Grand Prix. Monaco had emerged as the most high-profile and glamorous of all motor races and in 1955 Grand Prix seemed to be on the threshold of a golden age, with three competitive Italian teams and the return of Mercedes-Benz.

Ascari's Lancia shared the front of the grid with the two Mercedes of Moss and Fangio. Castellotti in another Lancia and Jean Behra's Maserati in the second row. As soon as the flag fell, all five thundered towards the first corner in tight formation until Fangio and Moss managed to pull away. The two Mercedes, circled in close formation until lap fifty, when Fangio's race ended on the Station Hairpin with a rare mechanical failure. With a sixty-four-second lead over Ascari, Moss, lapping most of the field, looked like the race was his until a plume of white smoke erupted from his Mercedes engine. Ascari, far behind, unaware of Moss's misfortune and struggling to shake off Behra's Maserati, had no idea he was now in the lead. In the pits, the ecstatic Lancia crew prepared a board that would alert Ascari to the good news, but he was never to see it. He stormed out of the tunnel under the Casino into blazing sunshine, down the ramp that led to the chicane on the quayside and at about a hundred miles an hour braked either late or not enough. The Lancia slewed sideways scattering hay bales, tore through a wooden palisade, passed – miraculously – between two solid iron mooring capstans, and flew over the harbour's edge some forty metres before it splashed down in a swirl of steam as red-hot metal hit the water.

There were ten anxious seconds before Ascari's blue helmet surfaced, the cockpit spacious enough for him to wriggle free, and he swam to the nearest boat, unhurt except for a broken nose. This punted Frenchman Maurice Trintignant's Ferrari into the lead, the remaining Lancias unable to catch him with their fading brakes, and Castellotti could have counted himself lucky to hold on to second, with Villoresi and Chiron fifth and sixth.

If Lancia was troubled by the superiority of the Mercedes, he could console himself with the fact that three of his cars had finished, and that Fangio no less had enquired about driving for Lancia the following year.

Hopes were now high for a clash of the titans at Spa in Belgium in a fortnight's time. Fangio and Ascari had each won there twice and though the field would be ripe with contenders, all attention would be on which of these two would come out ahead. But it was never to be.

Four days after Monaco, on the morning of Thursday 25 May, Ascari, back at home in Milan with his wife and children, headed off to the Monza Autodromo to watch the practice for the Supercortemaggiore 1,000km race. Since they were concentrating all their efforts on the Grand Prix, Lancia allowed his drivers to race other makes in sports car events. Ascari had agreed to share a Ferrari with Eugenio Castellotti in the race but, still recovering from his ducking and nursing his broken nose, did not intend to drive that day. He joined Villoresi, Castellotti and Gianni Lurani in the

Grandstand restaurant. As they were finishing, Ascari, according to Lurani, asked them whether they thought that after an accident it was good to get back behind the wheel as soon as possible. Evidently he already knew the answer as he left the table with Castellotti and headed to the paddock where the Ferrari team were preparing the car.

Ascari, like many racing drivers, was fiercely superstitious. His father had been killed while leading the French Grand Prix on 26 July 1925, so Alberto avoided driving on the 26th of any month. He also insisted on driving only in his lucky blue helmet and shirt. That day, however, he was in a suit and tie and as he climbed into Castellotti's car he put on a borrowed white helmet.

After three laps, emerging from the Curva del Vialone, one of the track's challenging high-speed corners, the Ferrari skidded and somersaulted twice, crushing Ascari as it threw him out onto the track, where he died minutes later from multiple injuries. Ascari's death had extraordinary echoes of his father Antonio's. They were almost exactly the same age, thirty-six years and ten months. Each had won thirteen Grands Prix and drove cars numbered 26.

For the second time that century, Milan was plunged into mourning for the death of a champion Ascari. On the day of his funeral, more than a million mourners are estimated to have lined the streets as his coffin was borne to the Cimitero Monumentale. Three days before he died, Ascari had told a friend: 'I never want my children to become too fond of me because one day I might not come back and they will suffer less if I don't come back.' After his death Fangio lamented that his title had lost some of its value because Ascari wasn't able to compete against him.

Modest, quick to praise rivals, Ascari was popular with spectators and drivers. Chubby, with a slight double chin, he was described as resembling a Milanese banker rather than an athlete. But his domination of Grand Prix during his time was unparalleled. His upright driving style was the opposite of Fangio's, seated close to the wheel, elbows out. Ferrari admired Ascari's precision and how when in the lead he was impossible to pass. 'Alberto was secure when playing the hare. That was when his style was at its most superb. In second place, or further back, he was less sure.'

Of his thirty-two race starts, he achieved thirteen wins, twelve fastest laps and became the first back-to-back winner of two championships, the only one to achieve that in the twentieth century. Despite his short career, having fewer Grand Prix starts than any other world champion, Ascari's performance during the 1952 season is considered one of the best single-year performances of all time.

Three days after the funeral, Gianni Lancia announced that Lancia was withdrawing from racing and, with his mother, boarded the *Andrea Doria* ocean liner bound for Brazil. It appeared that the decision was prompted by the death of their champion. In fact, Lancia was already in deep trouble.

50

Fall of the House of Lancia

Since the 1920s Lancia's road cars had been feted for their innovative design and groundbreaking performance, and under the guidance of the founder Vincenzo Lancia's son, the marque had maintained its reputation with two widely admired cars, the Aurelia and the Appia, clever designs from compact V-configuration engines to cunning construction that eliminated the need of a pillar between the front and rear doors. The performance of the production cars in road races and rallies proved the concept and set standards for performance and durability. Flushed with success, Gianni Lancia had taken on the most demanding test of automotive engineering – Formula One. And he went about it in some style, with Jano-engineered cars that were instantly competitive, and a professionally turned-out team travelling to races in a bespoke racing car transporter. Lancia was making all the right impressions, but even before the loss of Ascari his problems were beginning to mount.

After the war, the company did not get the same level of Marshall Aid as others. Whereas Alfa Romeo received $2.1 million, Lancia got only $800,000. The reason for this prompted claims that Gianni's alleged communist sympathies during the war had spooked Cold War-era Americans handing out the money. More plausible is that the nationalised Alfa Romeo was better placed to lobby for more. Although Lancia was led by a tight team of dedicated experienced car designers, the company lacked the equivalent production expertise of Fiat's Valletta or Alfa Romeo's Gobbato. In addition, Vincenzo Lancia's brother, Arturo, who had worked in American factories and set up a plant for the company in France, had hands-on experience of production but died in 1948. The cars themselves, priced above Fiats and Alfa Romeos, were popular enough, but costly to build and heavily reliant on skilled craftsmen rather than automated production.

Gianni Lancia, as the only son, was always destined to succeed his father, whose appetite for innovative engineering he shared. Doted on by his widowed mother, he was persuasive at getting his own way. His youthful installation as general manager rapidly bore fruit. His audacious bet on the clever V6 Aurelia paid off handsomely and maintained Lancia's reputation as a leader in road car design. And although it went against company policy to engage in motor sports, his move into racing met little resistance. Lancia succeeded in hiring Italy's most successful driver and his Grand Prix D50 showed such promise; it seemed that Gianni Lancia could do no wrong.

Only with hindsight does this view fall apart. Arguably he was an indulged, spoilt child whose vanity projects like the skyscraper office block and the Grand Prix venture were nodded through by biddable family members, who dominated a board lacking a sceptic looking closely at the balance sheet.

The death of Ascari, arguably Italy's greatest ever racing driver, seems to have been the catalyst for a dramatic change at the company. The family board members, Gianni's mother and sisters, had been growing increasingly anxious about the money disappearing into the racing programme. As Lancia's financial difficulties leaked, rumours spread through the motor racing world that Mercedes-Benz were exploring the purchase of Lancia's competition assets so it could neutralise them. What happened next would reveal how, not for the first time, Italian interests could be galvanised by the threat of foreign intervention.

Nineteen fifty-five had not been a good year for Ferrari. Although there were long waiting lists for his sports cars, his was a boutique operation from which most of the revenue went on racing. He cherished his independence. He had total control of his business and answered to no one else except – on occasion – his wife and his mother. He was also nearly sixty, an age when most men were thinking about retirement.

Although Fiat had not participated in Grand Prix motor racing since its abrupt departure in 1924, the Agnellis regarded themselves as guardians of Italy's industrial industry against foreign predators. Giovanni Agnelli, with the assistance of Mussolini, had seen off Ford in the 1930s, and a rumoured threat of takeover by General Motors had helped convince the National Liberation Committee to reinstall Valletta after the war.

Prince Filippo Caracciolo, the eighth Prince of Castagneto, third Duke of Melito, came from a long line of Neapolitan nobles, but he was no feckless aristocrat. Born in 1903, and with degrees in politics and commerce, he joined Italy's diplomatic service and while serving in Switzerland showed his anti-Fascist colours by becoming a key conduit between the British and Italy's resistance movement, the National Liberation Committee, on which he served as executive secretary. After the war he was appointed general secretary of the Council of Europe. He was also father-in-law to Gianni Agnelli, heir apparent to Fiat, and president of the Italian Automobile Club, governing body of the nation's motor sport. As well as his diplomatic skills, Caracciolo's family connections and interest in the fortunes of Italian motor racing gave him control of delicate negotiations to save Gianni Lancia's D50 racing cars for the nation.

There was no love lost between Enzo Ferrari and Gianni Lancia. An admirer of his father, Ferrari opined that, 'Only too often are the sons of such fathers handicapped from the start. Devoid of experience, they are often called to take their father's place too early, with the result that they fail to measure up to the same standards.' According to Ferrari, he only met Gianni Lancia once and was disappointed to find him uninterested in talking about the 'the great moral and technical inheritance to which he was heir'. There is no mention in his autobiography of any discussion about Lancia's future.

But like the much younger man, Ferrari was also guilty of having paid too much attention to racing results and not enough to his balance sheet. Poverty was part of Ferrari's own elaborate self-mythologisation, the small man pitted against the big interests.

But the bald fact was that in 1955 his racing cars were no match for the more sophisticated Mercedes and Lancias and struggled to beat Maserati. The Commendatore had also sacked his most gifted engineer, Lampredi. He badly needed new investment and expertise – and a competitive car.

Caracciolo identified a logic to the absorption of Lancia's racing team into Ferrari's own Scuderia. It would not be the first time it had taken delivery of race-winning cars that were suddenly surplus to requirement by a company in financial trouble. And there was a certain symmetry to the fact that Vittorio Jano, who had steered the creation of the D50 Lancias, had also been the designer of the Alfa Romeos that were passed on to Scuderia Ferrari almost twenty-five years before. Arguably, Ferrari was being dealt a favour, but the way he spun it was that it was more of a burden, an act of patriotic duty. A set of cars and spares was all very well but where would the resources come from to run the team? After his experience with Alfa Romeo, he was implacably opposed to selling any share of his company, and, given the Italian government's involvement in Alfa Romeo, it was hardly likely to take an interest in another challenging automotive enterprise.

Caracciolo had one other place to turn. But how could the fate of Gianni Lancia's racing cars matter to Fiat, a company that had emphatically exited from Grand Prix racing thirty years before?

By the middle of the 1950s Fiat was leading the charge of Italy's economic miracle. Centre stage with the highest profile of all Italian corporations, it had a reputation to maintain and a responsibility to be seen not simply as a corporate monolith.

On 7 July Prince Filippo Caracciolo, in his capacity as president of the Italian Automobile Club, displayed all his diplomatic cunning. 'With the intention of promoting the technical advancement of the building of racing cars, which are a glorious tradition of the Italian motor industry and add prestige to Italian products throughout the world, the President General of the Italian Automobile Club decided to intervene personally with Fiat and Lancia to enlist their aid in sustaining the efforts of the "Ferrari Automobili" of Modena, to which Enzo Ferrari has devoted his work . . .'

The way Caracciolo spun it played into Ferrari's mythology of the struggling artist labouring in the national interest, deftly skirting Lancia's dire financial straits. But the key piece of devilry came in the next paragraph. 'Fiat, which treasures the proud laurels won by its great drivers of the past, offers Ferrari an annual contribution of fifty million lire for a period of five years.'

Beside Caracciolo's finely crafted phrases, Enzo Ferrari's strain of self-pity and unctuousness borders on the crude, as shown in the telegram he sent that same day to Vittorio Valletta, president of Fiat:

'News just received surprises me and evokes my gratitude, I having only recently explained to President Prince Caracciolo my present situation consequent on prolonged stubborn isolated technical efforts in competition work. Glad to learn of warm comprehension and prompt generous significant gesture of solidarity made me by Lancia's offer of substantial technical contribution which comprises fruits of their latest experiments and by Fiat, fountainhead of all modern technical sports progress who generously will enable my small Firm to continue working.

'I earnestly hope that old and new collaborators will work happily together sharing sacrifices and anxieties in order to render even more worthy products of Italian work in the world thus honouring all those who have fallen in the extreme effort to keep the tricolore always to the fore. With respectful gratitude – Enzo Ferrari.'

Nineteen days later, on 26 July, a convoy of transporters arrived in Turin at the gates of Lancia's racing department on Via Caraglio. In the courtyard were lined up six Lancia D50s and a large consignment of spare parts and tools. Neither Gianni Lancia nor Enzo Ferrari attended the handover.

Faces were saved. The beneficiary was Ferrari, who was less interested in the cars than the injection of investment that came with them. And the expertise. Vittorio Jano was part of the package, the man who more than thirty years before he had been sent to Turin to lure away from Fiat.

As for Gianni Lancia, he began a new life as a rancher in Brazil. Later he settled on the Côte d'Azur with a second wife, French actress Jacqueline Sassard, who would star alongside Dirk Bogarde in Joseph Losey's *Accident*. Ever after he declined to talk about Automobili Lancia, which passed into the hands of Carlo Pesenti, a cement magnate who had supplied the concrete for Lancia's Turin skyscraper.

But by the time Lancia's cars were on their way to Maranello, any threat of a German takeover had already been eclipsed by a far bigger crisis that threatened the future of the whole of motor racing. For the first half of the year, nothing seemed to stand in the way of Mercedes-Benz's path to a glorious 1955. It was not so much a question of whether Mercedes would take the championship, but which of their drivers. As well as Formula One, the German team was going all out to win the sports car championship, taking the fight right into Italy's heartland with Stirling Moss's storming Mille Miglia victory in May, averaging almost 100 mph for ten hours.

As a gesture of fraternal goodwill, the Automobile Club de l'Ouest, the organisers of the 1955 Le Mans, had invited Count Aymo Maggi to flag off the start of the event on the Saturday afternoon of 6 June. And Eugenio Castellotti rewarded him by shooting into the lead in his Ferrari. But the race soon evolved into a battle between Jaguar and Mercedes, one of which was being driven by Frenchman Pierre Levegh.

But at 6.20 p.m., after thirty-five laps, Levegh's Mercedes, travelling at about 150 mph, clipped the rear of an Austin-Healey that swerved momentarily into his path, and took off cartwheeling through the crowd as it exploded into pieces, killing the driver and eighty-two spectators and injuring another hundred. The medical services at the event were completely overwhelmed; the difficult decision was taken to keep the race going or else the 200,000 spectators would start to leave, blocking roads that needed to be kept clear for ambulances. At midnight, a hastily convened Mercedes board meeting in Stuttgart decided to withdraw their team and pledged a million francs towards emergency relief. The day after, the West German parliament, the Bundestag, held a minute's silence.

For a time the future of motor sport hung in the balance. The next sports car race at Nürburgring and the Carrera Panamericana were both cancelled, several racing teams disbanded and the Swiss government placed a total ban on all forms of motor racing.

Mercedes decided to continue racing to the end of the season, taking the world championship for both sports cars and Formula One before they withdrew from motor racing altogether, not to return for many years. Rather to their dismay, the Italians were left very much in the ascendant.

51

British Racing Red

I n November 1955, after a dinner at the Royal Automobile Club
in Pall Mall, Stirling Moss asked a gathering of journalists for
a show of hands: should he drive a British car or a Maserati?

For the first ten years after the war, British cars were almost
nowhere to be seen on the Grand Prix circuit. Millionaire racing
driver Raymond Mays, his ERA (English Racing Automobiles)
having been sidelined by the all-conquering German Silver Arrows
during the 1930s, was raring to seize the opportunity that the end
of the war promised. Two months before VE Day, he issued a call
to action to Britain's motor and aircraft industries. Paying tribute to
their decisive role in the defeat of Hitler, he wrote, 'It is only fitting
that this superiority should be perpetuated as a gesture to the tech-
nicians and servicemen who made our victory possible.' Through the
British Intelligence Objectives Sub-Committee, a unit charged with
collecting technical intelligence from occupied Germany, Mays had
access to a wealth of data about the extremely advanced Mercedes-
and Porsche-designed Auto Union. Seduced by their technological
sophistication, buoyed by the hubris that had come with beating
'the Hun', he embarked upon the creation of a sixteen-cylinder supercharged machine.

He felt he had the full weight of Britain's motor industry behind
him – Rolls-Royce, whose Merlin engines had won the Battle of
Britain – would supply the superchargers. What he lacked in his
workshop, based in his family's woollen mill in the Lincolnshire

market town of Bourne, was the considerable weight of technical expertise of Mercedes and Porsche. Despite this, Mays forged ahead, his missionary zeal raising the hopes of Moss and his peers to fever pitch.

Moss, Mike Hawthorn and Peter Collins were well groomed to take them on. A home-grown, easily accessible amateur 500cc Formula, launched in the egalitarian post-VE Day atmosphere, meant it was no longer necessary to have a private income to go racing and provided an exceptionally useful training school. And some of those motorcycle-engined 500s had Italian DNA. John Cooper, who Enzo Ferrari would disparagingly dismiss as a *garagista*, created his first racing cars with a pair of crashed Fiat Topolinos from which he liberated Dante Giacosa's exceptional transverse-leaf front suspension.

But further up the hierarchy of motor racing formulae, British machinery was thin on the ground. BRM held out the only hope. In August 1950 it made its debut at a *Daily Express*-sponsored event at Silverstone. Seasoned French racer Raymond Sommer, who had driven for Alfa Romeo and Ferrari, was at the wheel and Tazio Nuvolari was given the honour of dropping the flag. But as the pack, which included nine Italian cars, roared away, Sommer was left stranded on the start line. Unable to cope with the prodigious torque produced by the BRM's supercharged sixteen cylinders, both driveshafts sheared.

Enzo Ferrari was always on the lookout for coming talent, regardless of nationality. A few months after BRM's very public humiliation, he made the 21-year-old Stirling Moss an offer he shouldn't have refused – a drive in the forthcoming 1951 French and British Grands Prix. But Moss, who was already committed to a British team, H.W.M., thought he should do the decent thing and not let them down. But he did accept an invitation to Modena, driving all the way in his Morris Minor. Ferrari offered him a drive in a Formula Two race later in the year, with the possibility of a seat in the Italian Grand Prix if things went well.

Moss, accompanied by his father, travelled by plane and overnight train to Bari on the heel of Italy and made straight for the Fiat garage where the Ferrari team was based for the F2 race. The car was all ready and Moss was about to try the driving seat when his way was blocked by a mechanic. The car had been reassigned to Piero Taruffi. There was no message from Enzo Ferrari, who was back in Modena and appeared to have changed his mind. Moss's humiliation was complete when, offered a drive in a British privateer's older Ferrari, the newcomer, unfamiliar with the traditional Italian pedal layout that put the throttle between the brake and clutch, missed his footing and crashed.

Another offer came after he was given a test at Monza in the Alfetta in which Fangio had just won his first world championship. Gianbattista Guidotti, Alfa Romeo's racing manager, took Moss for tea in Como and offered a place in the team for 1952, plus the appetiser of an Alfa 1900 Sports for personal use. But just days later, Alfa's bosses took the decision to pull out of Formula One. For the first of what would be many times, Moss found himself without a drive. He had shaken hands with Nuvolari when the great man was guest of honour at Silverstone; had he done his research he would have discovered how shamelessly ruthless the flying Mantuan had been, leaping from team to team with no notice in his quest for winning machinery.

By 1953, Moss's promise to the press that he would 'never go foreign so long as there is anything on wheels produced in England' was going to take some keeping. At the end of the year, Moss's manager Ken Gregory went to Modena and with the driver's family's savings bought a Maserati 250F for 9 million lire, about £5,500 then. The whole family chipped in, including his successful show-jumping sister Pat, who would go on to be a star rally driver. 'It was a big jump from the cars I had been driving up to that point and I was worried whether I could cope with it.' But it was all he had hoped for, faster than anything he had driven before and beautifully balanced. The car was painted British racing green and he drove a spirited season. Of the six Grands Prix he entered it broke down in five of them. 'We had gears shed their teeth, axle-tubes break, bearings collapse and oil pipes fracture.' In Belgium he managed third and at Monza he was twenty seconds ahead of Fangio's Mercedes when his engine seized. But for the young Englishman it was a valuable rite of passage. It showed the world what he could do.

What came out of it was the offer to drive for Mercedes-Benz in

1955. Despite Moss's Jewish roots – his grandfather had changed the family name from Moses – he could not possibly pass up a place in by far the strongest team, alongside the prodigiously successful Fangio, who had joined mid-season the previous year. Plus, the offer for Moss's services, £28,000, was double the figure his manager Ken Gregory planned to ask for.

At home, any residual anti-German resistance was overtaken by the general acceptance of the poor show British teams had put up. *Autosport* magazine placed the blame squarely on the British motor industry and 'their continued apathy to the importance of full-scale Grand Prix racing has virtually forced our best drivers to seek their fortunes with foreign products'.

Like Moss, Mike Hawthorn was deeply patriotic and according to his friend Neil McNab he 'hated the Krauts', and always placed a copy of *The Scourge of the Swastika*, one of the first books to document Nazi war crimes, on the parcel shelf of his car when he drove to races in Germany. A habitual pipe smoker, he adopted what was even for the 1950s a caricature Englishman pose, tweed jackets and caps off the track, bow tie and British racing green windcheater behind the wheel. But when Ferrari came calling, Hawthorn had no hesitation.

Although he never attempted to learn Italian, the two got along. But Hawthorn was never in awe of the great man and would not be bullied. Romolo Tavoni recalled Hawthorn complaining to Ferrari about a gearbox, which enraged him. '"You say my gearbox is no good? My gearbox is the best and if you say it is no good a second time you can leave." "Goodbye," said Mike, and walked out. Ferrari quickly called him back and all was forgiven.' But Mike only received a share of start and prize money; he was not on a retainer. And after a fiery crash in Syracuse, which gave him second-degree burns on his legs, Enzo Ferrari billed him for his hospital care in Italy.

Hawthorn clocked up seven wins in Grand Prix and sports car races with Ferrari in 1953, but life abroad in Italy took its toll on the young Englishman, as McNab recalled. 'Mike hated the Albergo Reale in Modena with a deep loathing. There was no crumpet, no beer and no decent food ... In the end he was glad to get away from Modena.' But a return to British teams, for Vanwall in 1955 and

BRM in 1956, was a great mistake and took him out of contention for two seasons. His hopes were briefly raised when, after Ascari's death, Vittorio Jano offered him a place, before the shock announcement came of Lancia's withdrawal from all racing. The following year he was back at Ferrari.

Stirling Moss's time at Mercedes-Benz was cut short by the team's decision to retire in the aftermath of the Le Mans catastrophe; he was once again looking for a competitive drive. The British teams BRM and Vanwall were showing more promise but were still no match for the perennially competitive Italians. So on that November evening, dining with journalists at the Royal Automobile Club, Moss put his choice, British or Italian, to a vote. Genuinely conflicted, he wanted to enrol the British press in his decision. Reason trumped patriotism; the decision went six–nine for Italy.

Gentleman Driver

With Lancia and Mercedes-Benz gone from Formula One, Ferrari was in a buyer's market for drivers. Among those without a seat for 1956 was none other than the now three-times world champion, Fangio. The Argentinian had it in mind to retire but events at home encouraged him to stay in Europe. Perón had been deposed. Although Fangio was not a slavish supporter of the exiled leader, Perón had backed the races that brought the driver's talents to world attention. Fangio decided it would make sense to let things cool down at home and stay in Europe.

After winning championships with Alfa Romeo, Maserati and Mercedes-Benz, Fangio had a keen sense of his value, which put him somewhat at odds with Enzo Ferrari. The Commendatore expected a certain subservience from his drivers and was accustomed to having them make their pilgrimage to Modena to kiss the ring while he dictated terms. Fangio sent an agent, Marcello Giambertone, to negotiate on his behalf and although the deal was done, the relations between the two giants of motor sport bordered on the toxic. Fangio bridled at Ferrari's refusal to name him his number one driver. 'For me the number one is always the one who wins.'

Much more to Ferrari's liking was his new British signing, Peter Collins. Like Hawthorn, Collins jumped at the chance to drive for Ferrari, but, unlike his fellow Brit, settled easily into life in Modena. Effortlessly charming and easy-going, he was also strikingly handsome, which may have helped. He loved the food and wine, rapidly learned enough Italian to converse easily with the mechanics and enjoyed long lunches with them in the recently opened Ristorante Cavallino opposite Ferrari's factory. The Commendatore, who believed that marriage could slow a driver down, also liked the fact that he was unattached. But that was not to last.

Early in the year, en route between races in America, Collins stopped over in Miami and went to the Coconut Grove Playhouse to see the stage version of *The Seven Year Itch*. Moss had met its dazzling American star, Louise King, and told Collins he should look her up. Louise was a free spirit who had passed up a film opportunity because she did not want to be tied to Hollywood. But Collins was another matter. Two days later, sunbathing beside his hotel pool, he proposed and a week later at the Coconut Grove Congressional Church, they were married.

At first the news did not please Ferrari but he came round when the couple announced their intention to live at Maranello and even lent them a house, Villa Rosa.

There was another reason for Ferrari's fondness for Collins: he had been a good friend to his son Dino during the last year of his life. They were two months apart in age and both enjoyed films. Romolo Tavoni recalled Dino urging Collins: 'If you go to the movies, tomorrow morning you can tell me about it. I cannot get out of bed. I am like a small bird in a big cage.'

Dino had been groomed to succeed his father, who, long after it was apparent to all that the boy had not long to live, was talking up his son's feel for engineering and his input on a forthcoming V6 Formula Two engine that was under development. 'I and my old friend Jano spent long hours at his bedside, discussing with him the design of the 1.5-litre engine. Dino argued that it should be a V6 and we agreed.'

Ferrari's only serious competitor was Maserati, who with Stirling Moss won at Monaco. Peter Collins, bursting with promise, was enjoying his first year on the front line of Formula One. Collins won in Belgium after Fangio retired with transmission failure and again in France after Fangio's fuel tank split, dropping him to third. But on the eve of the French Grand Prix, 30 June, came the day Enzo Ferrari dreaded. His cherished son Dino died from both muscular dystrophy and nephritis, at home in Modena. He was twenty-five.

'I had always deluded myself . . .' said Ferrari, 'that we should be able to restore him to health. I was convinced that he was like one of my cars, one of my engines.' For months his father had kept a daily record with graphs of his vital signs. But Dino's frame was beyond repair. The last entry read 'the game is lost'.

Ferrari's summing-up of his feelings for Dino speaks more of the character of a man who kept two households. 'The conviction has never left me that when a man says to a woman "I love you," what he means is "I desire you," but the only real love possible in this world is that of a father for his son.'

It was during Ferrari's prolonged grieving that Collins showed another rather more British side, as his wife Louise recalled: 'Eventually, Peter went to see Ferrari, and in effect told him to snap out of it. It made him angry that he was neglecting the company, spending so much time in this endless mourning. People couldn't believe that anyone would have the guts to say something like that to Ferrari but actually he accepted it, and was much lighter after that.' Five months after Dino's death, the V6 ran for the first time.

Ferrari was almost too grief-stricken to notice when Fangio won the next two Grands Prix at Silverstone and the Nürburgring, bring-ing the season to an almighty climax. At Monza, the final race in the calendar, three drivers had the championship in their grasp: Fangio, Moss and Collins. Fangio only needed to come third to take the title, and Luigi Musso and Castellotti, the two Italians on the team, would be desperate to win on their home circuit. Monza's combination of road and banked track was particularly tough on the Ferrari team's Englebert tyres, flailing and throwing their treads in practice. So just before the start, Fangio, knowing how badly the two Italians wanted to win, and that he didn't need to come first to bag another championship, told them that if they took it easy during the race he would let them through to fight it out in the closing laps. It was sound advice, given the problem with the tyres. Collins's roommate the night before the race had been woken by the young driver shouting, 'The tyres! The tyres!' But as soon as the race got going, neither of the Italians heeded Fangio's wisdom. From the start Castellotti and Musso roared off in a two-car duel and were in the pits for fresh tyres after only a few laps and, not long after, Castellotti retired after damaging his car in a spin. But then, on lap twelve, Fangio experienced a freak mechanical failure, his steering snapped and he limped into the pits with his front wheels splayed.

Moss was now in the lead and Fangio's title chances were vanishing fast. When Musso came in for his next pit stop he was asked to give up his car for Fangio, but he was having none of it. He had been obliged to do this once already earlier in the season and now on his home turf was not about to do it again. He remained seated behind the wheel, his gaze fixed on the track, pretending not to hear before he blasted off again. But then on lap thirty-four, Peter Collins in third place came in for a tyre inspection.

At first Fangio didn't realise what was happening when Collins stepped out of his car. If he finished first and drove the fastest lap, the young Englishman was in sight of becoming Britain's first ever world champion. But he all but bundled Fangio into the empty seat and the champion roared away to take up the young Brit's third place behind Moss and Musso, who was now, much to the excitement of the crowd, leading the race. But then, with three laps to go, Musso's Ferrari suffered the same steering failure as Fangio's. He was out of the race; Moss took the chequered flag for Maserati and Fangio collected his fourth championship – this time for Ferrari. Afterwards, Fangio confessed, 'I do not know whether in his place I would have done the same. Collins was the gentleman driver.' Collins had no regrets. 'I'm too young ... and Fangio deserves it anyway.' He didn't think he had earned it – and believed he had plenty of time to do that.

Ferrari was back on top, bathed in the glory Fangio and Collins – and Jano's Lancias – had delivered. But there was no rapprochement between the Commendatore and 'the Old Man', who celebrated by making his return to Maserati. Ferrari's sardonic observation about Fangio was that he did not remain loyal to any marque but always made sure he drove the best car available that season. Perhaps what Ferrari recognised was that, when it came to self-interest, he had met his match.

Ferrari's Primavera

In Maranello in 1957, Peter and Louise Collins were living the dream. Louise wrote home excitedly to her parents in New York, 'Mr and Mrs Ferrari have been wonderful to us. She has taken a liking to me and insists on going everywhere with me ... They have offered to let us have their villa at Rimini after the race in Naples so I hope we can go bake on the beach for a while. What a life!'

But in March, Louise Collins got her induction into the darker side of motor sport. Collins was one of what the Italian press were calling 'Ferrari Primavera', the new generation of drivers which comprised him, Hawthorn, Alfonso de Portago, Eugenio Castellotti and Luigi Musso, all of them in pursuit of Fangio. Within two years all five would be dead.

Castellotti's father was a wealthy land-owning lawyer; his mother, Angela, a 16-year-old housekeeper when the boy was born. Eugenio was twelve when his father died, leaving him a fortune with which he would finance his racing. In 1956 he distinguished himself by winning the rain-drenched Mille Miglia for Ferrari averaging an extraordinary 137 mph and beating Collins, Musso and Fangio. Handsome, with a bodybuilder's physique, his co-respondent shoes had built-up heels to disguise his short stature. Intense and publicity-shy, his courtship of ballerina and actor Delia Scala made the couple a magnet for paparazzi, all the more when they announced their engagement and a wedding scheduled for that April. But there were tensions, as Romolo Tavoni recalled.

'Castellotti took Delia home to meet his mother. She took Delia's arm and said, "You look like a waitress; the kitchen is this way." There was a terrible row.' Unlike Louise, Delia had no intention of giving up her career, which Eugenio was insisting on, and she wanted him to give up driving.

Ferrari offered his advice. 'Try to understand one another better and try, each of you, to understand yourself better.' With less than a month to the wedding, the couple took a break in Florence to try to resolve it. But after a few days, Ferrari called Castellotti back. Maserati had just broken the lap record at the Modena Autodromo. Castellotti set off at five in the morning and was at the track by eleven. Ten minutes later he was dead. On his first lap he lost control, was flung 90 metres from the car and died instantly of a severely fractured skull.

Ferrari observed that 'he was going through a confused and conflicting time emotionally, and it is probable that his end was brought about by a momentary slowness to his reactions'.

Motor racing was just one of the many extreme pursuits of Don Alfonso de Cabeza Vaca, the eleventh Marquis de Portago. Born into the Spanish nobility, at just seventeen Fon de Portago, as he was known, won a $500 bet by flying under London's Tower Bridge. He subsequently rode in two Grand Nationals and won a bronze medal in the 1956 Winter Olympics for bobsleigh. Ferrari judged him 'a rare and perfect gentleman despite the deliberate roughness of his outward appearance'. Not that this discouraged the attention of women, as Louise Collins noted. 'He really was extraordinary the way he got in and out of bed with an amazing number of females without others knowing about it. That man was so busy with women I don't know how he had any time for racing.'

That year he was dating Hollywood actress Linda Christian, technically the first 'Bond girl', having starred in a 1954 TV adaptation of *Casino Royale*. For his first Mille Miglia she arranged to see him at the halfway stop at Rome where paparazzi were on hand to catch what would be their last kiss, before catching a flight to Brescia for the finish.

Coming from Mantua towards the village of Guidizzolo, with only thirty more miles to go to Brescia, Portago and his navigator

Ed Nelson were doing an estimated 175 mph when a front tyre exploded, sending the machine cartwheeling through the air as it disintegrated before coming to rest in a ditch. Nine spectators were killed, two of the dead children hit by a concrete milestone torn from the ground by the car and thrown into the crowd. The body of de Portago was found in two sections, and co-driver Ed Nelson was badly disfigured beneath the upside-down vehicle.

Louise saw first-hand how those in the business responded back then. 'It was very strange to see the reaction of the racing people – it was almost as though they expected it and although he was a very popular guy no one could get upset about it. That night a group of us went out to a restaurant and after dinner we danced the night away ... it provided us with a sense of release after the race.'

Peter Collins told the *Sunday Times*. 'Things are getting pretty ridiculous. My car this year for example, a 4.1-litre Ferrari was capable of 310kph, nearly 200mph. And the crowds – you could see the road ahead solid with people, no gap at all, and they only get out of the way when you frighten them by weaving the car from side to side.' Days later, Ferrari was charged with manslaughter and causing grievous bodily harm by negligence, but an investigation could not conclusively pin the tyre burst on anything defective about the car and the charges were eventually dropped. But that was the last Mille Miglia.

Among the remaining Primavera, there were tensions. Luigi Musso had been Castellotti's great rival but with him gone he focused on Collins and Hawthorn, sensing in their closeness a plot against him. For Ferrari, such rivalry was grist to his mill; this, he believed, was how he got the best out of his drivers.

Like Castellotti, Musso along with his 21-year-old actor mistress Fiamma Breschi were great material for the gossip columns and paparazzi. A diplomat's son from Rome, he was privileged and, by reputation, lazy. He was already a figure of some notoriety having left his wife and two children and for attempting to get his marriage annulled while conducting a series of affairs. According to Tavoni, Musso loved racing, but even more he loved to gamble. Deep in debt after a venture to import American Pontiac cars collapsed, he was desperate for the prize money as well as championship points.

At the French Grand Prix at Reims that July, the organisers were offering 200 bottles of champagne to the first driver to lap at over 200 kph, which Mike Hawthorn had no trouble with, shaving two seconds off Fangio's 1956 record. At the start he took the lead, followed closely by Musso, determined to keep up. Collins had a disappointing race. An air scoop for the magneto had got detached and lodged itself under his brake pedal. He managed to bring the car to a stop with a deft controlled spin. But when he came to re-start, the gear lever jammed. Eventually he managed to free it by hitting it repeatedly with the offending air scoop and was back in the race, down to eighteenth. According to Gregor Grant, writing in *Autosport*, 'As he passed the pits in 18th position, mechanics ducked as the offending air scoop came flying through the air, chucked out by a furious Collins.'

The Ferraris had taken the first three places until lap ten when Musso, clinging onto Hawthorn's tail, lost control on the 155 mph right-hander after the pits and disappeared into a cornfield. Hawthorn was ecstatic about his victory, his first Grand Prix in four years as well as Ferrari's first since the 1956 Grand Prix, while Collins had to settle for fifth after running out of petrol and pushing his car to the finish. But the celebrations did not last long, for Musso, rushed to hospital after his crash, died from his head injuries that evening. As Louise Collins wrote later to her parents, 'It was quite a shock to everyone, but Peter said he saw Musso go off the road at the same spot about three times before he had his accident. So I'm afraid it was his terrific desire to be the great Italian hero and world champion that killed him. In this business common sense should be the most important thing, but it seems Musso let his dreams take over.'

Fangio having retired earlier in the year, the way was finally open for a British champion. And after Hawthorn's victory at Reims, Collins talked about helping his mate get there. At the British Grand Prix, he decided he would go all out to be the hare and tempt the competition until he either blew up or let Hawthorn through, but in the end Louise and Peter's family were all at Silverstone to witness a decisive win half a minute ahead of Hawthorn. After starting to find the Ferraris' hospitality claustrophobic, the couple abandoned Maranello for a rented boat in the harbour at Monaco, and had put down a £500 deposit on a dilapidated Georgian house near Peter's parents in Kidderminster. All the signs were there that they were starting to live beyond the moment. After the German Grand Prix at the Nürburgring, nothing in Formula One would be quite the same for Ferrari. Two British drivers came home first and second, Tony Brooks followed by Roy Salvadori. Each was in a different British-made car. Brooks's Vanwall was finally becoming a contender and Salvadori's revolutionary rear-engine Cooper-Climax was about to cause the biggest rethink of the century in racing car design.

Stirling Moss in his Vanwall had stormed into the lead, only to retire early with magneto failure, which put Collins and Hawthorn out in front. While the Ferraris were 10 to 15 mph an hour faster on the straights, the Vanwall's superior disc brakes and better springs made it faster round the Nürburgring's 170 corners.

After nine laps, Tony Brooks nosed his way ahead of Collins and into the lead, a thrilling moment for the lesser-known driver. Hawthorn, behind the two, had full view of what happened next as the three of them hurtled through a tree-lined dip in the track called the Pflanzgarten. 'Peter was fighting hard to catch Tony and he put his foot right down and in the heat of the moment he did not turn into the corner early enough. When he did turn it was obvious that he was going too wide: he was only a yard, maybe two yards, out of line but it was enough.' Hawthorn thought for a moment that Collins might spin and take them both out. 'I was just thinking up some choice words to say to him when we climbed out of the two bent Ferraris when, without the slightest warning, fantastically quickly, his car just whipped straight over.'

It was a while before Louise knew what had happened. 'I was in the pits, doing my lap chart as I always did and I finished it for the race. Someone told me Peter had had an accident and someone else said he was walking back so I was not worried. Then Tavoni came and told me that the accident was serious and that Peter was being taken to hospital in a helicopter.' He drove her the 78km to Bonn where they were told that Peter had died in the air. When they saw him, Tavoni recalled that he looked as if he was asleep. 'There was a bruise on one arm and the skin on the back of his neck was very red but that was all.'

After the funeral, Louise returned to Modena to see Ferrari, who she had never seen so upset. After the Mille Miglia, *L'Osservatore Romana*, the Vatican newspaper, put the blame for the drivers' deaths squarely on his shoulders and likened him to 'a modern Saturn, devouring his own sons'. He asked her to accompany him to Monza for the Italian Grand Prix which she agreed to. 'I'm sure he felt it would be good for me to go – rather like getting back on a horse right after a fall.' She made the journey, but Ferrari did not show up. Nor did a lot of other Italians, only 20,000 tickets were sold – a fraction of the usual turnout. Brooks won the race, another victory for the British Vanwall team. Louise's weekend was salvaged by an invitation from Peter Ustinov, who she had met in Monaco. He was touring his Broadway hit *Romanoff and Juliet*, a Cold War romance, and offered her a part which she jumped at, believing it would give her some discipline and purpose.

The championship now came down to a duel between Britain and Italy, Moss in his Vanwall and Hawthorn for Ferrari. In the Portuguese Grand Prix on the cobbled, tramlined streets of Oporto, Hawthorn found his brakes fading, no match for the discs on Moss's Vanwall, which won the race. On his final lap Hawthorn, his brakes gone, had to use an escape road and then stalled. Exasperated, he tried to push-start the Ferrari but there was a gradient. Moss, on his slowing down lap, came past and recognising his predicament shouted at him, 'Push it downhill; you'll never start the bloody thing that way.' Hawthorn restarted and managed to make it across the line, but with no idea where he was placed, until team manager Tavoni told him the good news. He was second, and having done the fastest lap, was leading the points thirty-seven to Moss's thirty-two.

However, a marshal had reported him for going against the direction of the race, which meant he could be disqualified. Moss came to Hawthorn's defence, pointing out that he was on the escape road at the time so could not have been going against the traffic, which the officials accepted. Moss's comradeship might cost him his championship, but he did not want to win it by default.

With one more race to go, in Casablanca, Ferrari pressured

Hawthorn to commit for another season, telling him, according to Romolo Tavoni, 'You can write your own contract and I will sign it without reading it.' But the Englishman resisted. After the loss of his friend Collins, the fun had gone. For the first time, a British driver was sure to be world champion; but in a British car or an Italian? Moss was eight points behind Hawthorn. To win the championship, Moss would have to come first and set the fastest lap. But even then, if Hawthorn came second the prize would be his.

But any British jubilation would be tempered by yet another fatality. Moss led from the start and stayed there, while his teammates Tony Brooks and promising young Briton Stuart Lewis-Evans tried to keep Hawthorn out of the first three places to secure Moss's championship. But Brooks's engine blew up and Lewis-Evans's Vanwall crashed. Engulfed by smoke and flames, Lewis-Evans managed to extract himself from the wreckage but died of his injuries six agonising days later.

Tavoni was on hand to congratulate Hawthorn as he climbed out of his car and it was then that he told his team manager he was going to retire. The world champion shunned the press and went straight to his hotel. Conscious of the part Peter Collins had played in his success, before he went to bed that night he cabled his news to Louise, who was on stage in Washington DC.

Hawthorn and Ferrari did not meet again. Ferrari, always economical in his praise for his drivers, pronounced the first British champion 'good on his good days'. Hawthorn was pleased to settle into a quiet life running his father's garage in Farnham, Surrey, and marrying his girlfriend, Jean Howarth, a Hardy Amies model. When *Romanoff and Juliet* arrived in the West End, he made a date to meet up with Louise. But en route to London in his much-modified Jaguar saloon, he encountered his old pal Rob Walker's Mercedes 300SL. Duelling at somewhere over 100 mph on the Guildford Bypass, Hawthorn lost control of the Jaguar, which was almost cut in half by a tree. He was pronounced dead at the scene.

For Louise, Hawthorn's death brought the final curtain down on a drama full of multiple tragedies, but she had no regrets. 'Racing was so different then. Much more dangerous, of course, and not highly paid. But it seems to me there was much more joy in it, and I'm so glad I experienced it. There was etiquette, if you like, rules by which the boys played – a feeling that they were all doing something they loved, and weren't they lucky? Peter and I weren't together very long, but it was the happiest time of my life.'

The Bombshell

America's auto industry had been emboldened by its contribution to the war effort. Mass-production expertise enabled it to turn out aircraft as fast as it had built cars; factories expanded to service lucrative military contracts which enabled Detroit to invest in ever more sophisticated plant.

Unlike in Europe, car production continued through the war, as did design and development, so that when American cars appeared at the first peacetime motor shows, their curvaceous pressed steel bodies made the Europeans look positively vintage. And when the first new French Peugeots and Renaults and Italian Fiats and Alfas finally appeared, they all resembled scaled-down versions of American models.

Studebaker, based in South Bend, Indiana, the oldest of all American auto makers, could trace its roots back 200 years to a wagon business. As the war was drawing to a close, their stylist Virgil Exner produced a game-changing design. The Studebaker Champion of 1947 had such a pronounced boot, almost as long as the bonnet, that critics said it looked like it was 'going both ways'. It also boasted curved window glass that wrapped around the sides of the roof. The Champion changed the silhouette of a typical family saloon car from 'two-box', bonnet and body, to 'three-box', bonnet, body and boot, or in American parlance 'hood, body and trunk'. Exner's popular silhouette would soon be adopted worldwide.

Flush with their wartime success, America's auto companies were locked in a bitter battle with each other for stylistic supremacy. Never before had fashion played such a critical role in car sales. Mirror-like chrome and revolutionary new paint colours were smeared over steel like pancake make-up. The results were both seductive and extreme. But Chrysler's more conservative leadership was wary of cosmetic innovation. In the 1930s it had been badly stung after betting on its radical 'Airflow' model. Its streamlined looks pleased no one and cost the company dearly in sales before it was rapidly replaced with a more conventional design.

The company's president K. T. Keller was an old-school engineer who believed that folk should be able to get into a car without taking their hats off. But he knew that Chrysler needed to change if it was to survive. So he hired Exner as his chief of advanced styling, with a brief to 'design the most beautiful car you can'. Exner, charismatic, with Cary Grant looks and prematurely silver hair, had dropped out of art school to work in advertising as an illustrator. Despite – or perhaps because of – his lack of engineering training he was open to new ideas that were not burdened by practicality. It was a brave hire for a corporation where engineers dominated.

Armed with a plan to build a series of 'Idea cars', Exner and Keller travelled to the 1950 Turin show in search of inspiration – and collaboration. Ahead of most Americans Exner was aware of Pinin Farina's Cisitalia, and the Ferrari Barchetta that was beginning to make its mark on America's race tracks. He also had definite views about European automotive style, finding the British 'too traditional and dated', the French 'fruity, effeminate and decadent' and the Italians 'a refreshing blend of smoothness with the classicism of a day long passed'.

On the Ghia stand he met Felice Mario Boano, who had trained with Pinin Farina. Exner was very taken with what he saw and Keller was amazed to discover that a one-off show car, which in Detroit would cost over $80,000, Ghia could produce for them for a mere $10,000. They were also impressed by the craftsmanship and build quality of the small and little-known *carrozzeria*.

Founded by Giacinto Ghia in 1915 after a serious accident ended his career as a test driver, it made lightweight racing car bodies as well as bespoke coachwork. But the works was destroyed by Allied bombing in 1943, and Ghia died shortly after. However, his widow Santina was determined to revive the business and offered it to two of her husband's closest associates, Giorgio Alberti and Mario Boano. It was to Boano that Exner gave the task of styling the XX500, a restrained, very European, four-door sedan scaled up to fit a full-size Chrysler chassis. When Exner flew back to Turin to inspect its progress he paid his first visit to what he thought would be Ghia's studio. He was flabbergasted to find the futuristic designs were taking shape in ancient stone sheds surrounded by a cobblestone courtyard. From his drawings an exact full-size rendering had been created out of wood, which on the inside, he noted, still had the bark attached. He had imagined the craftsmen would be elderly, but Ghia's were all teenagers, gifted and energetic. Around the wooden 'buck' were several tree stumps. Exner watched in awe as the panel beaters took sheets of steel in one hand, hammer in the other, studied a section of the shape and then beat the metal over the tree stump before taking it to the buck and offering it up to the allotted area. Once the shape was perfected, another man would approach with a welding torch and weld the pieces into one smooth, contoured form. Any changes needed were done in a matter of hours. Exner's visions of future cars were being brought to life by Piedmontese metalworkers, who a few centuries before had been using the same techniques to fashion breastplates for medieval knights.

While the Chrysler job was underway, Boano added a new man to the small Ghia team, Luigi Segre. Unlike most of the *carrozzerie* people of Milan and Turin, Segre was from Naples in the south. Born in 1919, he was working for his father's construction business when Italy went to war. In 1943 he took part in the Quattro Giornate di Napoli, a spirited and spontaneous uprising against the occupying German forces following the Italian capitulation. Barely armed or organised, they foiled the Wehrmacht's attempt to deport citizens and destroy the city in advance of the imminent Allied landings. When the Americans arrived, Segre asked if he could join them. After a brief training period he was parachuted into Canavese near Turin, where he became a liaison officer between the Italian partisans and the OSS. When the war ended he managed to get a job with Ford and an engineering qualification, and won the touring car class in the first post-war Mille Miglia.

Together, Segre and Exner developed a fruitful partnership. Exner was able to explore his 'ideas', which Ghia were able to turn into finished cars. Much admired, they embodied the dimensions and presence of the big American machines with distinctly Italian clean, harmonious curves, as the magazine *Torino Motori* observed. 'The Ghia lines of these cars bring a note of gracefulness to these elephantine American chassis, softening the intersections between the various elements of the car, wings, body, cockpit and reducing the mass of chromed components which characterise American cars.'

Chrysler sanctioned a production run by Ghia of 400 to sell in Europe. This expansion suited the ambitious Segre better than the more singular designer Boano, who preferred to cater for their bespoke market. When Boano left, Segre replaced him with Giovanni Savonuzzi, a stylist who was also a qualified aerodynamicist.

Back in Detroit the fruits of Exner's collaboration with Ghia led to him being given the go-ahead to restyle the entire Chrysler line-up for 1955. He made it a condition that the Chrysler stylists all reported to him and not the engineering department, who he feared would tone down his vision. With a synthesis of his own ideas and Ghia's, the results were a striking departure for Chrysler, who were feted for their 'forward look'. But this was just the beginning.

Savonuzzi's signature design was not an Exner collaboration nor ever intended for the road. Built purely as a showstopper for the 1955 Turin show, his Ghia Gilda was an almost entirely aerodynamic form. Early experiments using wind tunnels and streamlining had not always been a success, as Chrysler had discovered with the Airflow. But after the war, American stylists, excited by many features of their victorious fighters and bombers, had experimented with tailplane-like shapes sprouting from the tops of the rear wings. But Savonuzzi's Gilda went much further. As a lecturer at Turin Polytechnic, he had access to a wind tunnel and there he sought to reconcile aerodynamic principle with aesthetic preference.

The result was revolutionary. His Gilda was low, with wide, flat, horizontal planes, but its signature feature was a pair of dart-shaped fins that rose in a dead straight line right from the front of the car to sharp points at the rear. Savonuzzi called it Gilda after the 1946 film starring Rita Hayworth, whose tagline was 'There never was a woman like Gilda' – nor was there ever a car like the Gilda. As soon as he saw it, Exner adapted the shape for one of his own 'Idea' cars and, two years later, all Chrysler models included the Gilda-inspired 'swept-wing' styling, which amounted to the tallest fins ever to appear on production cars. They have gone into folklore as the ultimate expressions of Detroit at its loudest and most extreme, but the roots of that look have their origins in the cobbled courtyard of a Torinese *carrozzeria*.

A more lasting legacy of this Italo-American collaboration actually came from Germany. For the entrepreneurially minded Segre, Ghia's association with Chrysler was a calling card for commissions from other foreign car firms. Wilhelm Karmann's family business in Osnabrück built convertible versions of the Beetle for Volkswagen. Segre suggested Ghia come up with a coupé body that Karmann could build on the VW platform. Using a scaled-down version of one of Exner's collaborative Idea cars, the Chrysler d'Elegance, shorn of its radiator grille, they presented the coupé which Karmann used to win over VW's boss. Exner had no knowledge of the project until he saw the finished Karmann Ghia, as it became known. To his credit, rather than complain of plagiarism, Exner was amused and pleased that one of their designs had made it into mass production. And so it would seem were the customers: between 1955 and 1974, 440,000 Karmann Ghias were built.

Soon, other manufacturers across Europe were heading to Turin and Milan in search of style. While the rest of the world's coachbuilders were vanishing, killed off by the standardisation brought on by mass production and unitary 'monocoque' body construction, Italy's *carrozzerie* were en route to world domination.

Italy's Sweetheart

Alfa Romeo faced an existential problem. Through the 1930s, propped up by Mussolini's government, it had survived on military contracts for vehicles and aeroplane engines. The output of cars dwindled to a trickle, most of them hand-built to order, stylish, exotic and exclusive. For Alfa to survive as a car maker, a complete rethink was required.

In 1948, to manage the state-owned businesses inherited from the Mussolini era, the post-war government formed a holding company, Finmeccanica, and brought in Giuseppe Luraghi, an economist and management expert who had run the Pirelli tyre business. His secretary, Lidia Bongiovanni, was a champion skier and had also competed in the 4×100 metre relay at the 1936 Berlin Olympics. Soon after she started work for Luraghi, she introduced him to her fiancé, Rudolf Hruska. This meeting would have a dramatic impact on the fortunes of Alfa Romeo.

An engineering graduate from Vienna, just before the war Hruska had joined the team of Austrians led by Ferdinand Porsche who, with the help of expertise from Detroit, were fitting out the giant plant for the Third Reich in Germany which would eventually build the Volkswagen. The task had given him first-hand experience of American-style mass-production techniques. Luraghi made Hruska a Finmeccanica consultant to advise Alfa. At the time, they were producing fifteen to twenty cars a day, hardly mass production, but it was their first venture away from bespoke manufacture, and they were struggling.

Hruska's Volkswagen experience as well as his diplomacy helped trouble-shoot Alfa's problems and prepare Portello for mass production. Persuasive and disciplined, he instituted a drastic 'house-clearing' operation, which removed an extraneous stock of machinery to create more space and prepare the way for Satta's next car, the smaller 1300cc saloon.

Giuseppe Busso, back at Portello after his brief sojourn at Ferrari, was given the task of producing the engine, his first clean-sheet design. For Alfa's cheapest-ever car he nevertheless gave it a twin-cam, all-aluminium engine that owed much to his own training as an aircraft engineer for its lightness and high revving capability. And Hruska and Satta, themselves enthusiasts, could not help but egg him on.

But for the new model to be profitable, Hruska argued that they would need to build 200 a day, an unimaginable number for the company which, before the war, had struggled to build that many in a year. So he made the case to Luraghi that to properly mass-produce the smaller car, Finmeccanica had to come up with significant investment for new plant and machinery. Their response was to launch a public sale of interest-bearing bonds, with an added incentive – a lottery draw of the shares would award 200 Giulietta cars to lucky bond-holders. The offer was a great success: the bonds were snapped up and the lottery draw eagerly awaited. But there was a problem. With just months to go before the scheduled launch at the 1954 Turin show, the new saloon was running late. Hruska was determined to eliminate all the noise and vibration issues that were dogging the first production prototypes. But delaying the launch – and the much-anticipated lottery draw – could cause uproar.

Although the body needed more work, the 'platform' on which it sat, which carried all the moving parts, had been completed. Since it was traditional that Alfa models were also offered as coupés, Hruska proposed that they pre-empt the launch of the saloon with an outsourced coupé built by a local *carrozzeria* with the capacity to build enough bodies to cover the lottery winners and avert a crisis. Hruska and Satta chose Bertone.

Like Pinin Farina, Giovanni Bertone had fled rural poverty. As a child he had been apprenticed to a wagon maker and in 1912 he started his own workshop repairing carriages and making racing sulkies. Adept at choosing the best materials, he was known for carrying a hammer whose face bore his initials, which he would use to mark the timber he had selected, rather as a cattle farmer would use a branding iron. Bertone moved onto car bodies and in 1934 his son Nuccio joined him.

Although an enthusiastic designer at heart, he had been persuaded to study accountancy, which helped him put the business on a more profitable footing and concentrate on series production of bodies rather than individual orders. This made Bertone a useful partner for Alfa.

Two weeks ahead of its launch, a preview for the car, now christened Giulietta, was organised in the courtyard at the Portello plant in Milan. The Archbishop of Milan was on hand to bless the new model and two actors dressed as Romeo and Juliet leapt from a helicopter. When the Giulietta appeared at the Turin show, the reception was rapturous. The press hailed it as *la fidanzata d'Italia* ('Italy's sweetheart'). Seven hundred orders were taken in a single day.

To cope, Bertone had to call on master panel beaters working at small workshops all over Turin to help him complete bodies partly beaten by hand on wooden dies and partly made up of pressed panels, a very 1920s solution to an explosion in demand.

Max Hoffman, like Luigi Chinetti, had fled Europe for America in the 1930s and was now selling imported European cars from a plush showroom on New York's Park Avenue and enjoying a share of the runaway success of British sports cars over there. On first sight of the Giulietta, Hoffman approached Alfa with a deal to distribute their cars throughout America – on the condition that they produced an open version – the Spider. With Bertone already overwhelmed with producing the coupé body, the job was enthusiastically picked up by Pinin Farina. The combination of a twin-cam engine, Italian styling and features not yet found on equivalent British sports cars, like exterior door handles and wind-up windows, made the Spider an instant hit.

When the developed Giulietta saloon appeared a year after the coupé, the reception was similarly rapturous, but Satta and Luraghi's carefully crafted business plan for a stable of modestly priced saloon cars to help it transition to mass production had been blown out of the water by the explosion of demand for their sports cars. And while the rest of Europe's coachbuilders were disappearing, Bertone and Pinin Farina were having to expand into full-scale series production to meet international demand for Italian style.

The Ice-cream Makers

In the early 1950s, two of Britain's biggest car makers, Austin and Morris, were merged to form the British Motor Corporation, the fourth biggest auto manufacturer in the world. Its boss, Leonard Lord, a blunt, no-nonsense, night school-educated engineer, had made his name as a ruthless and gifted organiser of production. His show-piece plant, Longbridge, boasted such advanced tooling that teams from overseas firms came to learn from it. The Duke of Edinburgh, husband of Queen Elizabeth, also came to have a look and was invited to view their designs. 'They're no good,' he said. 'You'll never sell them.' When it came to bluntness, Lord had met his match.

Since before the war Austin's styling had been overseen by Ricardo Burzi, an Italian fugitive from fascism who had arrived in Birmingham from Lancia after he was caught drawing anti-Mussolini caricatures. But Lord had strong opinions and an abundance of self-belief, so the look of their cars from the mid-1930s onwards had been an amalgam of Lord's demands and the render-ings of the amiable, biddable Burzi, whom Lord frequently referred to as their 'ice-cream seller'. After the war they had struggled to find a style. Lord had hired in American consultants who produced shapes that he and Burzi would then 'anglicise' and name after English counties: Devon, Dorset, Somerset, Hampshire, Hereford, Cambridge. Their dowdiness reflected a British antipathy to flair that typified the rationed, restricted post-war years, but by the mid-1950s the world was moving on.

The arbiters of British automotive style had been the coachbuilders whose classical shapes were constrained by the traditional use of wooden frames. But with the advent of pressed steel and monocoque or unibody construction, they had almost all disappeared, leaving car companies struggling to find new forms. Ford and Vauxhall, Britain's two American-owned satellites, simply adapted Detroit styles, but bright colours and chrome were not always to the taste of the utilitarian-minded Brits. The only exception was Jaguar, whose founder, William Lyons, was a gifted stylist of glamorous designs inspired by Italy. The Duke of Edinburgh's devastating judgement stung the boss of the British Motor Corporation into action. The next day Len Lord made a telephone call to Turin.

Pinin Farina was surprised. 'My friends swore that Britain was still a hard island to conquer for continental coachbuilders and their scepticism was not totally misplaced.' Rolls-Royce and Bentley he regarded as 'national monuments' and therefore untouchable. It is likely that the choice of Pinin Farina was actually Prince Philip's idea. The two men had met the previous year when Farina was invited to become an honorary member of the Royal Society of Arts. At their John Adam Street headquarters, he recalled the duke bemoaning the fact that British cars seemed to be 'dressed in top hat and tails'. What Lord seemed to be asking for was a styling makeover for the entire BMC range. In the late 1940s, Pinin Farina's Cisitalia had become a template for other designers to follow. But by 1955 he had moved on. Unveiled at the Turin show, his Lancia Florida caused a further sensation and signalled another complete change of direction. Where previous shapes looked like – and indeed were – sculpted out of clay, the Florida looked more like it had been folded out of card. The roof, bonnet and boot looked almost flat; a straight line ran from the top of the headlight to the tapered tip of the tail light. The wheel arches, swept back to emphasise forward movement, looked as though they had been cut out of the otherwise entirely smooth, gently curved sheet metal. The radiator grille spread across the front of the car between headlights mounted in the tops of the wings.

For Austin, Pinin Farina produced a small, two-door car that owed much of its inspiration to the Florida and absolutely none to previous Austins. The A40 was a model of stylish simplicity. Barry

Brecknell, who worked in the design office at Longbridge, had been away on National Service when he was called in to see his colleagues who were preparing the A40 for production. '"Have you seen this bloody matchbox we're producing?" they asked. I couldn't believe it was an Austin. Previously we'd had rounded bodies, but this was square at the front, square at the back, square at the bloody sides. Amazing.'

Launched at the Paris Motor Show in 1958, the Italian-styled Austin was judged a hit, and Pinin Farina proceeded to work the same magic on the rest of the BMC range, whose Morris Oxford and Austin Cambridge even sprouted modest but very un-British fins.

BMC was not alone in seeking Italian help. Coventry's Standard-Triumph had been the only British company to use the services of an art-school-trained stylist, Walter Belgrove. But like Burzi, Belgrove had struggled to respond to the post-war era. His boss at Standard, John Black, instructed him to create a scaled-down version of an American Plymouth they had spied outside the US Embassy. But the result was an awkward attempt to bend Detroit-proportion curves around the Standard Vanguard's short chassis. Increasingly frustrated, in 1956 Belgrove abandoned the industry altogether to run a village post office, leaving Standard-Triumph's chief engineer Harry Webster with a problem – their frumpy, wilfully utilitarian small car, the Standard 8, was in urgent need of replacement. Launched at the start of the decade, it had no chrome, sliding windows, a single windscreen wiper and a boot which could only be accessed by folding down the back seat.

Coincidentally, in the spring of 1957 he was shown a prototype 200cc microcar called a Frisky Sport being made in nearby Wolverhampton. The tiny machine had an unexpectedly appealing shape, which had been commissioned from Carrozzeria Vignale, who had in turn given the job to a young freelance designer, Giovanni Michelotti. Despite its diminutive size, Webster was struck by how sharp and contemporary the Frisky looked. Webster decided to go direct to the stylist.

Giovanni Michelotti had grown up in the heart of Italy's automotive industry. He was sixteen when he started at Stabilimenti Farina in 1937, his father had worked for Itala in the 1900s and he could boast that he had machined the crankshaft for Prince Borghese's legendary Peking–Paris car. By the 1950s, he was working freelance for Vignale and other *carrozzerie* and in the process of forming his own business. He was known for his speed of execution; clients were directed to a nearby café and when they returned a fully completed sketch would await them.

In September 1957 when Michelotti presented his first ideas, not drawings but watercolour paintings, and quoted a price of £3,000 for a full-size mock-up, Webster decided to make a leap of faith. Three months later, just as the factory was closing for Christmas, a striking coupé, finished in black and silver, was delivered to Standard-Triumph. Webster was thrilled with it. 'We got it into the styling studio and put it on the turntable ... Everyone thought it was superb. Afterwards we all went down to the canteen and got gloriously drunk.'

Michelotti's sharp, sporty coupé was a world away from its Standard 8 forebear. Webster was also amazed at the quality of the Italian's work and the practicality of the design. There was nothing about it that could not be made by a press tool. Like the Pinin Farina Austin, the Triumph's Michelotti-styled Herald, as it was named, was a complete departure. It won widespread praise for its 'up-to-date Italian look', which had a chic sportiness about it. But the Herald was just the start. For the next decade all of Triumph's cars would be styled by Michelotti.

Pinin Farina's Austins and Michelotti's Triumphs brought the curtain down on the wholesome utilitarianism of post-war Austerity Britain and promised a brighter new direction that did not submit to American cultural imperialism, being appealing and fresh yet not brash or exclusive. They were affordable, modest machines that might be seen on any driveway in any suburb; most of their owners were probably not even aware of the Italian origins of the look of their cars. But one British car in particular, which became an icon of the era, as hip and British as the Beatles and Twiggy, also had its roots in Italy's *carrozzerie*. And the only hint was the discreet script on either side of its bonnet – Superleggera.

When Ian Fleming, a great patriot even though he drove a Ford Thunderbird at his retreat in Jamaica, exchanged his hero James

Bond's Bentley for an Aston Martin 'DB III' in his 1959 thriller *Goldfinger*, he could have been sure it would have fitted right in with 007's Savile Row suits and cigarettes by Morlands of Grosvenor Street. The bodywork of that Aston Martin had come from the pencil of Frank Feeley, a self-taught stylist whose coachwork had clothed Aston Martins and Lagondas since the 1930s. But by the time *Goldfinger* came out as a film in 1964, Aston Martin had moved on.

When Aston director John Wyer saw Feeley's renderings for their next car, the DB4, he was unimpressed. For a car that was going to be the fastest on sale in Britain, Wyer's benchmark was Ferrari's dramatic Barchetta, so he asked Touring in Milan for some renderings. What also appealed to Wyer was Touring's ultra-lightweight Superleggera construction, with alloy body panels fitted over a cage of thin metal tubes – impossible on a mass-produced car but fine for a boutique firm producing fewer than ten hand-built cars per week. A pair of prototype bodies were sent from Milan to the Aston Martin factory in Newport Pagnell from which their craftsmen could learn the art of Superleggera construction, paying a licence fee of £9 for each body they made.

Federico Formenti's vision was not radically different. It bore a family resemblance to the previous Astons, yet the car had extraordinary presence. As on Michelotti's Herald there was a straight line from the front headlamp to the rear light, and frameless door windows, but the body sides, like on Pininfarina's Lancia Florida, were completely smooth and gently curved at the top and bottom. A pronounced scoop to suck air into the engine bay stood proud of the bonnet. The windscreen was raked, curving round to where it met the door pillars and the roof sloped back in a near-straight line to the top of the boot. The overall effect was understated yet dramatic and eye-catching, so much so that when the single pale primrose DB4 was launched at the Paris Salon in October 1958, Marcel Blondeau, their French distributor, had tears in his eyes – because he knew Aston could never make as many as he could sell.

Those who thought of Italians as ice-cream sellers had been swept aside by a new generation who regarded all things Italian with respect. Until the 1950s, style in Britain was all about affluence and exclusivity. This was undercut by Italian products aimed at the wider public, and in particular the working classes who were beginning to enjoy some disposable income.

Italian espresso coffee bars with their chrome Gaggia machines became magnets for British youth, with Vespa and Lambretta scooters for many of them the gateway to motorised transport. Mods listened to American jazz but favoured Italian-styled suits. Like the scooter, these had emerged at the end of the war when Brioni opened its first shop in Rome in 1945. They refreshed the established English lounge suit with lighter materials, shorter, unvented jackets with narrower lapels and tapered hip-hugging trousers with a lower belt-line. Savile Row was no longer the arbiter of Western male dress.

As the 1950s rolled on, it seemed no item could escape the influence of Italian stylists. The most mundane products, from table lamps to typewriters, all received the attention of designers bent on improving the furniture of everyday life. After a brutal war Italy's designers and craftsmen had rebounded with dizzying energy and creative verve. Boosted by America's Marshall Aid, Italy's industrial base grew dramatically and delivered an economic boom that would bring not just cars but also fridges, vacuum cleaners and TVs within reach of ordinary Italians. And the explosion in the production of consumer goods provided plenty of work. In 1950, La Rinascente, Milan's pre-eminent department store, mounted an exhibition promoting 'the Aesthetics of the Product' and sponsored the Compasso d'Oro awards for good design. Along with a sewing machine, vacuum cleaner, clothes hanger and telephone were cars by Dante Giacosa and Pininfarina.

The Italian appetite for joyful pleasure in the good design of everyday things was a world away from the worthy wholesomeness that dogged traditional British style, the rarefied snobbery that surrounded Paris fashions, the earnestness that came with Germany's Bauhaus aesthetic. It is also striking that class and privilege were not a prerequisite for joining Italy's design revolution. While Dante Giacosa was a product of Turin's prestigious Polytechnic, Pinin Farina and Federico Formenti were entirely self-taught school leavers.

Il Boom

A t the beginning of the 1950s, Italy was on the cusp of the '*miracolo economico*', a consumer boom that would engulf the entire nation. But when Fiat boss Vittorio Valletta and chief designer Dante Giacosa began to plan the tiny post-war Fiats that would replace the ageing Topolino they were preparing for the worst.

Valletta's haste to modernise Fiat's plant and hurry on plans for a new small car was born out of fear rather than optimism, as he confided in Giacosa: 'We have to concentrate incessantly on finding work for our factories. The responsibility rests squarely on us, everything depends on us, remember that. Not for the sake of the shareholders but for the workers and ourselves.'

Having weathered three decades of economic turbulence, Valletta was not a natural optimist. Italy was a bruised and fragile country; the first signs of recovery could turn out to be a mirage. In 1950, cars in Italy were still essentially a luxury item. Smaller, cheaper cars could be more accessible to lower-income households. But they were just as much a hedge against the ever-present possibility of an economic downturn when people would stop buying bigger cars.

American support for post-war Italy through Marshall Aid helped put the country on the road to recovery, but the support was not unconditional. The onset of the Cold War at the end of the 1940s stiffened America's resolve to support Western European recovery as a bulwark against Soviet Russia. But it also heightened

American paranoia about Soviet influence, especially in Italy where the Communist Party was a force in domestic politics, local government and unions. Fiat's high-profile position as a major recipient of American financial support opened it up to scrutiny.

In March 1953, Claire Boothe Luce was appointed Washington's ambassador to Italy by the incoming Republican president, Dwight D. Eisenhower. A fervent anti-communist, Luce immediately aroused controversy in her first speech in Rome, warning of 'grave consequences for this intimate and warm cooperation we now enjoy' if communist sympathies were not reined in. It was more than a warning. A deal with the US Navy for a warship construction project in Palermo was cancelled along with a lucrative contract for munitions. Then, in February 1954, she summoned Valletta to Rome to express her concern that despite 'the great sacrifices America had made to come to Fiat's aid, Communism in spite of declining, seemed to be making continuous progress'.

Like Giovanni Agnelli, Valletta had distanced Fiat from party politics, accommodating rather than resisting the presence of Communist Party members in the workforce and maintaining cordial relations with Palmiro Togliatti, the Italian Communist Party leader. But Valletta saw the difficulty of justifying this to Luce, all the more since Washington was in the grip of its own anti-communist witch-hunt being pursued by Senator Joseph McCarthy.

Valletta reassured her that each year 300 workers trained 'the Fiat way' to be foremen were introduced into the workforce, that 'turbulent elements' were sacked and activists confined to the spare parts division. Luce was placated. Fiat had once again survived political interference. But Valletta was leaving nothing to chance. Italy's and Fiat's recovery still had a long way to go.

By the time Dante Giacosa came to design Fiat's new generation of small cars, he had evolved a whole theory of design around what he defined as a 'supreme principle of economy ... the art of justly ordering the parts within the whole, achieving the just relationship between dynamic qualities as well as between intrinsic and aesthetic ones'. His methodology left no room for any separate notion of 'style'. He shuddered at the sight of a tailfin, 'as ugly as they were useless ... expressions of a decadent aesthetic'.

The parameters set by Valletta for the new small car were even more daunting than what he was given for the Topolino. Like its predecessor it would be a two-door and although no bigger it had to be a four-seater. It also had to be *cheaper*. Giacosa considered his options. The Topolino had its engine in the front driving the rear wheels; to fit more passengers he would have to squeeze all the moving parts together, either in the front or the back. Front-wheel drive, he believed, posed too many challenges, not least Fiat's historic antipathy to innovation, so he opted for a more familiar rear engine right behind the rear axle. This posed a problem for any van or estate car version, variants of the Topolino which had been big sellers. So he devised an ingenious alternative body, leaving the engine where it was, but moving the front passengers forward, over the front wheels, and making the windscreen flush with the front of the car. This created a substantial space either for loads, or two more rows of seats accessed by a second set of doors. A measure of how profound the decision was, Valletta convened the entire board, including future chairman Gianni Agnelli, to approve the project. The 300 billion lire earmarked for production was far bigger than any previous investment.

Giacosa felt his life was on the line as each board member was invited to comment. Neither version bore any relation to a previous Fiat. But the vote was unanimous. It would be called the Seicento, or 600, and its load-carrying variant the Multipla. Launched in 1955, for a price starting at 590,000 lire, it would go on to sell more than 2.6 million over fourteen years, a huge leap from the 122,000 Topolinos Fiat produced. The investment Valletta secured after the war had been put to good use, with modern tooling. At Mirafiori between 1948 and 1956, productivity increased five times over. Labour as a proportion of costs dropped from 39 per cent in 1948 to 23 per cent in 1956 and man hours per automobile fell by 72 per cent. More than any other car, the Seicento put Italian households on wheels, but as an icon of the *miracolo economico* it was eclipsed by its even smaller sister, the Nuova 500, or Cinquecento.

Giacosa was fascinated by what he called a 'minimum auto', smaller, lighter and even cheaper than the Seicento. An admirer of the Vespa, he wondered if there was something one step up from the scooter. 'The Italians wanted to become auto-owners and would willingly put up with being a bit cramped provided they could travel on four wheels. However small it might be, an automobile would always be more comfortable than a motor scooter, especially when the weather was cold or wet.' Less than three metres long and only 1.3 metres wide, to save on cost and weight the engine had just two cylinders; the roof was partly fabric. Measured against any other car it was distinctly spartan. But it delighted the public who recognised it as a true successor to the Topolino. Although it bore some resemblance to the bigger 600, its more rounded and harmonious outline charmed the public. Giacosa, a shy man who preferred to share any credit with his team, was paraded on national television beside the production line as the tiny cars rolled past him. Pinin Farina pronounced it 'the light cavalry which is needed to launch the attack on our cities, most of which have medieval layouts'.

As with the equally simple Vespa scooter, the Nuova 500 expressed an almost uniquely Italian capacity to find beauty in utility. Never before had such functional, basic products, born out of austerity, come to represent the vanguard of national style. It was so well received that Giacosa became a national hero. In 1959, he received a prestigious Compasso d'Oro, the first awarded to a car designer. By 1958, Italy's one car per twenty-four inhabitants was about the same level as France and Britain in 1930. By 1965 there was one car per ten inhabitants in Italy.

The launch of the Cinquecento in 1957 coincided with another key milestone in Italy's post-war revival, when it hosted the signing of the Treaty of Rome, with France, Germany and the Benelux countries, which gave birth to the European Common Market.

Newly industrialised, low-wage Italy was perfectly positioned to reap the benefits with competitively priced cars, fridges, radios, sewing machines and other electrical goods. Italy's industrial revolution was not about coal and steam and steel but consumer goods. No other country offered such a wide range of cars, from the ultra-small, ultra-cheap Fiats to their larger siblings, but also affordable performance cars from Alfa Romeo to ultra-fast, ultra-glamorous Ferraris and Maseratis. Over the next five years industrial production more than doubled, as did investment in plant.

Nowhere was the impact of *il boom* felt more startlingly than in Italian households, where between 1950 and 1970 average per capita income trebled. Home life was transformed by an influx of consumer goods. In 1955, only 3 per cent of Italian homes had refrigerators and 1 per cent had washing machines compared to 8 and 18 per cent respectively in Britain. By 1975, Italy's percentages had pulled ahead of Britain's to reach 94 and 76 per cent respectively. When television began in 1954, RAI, the only channel, decided to put all its commercials into one, one-hour slot, which became the most popular show.

Between 1955 and 1970, 9 million Italians migrated from the impoverished agrarian south to the industrialised north. It became known in Italy as the era of *la valigia di cartone*, the cardboard suitcase, a misnomer since most of the migrants were too poor even to own a suitcase. Entire families hitched rides on northbound trucks on the newly opened Autostrada del Sole, often sleeping in railway stations until they found work and shelter. And they did not have to look for long. Demand for workers was high as car factories in the north entered a period of astonishing expansion, from 100,000 units in 1950 to over 500,000 by 1960 and, by 1966, one million.

In 1963, US president John F. Kennedy personally praised Italy's extraordinary economic growth at an official dinner in Rome with Italian president Antonio Segni, stating that 'the growth of the nation's economy, industry, and living standards in the post-war years has truly been phenomenal. A nation once literally in ruins, beset by heavy unemployment and inflation, has expanded its output and assets, stabilized its costs and currency, and created new jobs and new industries at a rate unmatched in the Western world.' Valletta, no doubt aided by Gianni Agnelli's friendship with JFK, found himself giving the American president advice on which of Italy's political parties should be given support.

On the basis that what was good for Fiat was also good for Italy, Valletta effectively pursued his own foreign policy that owed no allegiance other than to the company, and nowhere was this more apparent than in the most audacious deal of his career – to set up a car factory in Soviet Russia. His cordial relationship with the Communist leader Togliatti helped smooth the way but Valletta was also leveraging Fiat's association with Russia which predated its revolution. In the First World War it had supplied trucks to the Csar's Imperial Army and in the 1930s, provided expertise in the form of Ugo Gobbato to build a ball-bearing plant outside Moscow. In this deal, signed by Valletta at the Kremlin in 1966, Fiat would supply all the tooling for production of up to 600,000 cars a year in an entirely new factory in a new town, appropriately named Tolyatigrad after Italy's communist leader Palmiro Togliatti. Based closely on a Fiat 124, the car, the VAZ 2101, would become better known to the world as the Lada.

For a Western company to be aiding Soviet Russia might have looked controversial, but Valletta had already sought blessing from Washington. In an article headlined 'To Russia without Love', *Forbes* magazine caustically described Fiat as a 'middleman for the US machine industry' and noted that three quarters of the plant installed in the Russian plant would be of US origin.

L'Avvocato

Gianni Agnelli had a hard act to follow. His grandfather, who had led Fiat for almost half the century, had by some considerable margin been Italy's most successful industrialist. The early death of Gianni's father, Edoardo, in 1935 meant that from the age of fourteen he was first in line to the Fiat throne.

He studied law and although he did not take his final exam was ever after known as l'Avvocato. Like his grandfather, he attended the Pinerolo cavalry school and in the Second World War served in an Italian tank regiment on the Eastern Front and in the North African desert. But after the Allied landings he became a liaison officer with the US Fifth Army. When he returned to Turin after the war, his grandfather, only months away from death, advised him to take it easy and leave the business in the capable hands of Vittorio Valletta.

Gianni followed his grandfather's instructions to the letter; he embarked on what is best described as a seven-year-long party. He headed to the French Riviera, which since the 1920s had been a favourite gathering place for wealthy, influential Americans and their European counterparts. Pamela, the flame-haired daughter-in-law of Winston Churchill, on the run from her husband Randolph, had taken refuge at the waterfront villa of Prince Aly Khan, when Agnelli, stepping off his speedboat, spotted her. Fluent in English and charm, he whisked her away on a Mediterranean cruise. Together they moved into a twenty-bedroom villa in Cap d'Antibes. At a time when Italy's reputation was still somewhat compromised by two decades of Mussolini's fascism, the well-connected Pamela helped him build an influential social circle. She introduced him to Franklin Roosevelt Jnr, son of the late president, Hollywood moguls Darryl F. Zanuck and Jack Warner, Monaco's Prince Rainier, Greek shipping magnate Aristotle Onassis and newly elected Massachusetts congressman John F. Kennedy. Famously handsome, tall, poised, permanently tanned, with a Roman nose and a coolly penetrating gaze, Agnelli oozed natural, unforced charisma. Kennedy said 'he had the physiognomy of a king', but he was also attentive and naturally amusing in at least three languages. His flirtation with the cosmopolitan Riviera set enabled him to widen his horizons from the city of Turin and occasionally claustrophobic Agnelli family life.

His appetite for adventure was voracious; as well as skiing he became a devotee of the bobsleigh Cresta Run in St Moritz, and loved nothing better than to start a weekend entertaining friends in the sun by jumping into the Mediterranean – from a helicopter.

Lupo Rattazzi, Agnelli's nephew, bemoaned how after a visit 'the worst part was to go back to your life, it was terrible because when you were with that man you were living like James Bond. And when you had to get back to your life it was something disappointing.'

The party came to a sudden halt in 1952 when, intoxicated in the early hours and after an argument with Pamela, who had found him in another woman's arms, he crashed his Fiat station wagon into a butcher's van, breaking one of his legs in seven places. Doctors fought to save it and ever after he walked with a slight limp. During his convalescence, his sisters set about finding him a suitable wife.

In 1953 he married Marella Caracciolo dei Principi di Castagneto, a half-American, half-Neapolitan noblewoman, model and photographer whose work appeared in *Vogue*. Agnelli's friend William Paley, founder of CBS, observed that 'marriage may have been the wisest move Gianni ever made'. Marella's father, Filippo, a hereditary prince who had also been a member of the Italian resistance, and was now secretary general of the Council of Europe, brought further connections into post-war politics. A measure of how successfully Agnelli had embedded himself in international society is that according to Jackie Onassis it was he who introduced her and her first husband, John F. Kennedy, to Winston Churchill.

Another lifelong friend was Henry Kissinger, who enjoyed his wisdom and his attitude. 'Gianni disliked self-righteous posturing; in his view, the fundamental challenges spoke for themselves without the need for histrionics. Dealing with Gianni was like absorbing a Mozart symphony – frothy at the surface; serious, perhaps even somewhat melancholy, underneath.' He also did not suffer pomposity. His cook, Giulio Marconi, recalled a time when the president of Italy was coming to lunch. 'Let's have bulls' testicles,' Agnelli told him. Marconi tried to reason with him, but Agnelli would have none of it. 'My dear Giulio, when those people come over they should be treated as they deserve. What's more beautiful than serving testicles to a prick?'

Marella had supremely good taste and spent her new husband's fortune with great panache. She hired Lorenzo 'Renzo' Mongiardino, visionary Milan-based architect and interior designer, to transform their homes in Turin, Rome and New York. Marella also helped her husband become an international style icon. Fashion designer Nino Cerruti named Agnelli as one of his greatest inspirations, along with James Bond. *Esquire* magazine called Agnelli one of five best-dressed men in history. His unique style included pairing a Caraceni suit with brown hiking boots, wearing his wristwatch over his cuff, and tying his necktie with a loose knot. He personified the Italian art of *sprezzatura*, the art of doing something very clever or artful without appearing to try.

During his two decade-long apprenticeship for the role of Fiat supremo, Agnelli became a jet-setting ambassador-cum-poster boy for the new-look post-war Italy, a style leader sowing connections that would benefit the country and the family business. A supporter of NATO, he regarded American aid as fundamental to Italy's post-war revival. 'Without America,' he told his sister, Susanna, 'Italy would not exist.' But he also befriended Enrico Berlinguer, Italy's Communist Party leader, and never aligned himself with any political party. Just as his grandfather had managed his relationship with both Mussolini and the left-leaning trade unions and with both the Germans and the Allies during the war, Gianni Agnelli managed to achieve a similarly delicate balance. But unlike his grandfather and Valletta, he did not immerse himself in the details of manufacture, admitting to a *Time* magazine reporter, 'I haven't the slightest idea how to build a car.' He was content for Valletta to remain at the helm of Fiat long past retirement age. The arrangement suited them both.

Valletta was a uniquely capable executive, possessing all the practical knowledge of production organisation and political cunning needed to head up Italy's most important industrial enterprise. He made it his life's work and maintained his grip on it long after his contemporaries had retired. It was not until a board meeting in April 1966 that Valletta, aged eighty-three, submitted his resignation. Just over a year later he died. Italian president Giuseppe Saragat praised his command of Fiat and for making it 'the leading Italian industrial company, contributing more than any other to that economic miracle which placed our country among the first industrial nations of the world'.

Finally, it was time for Fiat to be led once again by an Agnelli. As it turned out, the timing for Italy's preeminent automotive brand could not have been better.

California Dreaming

U ntil the 1950s, motor racing in the United States and Europe had remained an ocean apart. Americans competed on banked oval 'speed bowls' like Indianapolis, running anti-clockwise in rugged machines built to survive at continuous high revs, or in modified production 'stock-cars'. Raw power and sturdy construction were the bedrocks of American race engineering, while the Europeans were ever in search of the right balance between power, weight and handling. Apart from Jimmy Murphy's 1921 French Grand Prix win in a Duesenberg and Maserati's victory at Indianapolis in 1939 and 1940, racing in Europe and the USA had gone separate ways.

Culturally they were also different. Where European competition was dominated by wealthy sportsmen racing in national colours, American racing was a wholly domestic and much more egalitarian business with a strong blue-collar subculture in a nation where car ownership was far more pervasive. Up to the Second World War, European cars in the USA were niche exotic toys exclusively for wealthy Americans with cosmopolitan tastes; the term 'sports car' was barely recognised. But by the time the war was over, Luigi Chinetti had divined that there was a sufficiently wealthy American clientele to put Ferrari on the road. His inspiration in the late 1940s coincided with the arrival in America of MGs, Austin-Healeys and Jaguars, as part of Britain's export drive to earn much-needed dollars to finance its recovery. MGs were cheap, not much more than a motorcycle – an ideal entrée to racing.

In 1951 the newly formed Sports Car Club of America launched a series of championship races with the unlikely help of US Air Force general Curtis LeMay. A European sports car fan, he sanctioned the use of the Strategic Air Command's bomber bases as weekend race tracks.

Growing up in Santa Monica, California, Phil Hill led a lonely existence. His home life with alcoholic parents was difficult and he was unpopular at the Hollywood Military Academy his father enrolled him in, where he was neither sporty nor sociable but played an alto horn in the orchestra. His only real interest was cars. For his twelfth birthday, his aunt bought him a Ford Model T which he overhauled, becoming an accomplished mechanic. One friend he did have was the grandson of William Randolph Hearst, whose family estate had a dirt track for horse racing, where Hill honed his skills behind the wheel. After dropping out of university, a job selling and repairing foreign cars brought him into contact with other aspiring racers. He worked his way up the hierarchy of the European cars that had begun to appear on the West Coast after the war, first with an MG TC then a Jaguar XK120, which he raced with the sort of success that got him noticed.

When both his parents died in 1951, he sought out Luigi Chinetti. The Italian émigré had made good his promise to Enzo Ferrari that he would find a market for his cars in the United States. He had established a clientele of wealthy customers and dealers who paid him a royalty on every car sold. Some customers tried their hand at racing; others, like racehorse owners, went in search of promising young men to race them. Hill blew $6,000 of his inheritance on a second-hand Ferrari 212 which came with some racing history. French driver Jean Larivière had been killed in it at Le Mans, decapitated by a strand of wire fence when he left the road. Rebuilt, the car had won another race in France before finding its way to America.

In 1953, with fellow sports car racer Richie Ginther, he entered Mexico's brutal Carrera Panamericana. 'We were on a twisty stretch over the mountains between Puebla and Mexico City. I was running so hard that on one turn I clipped a couple of big white boulders. We shot over a crest and there was a tricky, curling, downhill right-hander – with a lot of spectators hiding amongst the tall trees. I hit the brake pedal but the brakes were fading fast. I realised I wasn't getting enough to take the turn. In fact the darned brake pedal and clutch pedal pivoted on the same cross-tube, and I'd put so much load on the brake pedal I'd bent the tube and when I kicked the clutch to down-shift it didn't clear. All I found was neutral. So with faded brakes and the car out of gear it began to slide – still at high speed – towards the edge. I clearly remember wondering how far we were going to fall, because that's what we were going to do. We slid off the edge, and the car rolled.'

He and his mechanic were able to extricate themselves. 'We climbed up to road level amongst all these excited Mexicans. But there was the most terrific shriek of tyres and a stock-car class Cadillac came vaulting over the same bank and crashed down on the high-side of the stout tree behind which we'd just ended up ... A soldier told us Fangio's Lancia had nearly gone off just before we did. It turned out this was a notorious turn, and for entertainment the crowd had removed the warning sign.' The following year Hill was back and came home in second place.

Hill's cool, measured aggression was impressive enough for Chinetti to recommend him to Enzo Ferrari, who brought him to Modena. He took time to fit in. Diffident and earnest, he seemed lost among the demonstrative Italians. But he gained the team's re-spect because of his technical knowledge and the speed with which he picked up enough Italian to communicate. A classical music buff who travelled with his own record player so that he could listen to Beethoven and Mozart, he actually felt more at home in Italy than the rougher-edged Indy and NASCAR racing scene back home.

Enzo Ferrari thought of him primarily as a sports car driver, but Hill was determined to get into Formula One. By the end of the 1950s the team was under intense pressure. Dramatic changes in racing car design, the most radical in the history of the sport, had been forced on them by the newly triumphant British Lotus and Coopers. At first, Ferrari dismissed them as *garagisti* but their message was clear. Power alone was no longer enough. Rear engines, space-frame construction, disc brakes and aerodynamics, all new to Ferrari, had to be deployed.

In 1961, Ferrari came back with a vengeance. The 156, a complete departure with its V6 Dino engine mounted behind the driver and a dramatic double-nostrilled front end, earning it the nickname 'Sharknose'.

Ferrari were the favourites for the championship again – but which driver? Hill was pitted against Wolfgang von Trips, potentially Germany's first ever Formula One champion. Both of them were mature, committed racers. It would all be decided in Ferrari's heartland, Monza, on 10 September 1961.

Other than his teammate, Hill's only serious competition was from Lotus' Scottish wunderkind, Jim Clark. Hill led from the start with his teammate and Clark close behind. On the second lap as they decelerated into the Parabolica, a 180-degree corner that needed second gear, Clark and von Trips touched wheels, sending the Lotus into a spin. But von Trips's Ferrari slammed into the inside barrier, and cartwheeled across the embankment into a group of spectators protected by a flimsy wire fence. Unaware of the gravity of the accident, Hill cruised to victory and became America's first Formula One world champion. But it was a sombre moment. All the television screens were focused on the extrication of von Trips from the remains of his car and the helicopters sweeping in to take the dead and injured to hospital.

Hill tried to be philosophical. 'Everybody dies. Isn't it a fine thing that Von Trips died doing something he loved, without any suffering, without any warning? I think Trips would rather be dead than not race.' Once again, the spotlight was on Ferrari and the dangers of motor racing, but Hill's victory resonated all across America, even in the heart of Detroit, America's motor city, even up to the eighth floor of the Glass House, the Ford Motor Company's global headquarters, and into the office of Henry Ford II.

Italian Influence

Like Gianni Agnelli, Henry Ford II had also inherited the family business after the death of his grandfather, in 1947. But unlike Fiat, the Ford Motor Company had no Vittorio Valletta, no wise regent to oversee the business while the heir to the throne reached maturity. Henry II, married at twenty-four to his college sweetheart, had been obliged to take the helm at Ford at the tender age of twenty-nine, straight after military service.

The chubby, bullish young boss was as all-American as apple pie. The centre of his social universe was Grosse Pointe, the upmarket Detroit suburb where he lived. It was a conservative, Christian world where Ford's wife always said grace at dinner parties. Baseball and (American) football were the spectator sports of choice. Motor racing was frowned upon. Henry Ford I had competed once in 1901 and won, and ever after shunned all racing.

Henry II brought the family business into the modern age, but steered clear of any deviation from the mainstream. The Edsel sub-brand, launched in 1957 after extensive market research, had been a very public disaster. And Ford's tentative response to the influx into America of sporty British and Italian imports, the 1955 two-seater Thunderbird, was not even marketed as a sports car and rapidly grew into a four-seater cruiser. But by the 1960s Henry Ford's horizons began to widen.

'It was meeting Gianni Agnelli that did it,' recalled a member of the Ford family. 'Here was this man, who was just about the same age – handsome, macho, suntanned, dynamic – running a successful major business but also jetting from St Moritz to St Tropez. And suddenly Henry Ford realised, "Christ! This is what running a family car company is all about".'

In 1962, at an event at Maxim's in Paris to honour Princess Grace of Monaco, Henry Ford spotted Cristina Vettore Austin, a recently divorced Italian socialite, and switched the place cards on the dinner table so that he could get to know her. The ensuing affair introduced Ford to an exotic European jet set and scandalised the conservative, parochial Grosse Pointe social set. His sister-in-law referred to her as 'the Pizza Queen'.

For Lee Iacocca, Ford vice-president and general manager, his boss's infatuation was timely. Iacocca was living the Italian-American dream. His parents were émigrés from Campania in the south-west of Italy who had settled in Pennsylvania. After gaining a master's in engineering from Princeton, Iacocca joined the Ford Motor Company, moving from engineering into sales, where he excelled. He was just thirty-six when he got the vice-presidency in 1960, quite an achievement in a city where most Italian-Americans were to be found working on the factory floor, mocked by the *Detroit Times*'s popular columnist and 'poet' Edgar Guest.

> He smok' da cigar weeth da beega da band,
> Da diamond dat flash from da back of hees hand,
> Ees da beegest Giuseppe could find,
> For Giuseppe he work at da Ford.

But Iacocca's focus was elsewhere, on the future and America's youth. He discovered that in the next ten years America's population of 20- to 28-year-olds would grow by 50 per cent. Chevrolet had just launched a youth-focused car and called it the Monza, after the race track. Its low, clean lines had more than a hint of Italian style, but its rear engine was highly unusual, a legacy of the Corvair, a controversial car pilloried in Ralph Nader's 1965 exposé *Unsafe at Any Speed*. And Iacocca still wanted Ford to go younger and racier. The result was the Ford Mustang, a very affordable coupé with a long bonnet and short boot, whose styling and proportions had more than a hint of Italian *carrozzerie* about it. And, like the Ferrari, it had a silhouette of a horse on the front, albeit a galloping mustang rather than a prancing *cavallino*.

At the Mustang's launch in New York on 13 April 1964, Iacocca boasted that it came with 'all the flair of a high-priced, highly styled European road car'. It was a huge hit, selling more than 400,000 in its first year. Iacocca was feted as a visionary and featured on both *Time* and *Newsweek* front covers, but even he could not have foreseen what was coming next.

Pride and Prejudices

The message was deliberately cryptic and came by a circuitous route – via the German consul in Milan. Sent to Ford's German headquarters in Cologne, it advised that a small but internationally known Italian automobile factory could be for sale. Robert Layton, Ford's finance chief in Cologne, was only a little curious; there were plenty of boutique car builders dotted round Europe struggling to survive. But after making a few enquiries, enough to discover the identity of the firm, Layton passed the note on up to Ford's headquarters in Dearborn, Michigan, with his own comments attached: 'While I doubt whether this is of special interest, there may be angles I don't know of.'

When the memo arrived on Iacocca's desk he immediately dispatched his deputy Donald Frey and a posse of Ford executives to explore a deal. When they arrived at Maranello, what they found was a car factory in miniature, completely self-contained with its own foundry, body shop, tool room, design office and even a wind tunnel, albeit a miniature one for testing scale models. It even had its own restaurant, the Cavallino, across the road.

Having conducted a thorough inventory of the facilities, they concluded that the $18 million asking price was a steal and drafted a contract. But negotiations took their time and word soon leaked out that Italy's automotive crown jewels were about to be snatched by Detroit. Ferrari, a master of small print, scrutinised the translated text. He was not concerned about the fate of the road car business.

In his mind this was never more than a means to finance racing. What he was not willing to give up was his control of the Scuderia. At a climactic meeting with Ford's Donald Frey, Ferrari demanded to know where in the agreement was his freedom to make staff and investment choices, for the racing team. And what would happen if he decided to enter Indianapolis against Ford's wishes? Frey's reply was emphatic: 'You do not go.'

A tirade followed, full of traditional Ferrari theatrics. His rights, his integrity as an entrepreneur were being traduced, he would be crushed under the Ford bureaucracy and so on. The fact that Ferrari had not chosen to lay out his own terms in advance of the weeks of due diligence by the Ford team suggests that he had another agenda. A patriot and a cunning schemer, Ferrari, knowing that rumours of the negotiations would spread, was in all likelihood testing the water to see who else might come forward with a better deal, one that guaranteed him total control over the racing.

Donald Frey and his team went home empty-handed. Ferrari's pride, if not his finances, was secure. Back in Dearborn, when Frey and Iacocca delivered the bad news to their boss, Henry Ford II's response was succinct: 'We'll beat his ass.' If he couldn't buy Ferrari, he would defeat him – at Le Mans.

Ford was not the first American to think of taking on Ferrari. Briggs Cunningham, Luigi Chinetti's second Ferrari customer, spent a good part of his Procter & Gamble inheritance failing to build a car that would win Le Mans.

Carroll Shelby had started out racing an MG TC in the early 1950s. The son of a Texan mailman, by the time he started driving in earnest he had been an air force pilot, an oil-worker and a (failed) chicken farmer. Married with a family, he discovered he could make a better living as a driver for hire. His winning smile and the chicken farmer's overalls he always wore behind the wheel became his trademarks.

Confident and capable, Shelby set off for Europe in search of a drive with a professional sports car team, but spurned an offer from Ferrari, explaining that with three children to feed he could make more racing back in America. Ferrari, unaccustomed to being turned down, sent him away. Shelby got a better offer from John

Wyer, Aston Martin's team manager, with whom he won the 1959 Le Mans, but his racing career was cut short when he was diagnosed with angina, a condition that would eventually involve a heart transplant.

So Shelby focused on creating an American machine of his own, capable of taking on Ferrari. He found a little-known British sports car the AC Ace, which resembled the Ferrari Barchetta and approached Iacocca with a proposition – to fit the Ace with a Ford V8 engine. He needed $25,000 and a hundred engines on credit so he could build enough to qualify it as a production sports car. The famously persuasive Iacocca had met his match. 'Give him what he wants and get him out of here before he bites someone,' he told Donald Frey.

The result was the Shelby Cobra, displayed on the Ford stand in the 1962 New York Auto Show and first advertised in *Playboy* magazine, itself a departure for the conservatively minded company. Part of the Cobra's charm was its shamelessly Italian-inspired *barchetta* looks, but with its standard-issue Ford V8 it came in at less than half the price of a Ferrari. Purists dismissed it as a backyard hot-rod, but then it beat Ferrari in a race at Sebring in Florida. Phil Hill, still in recovery from his bittersweet time at Ferrari, enjoyed the moment: 'I loved being in an American car. I loved rubbing their noses in it.'

Unlike Ferrari, the team who would build Ford's first ever in-house racing car had unlimited funds. But what Ford couldn't buy, which Enzo Ferrari had in spades, was decades of road-racing experience, especially when it came to Le Mans, where his cars had won the previous four races. A team of Ford executives went on a fact-finding mission to the 1963 event and got a rude awakening as to what they were taking on. Ferrari dominated the race, taking the first six places. They touched speeds over 200 mph; in the twenty-four hours of continuous racing, they covered nearly 3,000 miles, six times that of an Indianapolis 500 and on a track made up of closed public roads.

But behind the first six Ferraris, a lone Cobra had come seventh. Carroll Shelby found himself drawn into Ford's project. They needed hands-on Le Mans experience. Shelby suggested they hire John Wyer, his Aston Martin team manager; he encouraged them to build the car in Britain where they could soak up some of the racing expertise behind Jaguar, Lotus and Cooper. Ford's people knew they had to deliver, all the more since rumours were beginning to circulate that Ferrari might be looking at a partnership with Henry Ford's great rival in Turin, Fiat's Gianni Agnelli. This was war.

At Le Mans in June 1964, the Ford GT40 made its debut. The name was inspired by the height of the car, just 40 inches, and beside the competition it looked stunning. Painted white and blue, America's racing colours, but built in England, it was powered by a 4.7-litre variant of the production V8 that went into millions of Fords, yet on the Mulsanne Straight it could easily reach 200 mph. The team led by John Wyer had a formidable line-up of drivers that included America's first world champion – albeit in a Ferrari – Phil Hill, and New Zealander Bruce McLaren.

The race started well enough, with a Ford leading a train of Ferraris for the first hour and a half until its Colotti gearbox, the only component sourced from Italy, gave out and by the end of the race all the Fords had retired. At the wheel of the first of the three top-placed Ferraris was Nino Vaccarella, a law professor from Palermo who would go on to win three Targa Florios, and French industrialist Jean Guichet, two old-school amateur 'gentlemen' drivers much like those who populated Scuderia Ferrari in the 1930s. But in fourth came one of Carroll Shelby's Cobras in the GT class, ahead of two Ferrari GTOs. All was not yet lost for the Americans.

When Ford returned the next year, Carroll Shelby had taken control of the factory Ford team and entered six GT40s, two of them fitted with 'big block' V8s of no less than seven litres, along with a further five Shelby Cobras. Phil Hill's record-breaking fastest practice lap of three minutes thirty-three seconds, touching 213 mph on the Mulsanne Straight, was a full five seconds faster than John Surtees' Ferrari.

Henry Ford and his wife Cristina flew in from Detroit to watch his cars from above the pits. Also present was Luigi Chinetti, three-time Le Mans winner and the first to do so in a Ferrari, now fielding his own team. As was his custom, Enzo Ferrari remained in his office in Modena with the TV on. Despite their prodigious power and speeds that touched 220 mph, by the time night set in, all the Fords were gone. To Chinetti's enormous satisfaction, victory went not to a works Ferrari but one of his own.

Henry Ford went back to Detroit empty-handed, but not his wife Cristina, who had won a bet that a red car would win.

Ford had to win or heads would roll. He ordered the creation of a Le Mans committee, headed by one of his lifelong lieutenants. Carroll Shelby was once again in charge of the company team, but this time there would be two more Ford teams, one fronted by NASCAR perennials Holman-Moody, and another pair of GT40s leased to the British Alan Mann team. Enzo Ferrari's response to this onslaught was only to be expected. During a rare visit to the paddock at Monza when Ferrari were testing their latest Le Mans contender, he was spotted by John Wyer, who introduced him to a Ford executive, Bill Geddes. 'I would like you to know, Mr Ferrari, that we at Ford have great respect for you,' said Geddes.

Ferrari listened while someone translated, then responded: 'Yes, I know, like America respects Russia.' For all his bluntness and seeming indifference to human emotion, Ferrari was a master manipulator of the public mood, especially when casting himself as the underdog. In the Italian magazine *Autosprint*, he wrote, 'Nothing can be done to resist the steamroller of the Americans.' The race, he warned, was already lost; Ford was effectively buying his way to victory, throwing everything at the task that his vast corporation could muster.

In a laboratory at the Ford complex in Dearborn, the air intake of Ford's Le Mans engine was analysed so that an extra 35 bhp could be extracted; the temperatures of up to 275 degrees Fahrenheit the electrical wiring needed to withstand were also measured. Another lab investigated how brake discs could absorb the 12.5 million ft/lb of energy every time they brought the car down from 200 to 35mph for the corner at the end of the Mulsanne Straight. Windscreen wipers for clearing rain at 200 mph were sourced from Boeing jet airliners. Nothing was being left to chance.

For the thirty-fourth Le Mans in June 1966, a record-breaking 350,000 fans converged on the circuit. Shortly before the start, Henry Ford II's helicopter touched down. Anointed honorary grand marshal, it was his task to drop the flag for the start. Parked down one side of the track were the cars and, standing on the other side, their waiting drivers. In total, thirteen Fords stood ready to battle fourteen Ferraris. Not since 1921, when Jimmy Murphy's Duesenberg won the French Grand Prix, had an American car won a race at Le Mans. And never before had two teams, one from the Old World the other from the New, squared up to each other in such numbers.

Despite the weight of a full tank of fuel, on the first lap, Ford broke the lap record – three minutes 34.3 seconds – and took charge of the first three places, their lap speeds averaging over 140 mph. But by the time dusk fell six hours into the race, the lighter, nimbler and less thirsty Ferraris had taken the first two places.

Ferrari's team lacked the regimented harmony of the Fords and was in the midst of a drama all of its own. John Surtees, a British driver of exceptional talent, a multiple motorcycle world champion – all on Italian machines – was already a hero in Italy before he moved on to four wheels, winning the world championship for Ferrari in 1964. But a long recovery from a bad accident and a poor relationship with Ferrari's team manager had disturbed the equilibrium. When he arrived at Le Mans, he discovered a different name painted on the door of his car. Ludovico Scarfiotti was a capable driver of nowhere near the same calibre. Not only was he Italian, but his grandfather had been chairman of the original group who formed the original Fiat enterprise with Giovanni Agnelli, in 1899. He was also the nephew of Gianni Agnelli, who, as it happened, would also be attending that year's Le Mans.

Scarfiotti did not make it through the night, crashing in heavy rain into an already abandoned competitor's car. By dawn, all the Ferraris were out of the race, comprehensively beaten, and the remainder of the race became something of a procession. At four o'clock on the Sunday afternoon, the three leading Fords took the chequered flag in tight formation, posing for the photograph that would appear on the front page of newspapers across the world. The full force of American dollars and muscle was more than the Italians could match. Stirling Moss, who despite being snubbed by him years before, felt for Ferrari. 'It's sad to see a man like this beaten by a big company, especially when you realize [Ford's] decision to race is really just another marketing decision.' But Henry Ford's mission had become personal; if Ferrari wouldn't join him he would beat him. And he had proved his point. Cristina Ford lost the $1,000 she had put on Ferrari, but Henry Ford's victory cost him a whole lot more. No one ever put a figure on the American Goliath's bid to beat the Italian.

But if he was hoping Ferrari might experience some remorse for spurning his offer, he would be disappointed. In his mind, Ferrari had already written off Le Mans 1966 as a foregone conclusion. The presence of Agnelli at the race and the choice of Scarfiotti over Surtees as his lead driver suggested that Ferrari had other priorities and fresh challenges.

Palace Revolt

By the 1960s Italy's motor industry was building an enviable variety of cars, from Fiat's tiny Cinquecento and Seicento to innovative, sporty Lancias and Alfa Romeos, exotic Maseratis and Ferraris. All of them came with a pedigree that dated back to the earliest days of the industry. Hardly room for a new-comer – and yet the one machine that came to be the automotive icon of the decade came from a company that until the early 1960s had yet to build a car.

Born in April 1916, Ferruccio Lamborghini was the first of five brothers. His father was a grape farmer in Renazzo di Cento, not far from Modena. When he was still a boy, he decided he was much more interested in motorcycles and cars than farming. 'I fixed every mechanical thing on the farm to save my parents money.' He per-suaded his parents to let him attend a vocational technical school, the Fratelli Taddia institute in Bologna, after which he became ap-prenticed to a blacksmith before being called up for military service. Stationed on the occupied Greek island of Rhodes, his maintenance unit repaired all kinds of vehicles and munitions. An opportunist at heart, when the Germans seized control of the island in 1944 after the Italian armistice, Lamborghini managed to avoid becoming a prisoner of war, acquired some civilian clothes and offered his services to the Germans, so successfully that he was eventually al-lowed to have his own small workshop. With the Allies' liberation of the island in 1945 he was briefly imprisoned as a collaborator before being sent home to Italy. His five years' experience of vehicle maintenance was put to good use when he opened a small garage in Cento, mostly mending trucks and tractors.

His first car was a Fiat Topolino which he modified, fitting his own overhead valve cylinder head, christening it the Testa d'Oro. He entered the 1948 Mille Miglia but his race ended ignominiously in a bar near Fano, 'which we entered by driving through the wall'. After that he decided to try his hand at building a tractor for his father, using a variety of Allied war surplus parts: a British Morris truck engine, an American General Motors gearbox and a Ford differential. He christened it the Carioca, meaning a song for many parts. Soon his father's neighbours were all asking for one, so he decided to go into production. An able self-publicist, he saw to it that local market days featured a tug-of-war between one of his tractors and a competitor's, with the winners usually being Lamborghinis. By the end of the 1950s, having branched out into domestic heaters and air conditioners, he was a wealthy industrialist.

As his business grew so did his appetite for cars; enough so that he used a different one every day of the week. A demanding and critical driver, he found the Maserati too heavy and not fast enough, the E-Type Jaguar's handling 'nervous' and the Aston Martin DB4 'noisy and choppy'. But his most searing criticism he reserved for the products from down the road at Maranello. 'All my Ferraris had clutch problems . . . when you were going hard, the clutch would slip under acceleration; it just wasn't up to the job. I went to Maranello regularly to have a clutch rebuilt or renewed, and every time, the car was taken away for several hours and I was not allowed to watch them repairing it. The problem with the clutch was never cured, so I decided to talk to Enzo Ferrari. I had to wait for him a very long time. "Ferrari, your cars are rubbish!" I complained. Il Commendatore was furious. "Lamborghini, you may be able to drive a tractor but you will never be able to handle a Ferrari properly," he said.'

He decided to modify the car himself at his tractor factory, replacing the clutch, then putting in new cylinder heads and adding six carburettors. He enjoyed encountering Ferrari test drivers on the Via Emilia and blasting past them. '"Hey, Lamborghini, what have you done to your car?" they would ask me later. "Oh, I don't know," I used to answer with a grin!'

Emboldened, he decided to build his own Gran Turismo. Uniquely for a prospective builder of such machines, he had owned and driven all the competition and knew all their shortcomings, especially the Ferraris'. Being derived from racing machines, in Lamborghini's view, compromised their all-round performance as road cars; it made them highly strung and temperamental. He also thought their interiors were too basic. Lamborghini wanted his cars to be more forgiving, easier to drive, but also more technologically sophisticated. Where Ferrari road cars had single camshafts and live rear axles, his would be twin-cam with independent suspension all round. Although he had never built a car before, he was down the road from the rich talent pool around Modena, somewhat swollen by a recent mass departure from Ferrari.

Just before Christmas 1961, eight key members of staff left Maranello. In a press release, Enzo Ferrari's explanation was marvellously opaque, explaining it as 'a matter of the over inflation of marginal issues'. The issue was Ferrari's wife, Laura, who, as a de facto shareholder, had begun to take an active interest in the business, creating friction in the otherwise all-male environment. Matters came to a head when, in the midst of an altercation, she slapped one of the mechanics across the face. 'She was criticising us to Mr Ferrari,' recalled Tavoni. 'We had a big discussion and we were all so unhappy that we wrote a letter to Mr Ferrari asking that Mrs Ferrari should stay out of the factory. He was very offended and at our weekly meeting he said, "If this is how you feel, there is the door, here is your money – OUT!"' Tavoni and eight of Ferrari's key staff resigned, including his chief engineer, Giotto Bizzarrini.

The timing could not have been better for Lamborghini. Nearly forty years old, Bizzarrini had a wealth of experience creating Ferrari's hallowed 250 GTO and the Testa Rossa sports racers but had yet to design an engine from scratch. The result was an astonishingly powerful all-aluminium V12 with a potential 400 bhp, capable of over 10,000 rpm. Although it outclassed Ferrari's engines by some margin, it did not meet Lamborghini's other requirement: that it could be driven to Bologna averaging no more than 40 kph.

Bizzarrini knew all about how to get high speed out of an engine; long distances at low speed was another matter.

The original prototype of the 350 GTV (Gran Turismo Veloce) was shown at the October 1963 Turin Motor Show, styled by former Bertone designer Franco Scaglione. It received a mixed reaction because of its slightly eccentric amalgam of styles, rounded at the front with an angular rear. Eye-catching details included hidden headlamps and six exhaust pipes protruding under the rear bumper. Bizzarrini's outrageous new engine was exhibited separately – because it did not fit under Scaglione's low-angled bonnet. The reception was enough to convince Lamborghini to go into production – even though the car had yet to run.

To sort out the numerous issues, Lamborghini hired another Ferrari exile, Giampaolo Dallara, just twenty-four years old, whose task it was to domesticate Bizzarrini's engine for everyday use, to be smoother running, more docile at low speeds and capable of going 40,000 miles between services. Dallara also dispensed with the racing car-style tubular space frame which obstructed the door openings in favour of a more conventional platform. The body was restyled by Touring Superleggera in Milan.

Launched at the 1964 Paris Motor Show, the 350GT was advertised at 5,500,000 lire, 300,000 cheaper than Ferrari's new 275 GTB with its live axle and single cams. Wholly committed to the project, Lamborghini bought a greenfield site at Sant'Agata Bolognese, near Bologna, and built a new factory exclusively for car assembly.

The 350GT was launched successfully. A hundred and twenty of them were built over the next two years. But its impact on the world was completely eclipsed by what Lamborghini did next.

Raging Bull

E nzo Ferrari was by nature conservative. Over the years, the most dramatic changes he made to his cars were forced on him by the competition he met on the track. Independent suspension, disc brakes and relocating the engine behind the driver – so the ox *did* push the cart – only happened at Maranello under duress. So for the young Giampaolo Dallara, his new boss was a revelation. 'Lamborghini was completely on board to try something new. Every day there was a new lesson to be learned.

'Fortunately we were so inexperienced that we didn't realise the enormity of the task we were taking on. There weren't many of us anyway and most of us were in our 20s.'

The mid-engined Ford GT40 racer had made a deep impression on him. No road car existed with that configuration of the engine behind the driver. Dallara recognised that replicating this configuration for a Lamborghini would be problematic. Ford's engine was a V8. Mounting Bizzarrini's much larger V12 behind the driver would make the rear of the car unfeasibly long.

Dallara drew his inspiration from far and wide. One of his engineering heroes was Alec Issigonis, creator of Britain's Mini with its engine mounted sideways between the front wheels. Could Lamborghini's V12 be persuaded to fit between the rear wheels, with a gearbox beneath it just like the Mini?

This was a huge risk with all kinds of implications for the balance, handling and shape of the car. But Lamborghini liked the idea and gave him the go-ahead to create a full-size chassis. But what would it look like? Its tall rear engine and short front end demanded an entirely new shape with different proportions. Touring's Federico Formenti produced drawings and a scale model based around the dimensions of Dallara's chassis but the *carrozzeria* was about to go out of business.

Lamborghini was now used to exhibiting works in progress at motor shows. He decided to throw down the gauntlet and display the bare chassis at the 1965 Turin Motor Show, alongside his 350GT. If anything, the lack of a body on Dallara's radical chassis caused more of a stir than if it had been fully clothed. The V12 slotted between the back wheels, showing off its two twin-cam heads and four Weber triple-choke carburettors with their twelve 'trumpets' pointing skywards. It stole the show.

All the major body designers came to inspect it but many of them had prior relationships with manufacturers. Ferrari would look askance at Pinin Farina working for his new rival. Bertone had no such inhibitions about taking up the challenge. 'I'm the one who can make shoes for your feet,' he told Lamborghini, and immediately got to work. Dallara recalled that 'at some point between Christmas and the first of the year when the factory was closed, Lamborghini called and said, "Tomorrow Bertone is coming with the proposals."'

The men met in the silent factory, and when Nuccio revealed the renderings, 'We immediately realised that this was something unique, something that happens once. Really, it was superb. So Ferruccio Lamborghini said, "Go ahead. Don't change anything, just go ahead."' Having revealed his chassis, Lamborghini now needed to show a finished car as soon as possible. By March 1966, in time for the Geneva Show, the car was complete. Lamborghini had recently visited the Ganadería Miura in Seville where fighting bulls were bred. He decided to make a bull his emblem and give his car a name this time – the Miura.

For decades, the motor shows of Turin, Geneva and Paris enjoyed revealing show cars, visions of the future, explorations of new shapes and configurations. Traditionally they were one-offs, dream cars that would never see the streets. The Miura, painted a provocative blood-orange, looked like one of those cars – but it was destined for production. Nuccio Bertone had driven the Miura to Geneva himself.

No road car came close. No other car was so low to the ground. At just over one metre, it was lower even than the Ford GT40. Its front end was short and shallow, its headlamps reclined flush with the bodywork and surrounded by black-painted grilles, which gave the impression of eyelashes and cooled the front brakes. The windscreen was steeply raked. Instead of a rear window it had a series of slats to allow the engine beneath to cool. Instead of the traditional Borrani wire wheels, the Miura rode on Campagnolo magnesium alloys. It completely upstaged the Ferrari 330 GTC that was launched at the same show.

The experience of driving the Miura was equally different. Its top speed was almost 175 mph. Being seated so low to the ground and so near to the front of the car increased the occupant's sense of speed, like a large ultra-fast go-kart. Motoring journalist Paul Frère told Lamborghini, 'You're mad to sell this car to a person who may only have a modest experience of driving.'

It was widely expected that the Miura was destined for the race track, but Lamborghini was not interested in competition. 'Every one I build [will be] like winning a Grand Prix, and people will talk about it for long after they have forgotten who won the race.'

Karl Ludvigsen tested the car for America's *Car and Driver* magazine: 'At 60 mph you can cruise in any of the top four gears,' he wrote, 'depending on what you think you may have to do next; it makes no difference to the Miura. In traffic there is no temperament, none at all. When you leave the city limits you step on it and away it goes.'

Another fan was Frank Sinatra, who observed caustically, 'If you want to be somebody you buy a Ferrari, if you already are somebody, you own a Lamborghini.' Despite his natural optimism, Lamborghini never imagined he would build more than fifty Miuras. He ended up making 762.

What Enzo Ferrari thought of Ferruccio Lamborghini's assault on his citadel has gone unrecorded. Any attempt at a rapprochement was rebuffed. 'One day in Modena I was entering a restaurant when I recognised Ferrari sitting at one of the tables. As I passed I tried to greet him, but he turned his head away and pretended to be talking to the person next to him. He was ignoring me! ... Ferrari never spoke to me again. He was a great man, I admit, but it was so very easy to upset him.'

A Question of Attribution

W hich of Bertone's pupils was responsible for the Miura? At the time the design was taking shape, Bertone was in the process of parting with one protégé and bringing on another. He had a reputation for finding new talent, giving opportunities to designers at the start of their careers. 'I pick people for what I feel about them, for what they will do rather than what they have done already.'

Giorgetto Giugiaro's father, his grandfather and great-grandfather were all artists from the spa town of Garessio, in the Ligurian Alps. They painted frescoes and decorative work in churches and palaces. Watching his father, Mario, and sometimes helping, Giugiaro began to understand how colour and shade changed according to how the light fell on surfaces at varying angles, invaluable knowledge for a future car designer.

At first, Mario was determined to train his son. 'He wanted me to draw a landscape or a portrait every day and every evening I had to present my work. I was like all children of my age; I would have liked to play ball. It was at that time that I learned to draw quickly and efficiently. I made several drawings in one evening that I presented to him day after day; that gave me a little time to go and hit the ball!'

Although he had every intention to follow the family tradition and be a painter, his father warned him off. 'A bohemian lifestyle is satisfying when we're young,' Mario told him, 'but it ends up being depressing.'

At fifteen he was sent to Turin, to the Academy of Fine Art, but Mario also signed him up for technical drawing classes. 'The artistic and the technical were quickly linked in my life.' One of his teachers, Eugenio Colmo, pen name 'Golia', was a famous illustrator who had done artwork for Fiat publicity as early as 1919. Colmo was also the uncle of Cinquecento designer Dante Giacosa, and after showing him some of Giugiaro's watercolours that featured cars, the Fiat chief engineer found him a place in the Fiat drawing office. But in the vast Mirafiori complex and still in his teens, he went unnoticed, and on occasion was reduced to painting portraits of Fiat directors. He wanted to make some money, 'enough to buy a pair of skis', so when he was twenty-one he approached Nuccio Bertone with a selection of his drawings. Bertone was suspicious that a mere 21-year-old could have produced such mature and original work. So he sent Giugiaro away with a task, to draw a coupé design for Alfa Romeo's new larger car. He worked overnight on the colour renderings, and the following day handed them in to Bertone.

'Bertone sees them and the next day calls me and tells me that Alfa wants the car. He asked what Fiat paid; it was 80,000 lire at the time. He offered me 120,000! Fifty per cent more. *Ma, va bene!* I signed in November; I got my skis.'

Bertone ran a tight ship. Giugiaro found himself working alone. His new boss was also fanatical about waste and refused to have the lights on during the day. The tracing paper he used was expensive and had to be used sparingly, so he used pencils and rubbers, only tracing onto a fresh sheet when the first was 'black with corrections'. He worked such long hours, sometimes seven days a week, that he discovered he was making less per hour than he was getting at Fiat. 'But at Bertone's, I understood and loved that I could see my projects come to fruition in the wake of the drawing. It was marvellous.'

After three months, Giugiaro was called up for military service in the Comando Truppe Alpine stationed at a barracks in the Piedmont town of Bra. Bertone rented him a room so he could continue his work. Despite his military duties, it was an extraordinarily prolific time when he produced renderings for a Ferrari, a Maserati and what would be one of his most feted designs, Alfa Romeo's Giulia coupé. In his six years at Bertone he produced twenty-six designs and, thanks to him, the *carrozzeria* enjoyed huge success. The young designer's transformation of Fiat's modest rear-engined 850 into a chic two-seater Spider won Bertone the job of building over 100,000 bodies for the popular little car, most of which were exported to America. Flushed with success, Bertone considered bringing in an understudy alongside Giugiaro to help with their burgeoning workload.

Marcello Gandini was just nineteen days younger than Giugiaro but his life up to then had taken a very different course. The Torinese Gandini family were steeped in the world of classical music. His father, Marco, was an orchestral conductor and composer and his grandmother was noted for having introduced the French composer Debussy to Italy. Marcello was expected to follow the family tradition but when music lessons started – he was four – the plan went awry. 'I refused to play the piano because I was forced to do it when everyone else was outside playing games.' A box of Meccano given to him for his fifth birthday further derailed his parents' plans, setting off a passion for engines, mechanics and technology. At eight, he was sent to a boarding school which his parents hoped would bring him round, but at sixteen, with money he had been given to buy a Latin textbook, he chose instead Dante Giacosa's celebrated masterwork *Motori endotermici*, his book on the internal combustion engine. From then on, he said later, 'engineering, applied to car design, was my first passion'.

When he abandoned the Turin Liceo his despairing parents cut him off, so, armed with what he described as 'a strong, stubborn and constructive sense of rebellion', he set about trying to make it as a freelance designer. 'I made drawings of anything, sketches for advertising, cartoons, furniture, and little by little drawings of cars for small body shops.' Eventually he managed to get an audience with Bertone, who immediately recognised his talent.

Bertone was impressed enough with Gandini to suggest to Giugiaro that he be taken on as his assistant, but Giugiaro was not looking for an assistant. However, in October 1965 he departed, leaving behind several unfinished projects. Gandini started one month later.

'I must admit that the Miura was already quite advanced before

Gandini arrived,' Giugiaro claimed later. Some credence to this claim can be derived from the fact that a full-scale rendering of the Miura was finished by Christmas, little more than a month after Gandini's arrival. Much of the Miura's shape was determined by Dallara's unique chassis layout, on which Formenti's early clay model was created just as Touring was closing its doors. Both Giugiaro and Gandini were contributors, with Bertone adding his own finishing touches.

What is beyond dispute is that Giugiaro and Gandini were two of Italy's most talented and prolific car designers, who for the rest of the century would produce a stream of outstanding designs from the most outrageous show cars to the most functional everyday machines. Gandini, whose subsequent Lamborghinis make the Miura look tame, suggests that his first effort was something of a compromise. 'It was important for me and Bertone to do something new that was acceptable to everyone. The Miura was aggressive but had a softness, it was more easily assimilated because it was in the tradition of great Fifties and Sixties sports cars.'

However, Ferruccio Lamborghini was unequivocal. 'For the rest of my life I'll feel happy whenever I look at my Miura. This car left its mark on its age, and I say that nobody has built anything better since.'

Marriage of Convenience

'My marriage to cars is an indissoluble one. I've never got tired of them. The thought of us having to separate makes me unhappy. It's the only thing that saddens me.'

After the death of his beloved son Dino, Enzo Ferrari had abandoned all thoughts of retirement, but he knew that he had to secure a future for his creation. Ford had failed to meet his demands, but how could he carry on without some support – yet still keep his independence?

Gianni Agnelli's interest in Ferrari dated back to the Turin Motor Show of 1948 where, like many other visitors, he had been entranced by Ferrari's 166 Barchetta. Soon after, he became one of the first to own one in Italy, with his personal choice of metallic green and blue paintwork. In 1952 he ordered a second, a 212 Inter, in blue with a magnolia roof, specially fitted with two additional headlights for fast driving at night. Several more followed, culminating in one of the first mid-engined road cars Ferrari was persuaded to build, a unique three-seater with a centrally positioned steering wheel.

After his very long apprenticeship, by the mid-1960s Agnelli was beginning to exert more influence over the family's core business. Overseen by design supremo Dante Giacosa, Fiat had launched a succession of enormously popular small to medium-sized cars that put Italy and many other parts of the world on wheels. But Fiat had no prestige model. Was there more to be gained from Agnelli's interest in Ferraris?

For the 1964 season, new FIA regulations introduced for Formula Two required the use of production car engines. 'Production' was defined as a minimum number of 500, way beyond what Ferrari could produce. A deal between Fiat and Ferrari solved the problem. Named after Enzo's son, with a coupé body by Bertone and a roadster from Pinin Farina, Fiat got a prestige model to grace its showrooms, made in sufficient numbers to qualify for Formula Two. The fact that Agnelli agreed to be photographed at the wheel and allowed the image to be used in the launch publicity indicated that he was easing into his new role as Fiat's boss.

But the birth of the Fiat Dino was a painful one. Ferrari's racing engine had to be heavily modified to make it conform to Fiat's expectations for a mass-produced car. But this first joint venture between Italy's most famous marques was the first step towards the kind of arrangement Enzo Ferrari was seeking.

After Ford's triumph at Le Mans in 1966, Ferrari hit back on Ford's home turf. At the Daytona Raceway in Florida the following February, for the opening twenty-four-hour endurance race of the 1967 World Sports Car Championship, the press were treated to another choreographed photo opportunity and a rebuke to Ford's finish at Le Mans in '66, when three Ferraris crossed the finish line in a tight victory formation. The highest placed Ford, one of thirteen entered, only managed sixth place. Ferrari would win the championship, beating both Ford and the increasingly threatening Porsches. But it was the win at the start of the season that brought Enzo Ferrari the most satisfaction and to commemorate it he named his next road car the Daytona.

But as he approached his seventieth birthday, Ferrari faced challenges on all fronts. Racing demanded ever more sophisticated technology, which needed ever more investment. His road cars for the first time now faced serious competition from Lamborghini. Selling a few hundred a year was not going to keep him afloat and making the business more efficient and profitable just did not interest him. 'The demands of mass production are contrary to my temperament, for I am mainly interested in promoting new developments. I should like to put something new into my cars every morning – an inclination that terrifies my staff.'

Dino's death had deprived Ferrari of an heir and as long as his wife was alive he could not publicly acknowledge Piero, his son with Lina Lardi. Despite his age, with no one to hand the business on to, he remained as single-mindedly focused on racing as he had ever been. He just needed the means – and the freedom – to continue in his own unique way.

The arrangement with Gianni Agnelli took four years to complete. When the time came to sign, Ferrari broke the habit of a lifetime. Perhaps out of respect for his saviour, and the favourable terms he had wrought for himself, he made the journey to Fiat's headquarters in Turin's Corso Marconi, and, because lifts gave him claustrophobia, took the stairs to Agnelli's private office on the eighth floor.

The two giants of Italy's auto industry had only met a few times before, but Ferrari was ready to bare his soul. 'I told him of my past and my present, of the things I wanted for my factory, and I was able as never before to express what I really thought about things.'

'Well, Ferrari,' Agnelli said, 'I suppose we should have come to this agreement before now. Perhaps we've wasted time. So we'd better start making up for it.'

Ferrari, who did not impress easily, was in awe. 'Twenty years younger than me, he exuded all the power of a thoroughly modern man, of the businessman, politician and diplomat, an alertly intelligent observer of the world he lived in. His questions were short and to the point, in the manner of a man who needed to know and to understand. Eventually he brought in his people and summed it all up ...'

The terms were respectful of Enzo Ferrari's unique position and his ambition for the remainder of his life. Fiat would buy 40 per cent and Ferrari would retain 50 per cent, which would pass to Fiat on his death, with the remaining 10 per cent given to his second son, Piero. Fiat would take over control of the Ferrari road car business and the racing team would remain his own for the remainder of his life.

A few years before, in 1961, Pinin Farina handed his business over to his son Sergio. At the same time, authorised by the president of Italy, the name of both the family and the firm was changed to Pininfarina. But Pinin showed no loss of interest in design. Before he died in 1967, he oversaw his last creation, Alfa Romeo's Duetto.

Based on the Giulia saloon's platform, the two-seater was distinctively aerodynamic, rounded and tapered at each end, with striking, scalloped flanks, its headlamps faired into the bodywork under clear Perspex curves. It showed that after more than half a century's work, right up to his last days, the entirely self-taught designer never lost his eye for style.

Inspired by the publicity success of the lottery for its predecessor the Giulietta, Alfa Romeo launched a nationwide competition to find a name for the new sports car, to be judged by the poet Leonardo Sinisgalli. Out of 140,000 suggestions, Duetto was chosen, but not long after the winner received his prize car, Pavesi, the confectionery company, revealed that they had already registered the name for their forthcoming vanilla and chocolate snack bar. So the Alfa remained simply the 'Spider', until the Americans found another name for it.

An elaborate launch was planned for the car involving a cruise on Italy's ocean liner, the *Raffaello*, with select members of the European jet set, accompanied by a trio of Alfa Romeo Spiders in red, white and green, the colours of the Italian flag, finishing in New York for the car's official US launch.

But just as the Vespa had almost upstaged the stars of *Roman Holiday*, a burnt-orange Alfa Spider racing through California to the sound of Simon & Garfunkel propelled the previously unknown Dustin Hoffman to stardom. *The Graduate* became the highest grossing film of 1967 in North America. It was only a matter of time before popular opinion prevailed and the car was rechristened the Alfa Romeo Graduate.

Because Italy's industrial revolution came so much later than those of other European countries, and since the country had not long been unified, small family businesses and artisanal workshops survived well into the twentieth century, co-existing often alongside pioneering manufacturers. Nowhere was this more striking than in *carrozzerie* as the motor industry developed. While the advent of pressed steel and increasing standardisation squeezed out coachbuilders in other car-making countries, Italy's *carrozzerie* rose to the challenge of building stylish bodies for even the smallest, most affordable cars.

Adaptable and flexible, those like Pininfarina, Touring, Zagato, Ghia and Bertone combined the creation of one-off show cars that pushed the frontiers of modern design with supplying batches of bodies to meet often last-minute, unplanned needs of manufacturers. Having survived the war, in the 1950s their designs, often from self-taught artisans like Federico Formenti and Giovanni Michelotti, were in worldwide demand.

In 1950 an exhibition, Italy at Work, at the Brooklyn Museum in New York celebrated all aspects of the nation's enduring craft culture. Introducing the show, Italian-American Max Ascoli explained: 'You are not going to see masterpieces by Leonardo or Michelangelo tonight. Most of the work has been done by simple artisans, poor, unsophisticated craftsmen. There are thousands and thousands of them in Italy – people who are haunted by a sense of beauty, and gifted with an almost immemorial skill in expressing with the work of their hands what they feel inside. This exhibition and the whole series of efforts that led to it have been inspired by the belief that this sense of beauty is something contagious.'

Although Pinin Farina was honoured that his car featured in New York's Museum of Modern Art, he dismissed attempts to describe what he did as 'art'. But he and his like belonged to a uniquely Italian tradition that had deep roots in the nation's artisan heritage. And when called upon to deliver on a grander scale, as Bertone was when Alfa Romeo faced its Giulietta lottery crisis, they were nimble and adaptable enough to rise to the challenge, tapping into an available talent pool of skilled craftsmen.

Art, craft and engineering converged in the creation of the Italian car. 'The automobile has become a mobile living-space,' wrote Dante Giacosa in 1970 at the end of his long career as Fiat's chief engineer. 'The car designer is now comparable to an architect.' Bertone's pupil Giugiaro went on to produce the Fiat Panda and the original VW Golf, each of them masterpieces of ergonomic functional form.

If it seemed Italy's car designers had a head start over their peers elsewhere it could be down to the responsibilities they were handed so early on in their careers. Pinin Farina was a teenager when he shaped the Fiat Zero for Giovanni Agnelli. Giacosa was still in his twenties when he was given the brief to create Fiat's Topolino, as was Giampaolo Dallara when he created the Lamborghini Miura's revolutionary chassis. 'Being so young,' he said, 'you didn't realise how many problems there are, and they didn't come all together so you didn't have time to think too much.'

'We Are a National Army'

The end of the 1960s was a high-water mark for Italy's automotive industry. Fiat was on the cusp of becoming Europe's biggest car producer, Ferrari was the premier global racing car name. Lancia and Alfa Romeo were delivering attractive, family cars alongside exciting and innovative sports models which showcased the best of Italy's unique *carrozzerie*.

However, with the so-called *autunno caldo*, the 'hot autumn' of 1969, came the beginning of what looked like the end of Italy's automotive renaissance. A wave of strikes and demonstrations starting at Fiat's Mirafiori plant in Turin heralded a decade of violent industrial unrest. *Il boom*, the twenty years of dramatic economic growth that had lifted millions of Italians out of poverty, had swollen the populations of Turin and Milan. Inadequate housing and punitive rents fuelled demands for better pay and conditions.

Industrial unrest was one of a succession of challenges that would engulf Italy's car industry. During the 1970s, oil crises dramatically increased the price of fuel, legislation demanded cleaner and safer cars and competition from Japan piled pressure on established manufacturers. Smaller firms either closed down or were swallowed up, while a series of cross-border mergers and takeovers consolidated the industry in America and Europe into fewer bigger corporations. By the end of the century, most of Britain's surviving car makers were under foreign control.

Gianni Agnelli found himself having to steer Fiat through

existential crises every bit as challenging as those his grandfather had faced. On more than one occasion he could have made an exit but as his longtime friend Henry Kissinger observed, 'Gianni had many opportunities to sell Fiat to his great financial benefit. Though he played with the idea, he always shrank from it in the end. "We are a national army," he said: "I can't bring myself to turn it into a foreign legion."'

And as general of that army Agnelli went to war, embarking on a wholesale revamp of Fiat's plants and working practices to keep the business competitive. But more than his company was at stake. The position he had inherited came with responsibilities that were more than merely commercial. In 1969, when Lancia became insolvent, Agnelli took it over. Other than the name, there was not a lot in it for Fiat; Lancia was deeply in debt, its products and plant all in need of investment. But in acquiring it for a symbolic one lira per share and the assumption of all its debts, Agnelli claimed he was acting 'out of a sense of duty' towards the city of Turin.

In 1986, the Italian government, Alfa Romeo's ultimate owner, received a tempting offer from Ford. Since the Second World War, Alfa had thrived as never before, delivering a succession of charismatic cars. With generous government investment it boasted production capacity of over 400,000 cars a year, but by the mid-1980s it was producing less than a third of that and was haemorrhaging money. But once the government's negotiations with Ford leaked, Agnelli's response echoed that of his grandfather to Ford's previous bid to get a foothold in Italy in the early 1930s. As *L'Espresso* reported, 'Gianni Agnelli came to Rome. He popped into the Palazzo Chigi, he sent his ambassadors to see the Communists and the Christian Democrats, and in a flash, the wind had changed direction.'

'We were warned about going into Italy,' admitted the boss of Ford Europe, Kenneth Whipple. 'We were warned that we should look out or we'd get skinned.' Alfa Romeo passed to Fiat. It was the third time Ford had been outmanoeuvred by the Italians.

Agnelli's critics accused him of monopolistic practices and claimed he was depriving the industry of healthy competition. But his successful bid to save Alfa Romeo for the nation was vindicated when, two decades later, Ford offloaded all the other celebrated European car brands it had bought: Jaguar, Aston Martin and Volvo. The only Italian name the American giant successfully secured was Carrozzeria Ghia, which it reduced to no more than a premium badge on Fords made elsewhere in Europe. Meanwhile, after acquiring Maserati in 1989, Agnelli was confirmed as the supreme guardian of Italy's automotive crown jewels.

By the time of his death in 2002 he was an Italian hero. His funeral was a national day of mourning. Even Turin's communist former mayor, Diego Novelli, paid his respects. 'They brought the coffin on the roof of Lingotto and 500,000 Torinese went up to the famous circuit where Agnelli's coffin was, like Muslims go to Mecca.' His funeral, broadcast live on Italian main TV network RAI 1, was attended by both the president and prime minister. The Pope pronounced him 'an authoritative protagonist of Italian history'.

Heritage weighed on Agnelli. That group of philanthropically minded Torinese luminaries his grandfather joined to create Fiat a century before had hoped to create employment and opportunity as a means of escape from the poverty and servitude which had trapped the Piedmontese. The opportunities they created surpassed their wildest dreams.

Like Agnelli, Enzo Ferrari made his business his life's work. He was often a ruthless task master when it came to the treatment of his staff, and even his drivers. The self-confessed 'agitator of men' prided himself on spotting talent, regardless of youth and inexperience. Brenda Vernor, the English woman who became his secretary for the last twenty years of his life, likened the job to being part of an all-consuming family. Asked why he never took time off, Ferrari said, 'a man has no need for entertainment. Entertainment only distracts from his duty. If a man has his duty, that is enough.'

The blend of paternalism and duty was what also led to Giovanni Agnelli's creation of a company 'welfare state' for his workers, indicating that he measured success as something more than the bottom line. Although neither Ferrari nor the Agnellis were overtly patriotic or nationalistic, having weathered the nation's turbulent upheavals they found themselves embedded in its history.

Nowhere more than in Italy did the motor car become an agent of social and economic change. Where coal and steam powered the industrial revolutions of Britain, France and Germany, the automobile was the force behind Italy's, embedded in the nation's culture as an instrument of liberation.

The Futurists had been the first to recognise this, celebrating the speeding car as the expression of energy and enterprise, and the means of escape from the oppressive forces of convention. From the outset, Italy's car makers embraced motor racing as a means of both development and marketing. Where America's races were confined to 'speed bowls' open only to ticket holders, Italy's competitions ranged across the landscape past the doorsteps of thousands of Italians who could not but help get caught up in the drama, thrilling at the exploits of Nazzaro and Nuvolari, humble men propelled to national stardom.

Another quarter of a century on and the motor industry is reinventing itself again. In the process, Agnelli's successors did forge alliances with some of their oldest rivals across borders and overseas. The consequence is Stellantis, a Franco-Italian-American agglomeration of brands, whose name, derived from the Latin verb 'stello' implies a sparkling constellation of brands. Registered in Holland, with a Portuguese CEO, it owes no obvious national allegiance. Though it is perhaps fitting that its chairman, John Elkann, is the great-great-grandson of Fiat founder Giovanni Agnelli.

ENDNOTES

Prologue: *Sprezzatura*

3 '"Thus early the race is robbed ..."' 'The Royal Silverstone Meeting', *Motor Sport* (June 1950), p. 265.

3 '"I saw a man motor racing ..."' Philip Porter, *Stirling Moss: The Definitive Biography* (Porter Press International, 2016), p. 78.

3 '"*Ce diable de Farina* ..."' Ernesto Caballo, *Pininfarina: Born with the Automobile* (Automobilia, 1993), p. 94.

Chapter 1: A Car Is Not a Poem

6 '"Gripped by a sort of automotive euphoria."' Carlo Biscaretti di Ruffia in Arnoldo Mondadori, ed., *'Fiat': A Fifty Years' Record* (Mondadori, 1951), p. 41.

6 'Between 1876 and 1914, 14 million people emigrated, two thirds of them men.' Figures from Robin Cohen, *The Cambridge Survey of World Migration* (Cambridge University Press, 1955), p. 114.

7 '"Grass grew green ..."' Mondadori, *'Fiat': A Fifty Years' Record*, p. 231.

7 '"One of the few men in Turin ..."' Karl Ludvigsen, *Italian Racing Red* (Crecy, 2008), p. 14.

7 '"A small car ..."' Mondadori, *'Fiat': A Fifty Years' Record*, p. 14.

8 '"Taking revenge against those classmates ..."' Valerio Castronovo, *Giovanni Agnelli* (UTET, 1993), p. 3.

9 '"Here is my signature ..."' Mondadori, *'Fiat': A Fifty Years' Record*, p. 34.

10 '"Unsuitable for one who could still feel the country ..."' Ibid., p. 91.

Chapter 2: Art of the Car

12 '"Whether he used the brush ..."' W. F. Bradley and Ettore Bugatti, *Bugatti: A Biography* (Motor Racing Publications, 1948), p. 10.

12 '"I really tried very hard ..."' Ibid., p. 22.

12 '"Artistic effort is of no use ..."' L'Ebé Bugatti, *The Bugatti Story* (Vintage, 1967), p. 22.

12 ‘“Just by looking at the machine …”’ L'Ebé Bugatti, *The Bugatti Story*, p. 24.

12 ‘Carlo Bugatti “lived in a world of art …”’ Bradley and Bugatti, *Bugatti: A Biography*, p. 13.

13 ‘“I very quickly thought …”’ Ibid., p. 14.

13 ‘“Having something to create …”’ L'Ebé Bugatti, *The Bugatti Story*, p. 24.

14 ‘“For the car of private construction …”’ Griffith Borgeson, *Bugatti by Borgeson: Dynamics of Mythology* (Osprey, 1981), p. 41.

14 ‘“Bugatti was an artist …”’ J. A. Gregoire, *Best Wheel Forward* (The Sportsman's Book Club, 1966), p. 191.

Chapter 3: Know Thine Enemy

17 ‘“Before it's too late …”’ Paul Mayen, *La France Automobile*, 1901.

Chapter 4: The Littlest

21 ‘“There were grey fields …”’ Caballo, *Pininfarina: Born With the Automobile*, p. 9.

21 ‘“They weighed income against expenditure …”’ Ibid., p. 12.

21 ‘“Playing hide and seek amongst the carts …”’ Ibid., p. 12.

21 ‘“Women in long outfits …”’ Ibid., p. 18.

22 ‘“My first impression …”’ Ibid., p. 12.

22 ‘“What really annoyed me …”’ Ibid., p. 12.

22 ‘“It was a grand unforgettable day …”’ Griffith Borgeson, *Thoroughbred & Sportscar*, June 1977.

22 ‘“I was looking for something …”’ Caballo, *Pininfarina: Born With the Automobile* (Automobilia, 1993), p. 16.

22 ‘“Slim elegant simplicity …”’ Ibid., p. 17.

23 ‘“Who wanted to complicate …”’ Ibid., p. 21.

23 ‘“It was a question of the car's anatomy …”’ Ibid., p. 19.

Chapter 5: Florio and the Targa

25 ‘“If we lose money …”’ W. F. Bradley, *Motoring Racing Memories* (Motor Racing Publications, 1960), p. 77.

26 ‘“Literally covered with all sorts of weapons …”’ Frances Elliot, *The Diary of an Idle Woman in Sicily* (Bentley and Son, 1881), p. 108.

27 ‘“Very seldom do we see …”’ *La Stampa Sportiva*, 28 October 1902.

Chapter 6: *Pechino–Parigi*

32 ‘“His habits were extremely frugal …”’ Luigi S. Barzini, Peking to Paris (Open Court, 1973), p. xvi.

32 ‘The Ceiranos operated …’ Caballo, *Pininfarina: Born With the Automobile*, p. 23.

33 ‘“The three men …”’ Luigi S. Barzini, *Peking to Paris* (Open Court, 1973), p. 27.

34 'He "always made it his rule ..."' Ibid., p. 351.

34 '"This is one of his favourite pastimes ..."' Ibid., p. 122.

34 '"It seemed to confirm ..."' Ibid., p. xiv.

34 '"The crew somehow gave ..."' Ibid., p. xx .

35 '"These two months ..."' Ibid., p. xx.

Chapter 7: Three-card Trick

37 '"The drivers who stood out ..."' W. F. Bradley, *Targa Florio* (G. T. Foulis, 1955), p. 44.

38 '"If you put the blame on me ..."' Ibid., p. 46.

38 'Kaiser Wilhelm had been unimpressed ...' J. Sloniger and H. H. von Fersen, *Performance Cars from Germany* (Robert Bentley, 1966), p. 32.

39 '"He handled his cars ..."' Michael Sedgwick, *Fiat* (Batsford, 1974), p. 68.

40 Production statistics (France and USA) from James Laux, *In First Gear* (McGill-Queen's University Press, 1976), p. 210, and (for Italy) Anfia. *Industria Automobilistica Mondiale Nel 1982* (Anfia, 1983), p. 5.

41 '"We are at the beginning ..."' Ludvigsen, *Italian Racing Red*, p. 23.

Chapter 8: Cavalier Attitude

45 '"Pinin is our designer ..."' Caballo, *Pininfarina: Born with the Automobile*, p. 28.

46 '"In those days ..."' Ibid., p. 31.

47 'Pinin was entranced ...' Ibid., p. 36.

Chapter 9: The Futurists

48 '"From that moment ..."' Peter Miller, *Conte Maggi's Mille Miglia* (The History Press, 1988), p. 18.

48 '"Modernity bursts onto the streets ..."' *Il Resto del Carlino*, Bologna, 6–7 September 1908.

48 'Filippo Tommaso Marinetti', *The Futurist Manifesto*, in *Critical Writings: Filippo Tommaso Marinetti* (Macmillan, 2007).

50 'Marinetti berated Ruskin ...' Stephen Bayley, Philippe Garner and Dejan Sudjic, *Twentieth-Century Style & Design* (Van Nostrand Reinhold, 1986), p. 84.

50 '"Don't expect to be invited ..."' Cesare De Seta, *L'architettura del Novecento* (Garzanti, 1981).

Chapter 10: 'I Would have Remained a Nobody'

53 '"If my father ..."' Michael Frostick, *Lancia* (Dalton Watson, 1977), p. 12.

55 '"With the precision of a surgeon ..."' Caballo, *Pininfarina: Born with the Automobile*, p. 28.

56 '"We have never seen anything ..."' *The Autocar*, 23 April 1910.

56 '"Our experience had proved ..."' David Owen, *Lancia,* Part 1, *The Vincenzo Years,* in *The Automobile Quarterly,* vol. XII, no. 4, p. 348, 1948.

58 '"With an almost perfect suspension ..."' *The Autocar,* 18 October 1922, p. 15.

58 'From an output of 472 cars ...' Figures quoted in Niels Johansen, *Lancia Aurelia in Detail* (Herridge and Sons, 2006), p. 17.

59 '"I am more frightened ..."' Nigel Trow, *Lancia: The Shield and the Flag* (David & Charles, 1980), p. 49.

59 '"I found him busy ..."' Trow, *Lancia: The Shield and the Flag,* p. 67.

59 '"I behaved like a pupil ..."' Caballo, *Pininfarina: Born with the Automobile,* p. 18.

59 '"A cross between a motorcycle ..."' Ibid., p. 60.

Chapter 11: The Years of Blood

62 '"A growth of moral tiredness ..."' Caballo, *Pininfarina: Born with the Automobile,* p. 45.

63 '"Social hierarchies ..."' Quoted in https://www.workersliberty.org/blogs/2019-04-11/turin-gramsci-and-italys-red-years

64 '"There is no shame ..."' 'Men of Flesh and Blood', *L'Ordine Nuovo,* Turin, 8 May 1921.

64 '"Like a language ..."' Caballo, *Pininfarina: Born with the Automobile,* p. 59.

65 '"He used to cut them off ..."' Ibid., p. 75.

66 '"I will be comfortable ..."' Lorenzo Gianotti, *Gli Operai della Fiat Hanno Cent'Anni* (Editori Riuniti, 1999), p. 31.

66 '"Nearly every family ..."' Caballo, *Pininfarina: Born with the Automobile,* p. 59.

Chapter 12: Tears in the Park

67 '"I was alone ..."' Enzo Ferrari, *My Terrible Joys* (Hamish Hamilton, 1963), p. 18.

70 'Capital of 1.8 million lire ...' Figures quoted from Griffith Borgeson, *The Alfa Romeo Tradition* (Automobile Quarterly, 1990), p. 34.

73 '"As soon as possible ..."' Ibid., p. 23.

75 '"Ferrari, where are the competent people?"' Borgeson, *The Alfa Romeo Tradition,* p. 46.

75 '"A man of great worth ..."' Ibid., p. 68.

Chapter 13: *Garibaldino*

77 '"The singing of the engine ..."' Giovanni Canestrini in *La Gazzetta dello Sport,* reported in Giulio Schmidt, *The Roaring Races* (Libreria dell'Automobile, 1988).

77 '"It was curious ..."' Caballo, *Pininfarina: Born with the Automobile,* p. 53.

78 '"On several occasions ..."' Arnaldo Fraccaroli, 'Quadruploci vittoria

Italiana all'autodromo di Monza', in *Corriere della Sera*, 20 October 1924, pp. 1–2.

Chapter 14: Fallen Hero

80 '"I didn't sleep ..."' Ludvigsen, *Italian Racing Red*, p. 57.

82 '"Who had died on the battlefield ..."' 'Ascari', *Il Popolo d'Italia*, 28 July 1925, p. 2.

Chapter 15: The Scuderia Assembles

86 Note on *la cavallino rampante*: how Baracca came by the *cavallino* is open to speculation. It can be seen in a photograph of him with his aircraft, on the side of the fuselage. As it happens, the Porsche badge, designed in the 1950s, also carries a black on yellow prancing horse, along with the name of its hometown, Stuttgart, whose emblem it is. To confirm their 'kills', pilots in the First World War would land near their victim's downed aircraft and cut an emblem from the wreckage, which they then displayed as a warning to their enemy. The emblem on the side of Baracca's aircraft, with a haphazardly jagged-edged background, has led to speculation that it was cut from a downed enemy aircraft whose pilot hailed from Stuttgart.

87 '"A great dilettante ..."' Enzo Ferrari, *Una Vita per l'Automobile* (Eredità Enzo Ferrari, 1998), p. 46.

87 '"It's worse than Didi's shoes."' Caballo, *Pininfarina: Born with the Automobile*, p. 1.

Chapter 16: Back to Brescia

92 '"Running over dusty roads ..."' Anthony Pritchard, *The Motor Racing Merchants* (Leslie Frewin, 1976), p. 59.

92 '"It took just under ..."' *Corriere della Sera* report quoted in https://1000miglia.it/storia-della-1000-miglia/la-prima-1000-miglia/

Chapter 17: *Extraleggera*

96 '"Even on gravel ..."' Ludvigsen, *Italian Racing Red*, p. 46.

Chapter 18: The Rivals

98 '"Varzi operated the wheel ..."' Caballo, *Pininfarina: Born with the Automobile*, p. 71.

99 '"I noticed he never ..."' Ferrari, *My Terrible Joys*, p. 60.

Chapter 20: *L'Auto del Popolo*

107 'Agnelli wrote congratulating him ...' Valerio Castronovo, *Giovanni Agnelli* (UTET, 1993), p. 3.

107 'Zerbi "suggested tactfully ..."' Dante Giacosa, *Forty Years of Design with Fiat* (Automobilia, 1979), p. 51.

Chapter 21: Putting the Clocks Forward

112   '"*They've put the clocks forward* ..."' Caballo, *Pininfarina: Born with the Automobile*, p. 37.

112   '"Easter eggs wrapped ..."' Ibid., p. 44.

112   '"An earthly paradise ..."' Ibid. p. 44.

112   '"In four or five hours ..."' Ibid., p. 46.

113   '"So we have ..."' Ibid., p. 46.

113   '"Where else would the farmers ..."' Ibid., p. 44.

113   '"America is the car's nursery ..."' Ibid., p. 46.

114   '"A single unit ..."' Ibid., p. 69.

115   '"Your proposal ..."' Ibid., p. 66.

115   'A "stern and high-principled environment."' Carlo Felice Bianci Anderloni and Angelo Tito Anselmi, *Touring Superleggera* (Autocritica, 1983), p. 11.

117   '"The Flying Star ..."' Ibid., p. 58.

Chapter 22: Gran Turismo

119   '"Chiseller of arms ..."' Bonvesin da la Riva, *De Magnalibus urbis Mediolani* (On the Marvels of Man), believed written in 1288.

119   'The "*balla*" test.' Anderloni and Anselmi, *Touring Superleggera*, p. 121 'Going to the mountains ...' Caballo, *Pininfarina: Born with the Automobile*, p. 64.

120   '"I was tired ..."' Ibid., p. 65.

121   '"I do not want to talk ..."' Ibid., p. 60.

121   '"I was irritated ..."' Ibid., p. 76.

121   '"To avoid all precocity."' Ibid., p. 77.

Chapter 23: 'O sole mio'

123   '"The maker of the best ..."' Borgeson, *The Alfa Romeo Tradition*, p. 99.

Chapter 24: Master Racers

128   '"Once Hitler had ..."' Chris Nixon, *Racing the Silver Arrows* (Bloomsbury, 1986), p. 295.

128   '"With his arrival ..."' Borgeson, *The Alfa Romeo Tradition*, p. 100.

130   '"*Quelques de nos autres* ... "' Ibid., p. 305.

130   '"To Tazio Nuvolari ..."' quoted in Richard Williams, *Enzo Ferrari* (Yellow Jersey, 2001), p. 82.

132   '"Even now no one seriously thought ..."' 'The German Grand Prix', *Motor Sport*, September 1935, p. 487.

132   '"Not even Nuvolari ..."' Ibid., p. 487.

Chapter 25: Racing Demons

134   '"Neither unhappy with ..."' *The Motor*, 4 August 1936.

137   '"What would the team do without you?"' Ibid., p. 492.

138   '"He lived life at 3,000 rpm at least ..."' Caballo, *Pininfarina: Born with the Automobile*, p. 53.

138   '"The concern of the hierarchy ..."' Gioachino Colombo, *Origins of the Ferrari Legend* (G. T. Foulis, 1987), p. 12.

138   'A "great confusion of roles ..."' Ibid., p. 13.

140   'Gobbato "was no believer ..."' Ferrari, *My Terrible Joys*, p. 30.

140   '"When he shook hands ..."' Ibid., p. 35.

Chapter 26: Detente

142   '"He would go to his room ..."' Susanna Agnelli, *We Always Wore Sailor Suits* (Viking, 1975), p. 36.

142   '"The Roman children ..."' Ibid., p. 17.

143   '"My father is gay ..."' Ibid., p. 25.

144   '"He walked in ..."' Ibid., p. 27.

146   '"An unusual talent ..."' Ferrari, *My Terrible Joys*, p. 37.

146   '"Agnelli expressed feelings ..."' Piero Bairati, *Valletta Vittorio* (UTET, 1983), p. 80.

Chapter 27: The Shadow of War

147   '"On June 10th ..."' Giacosa, *Forty Years of Design with Fiat*, p. 66.

147   '"Fascism is too strong ..."' Ferrari, *My Terrible Joys*, p. 121.

Chapter 28: Resistance

151   '"Huge illusions surrounding ..."' Edmonod Schmidt, *Il Caso Schmidt, Da Berlino a regina Coeli* (Centro Studi PIedmontesi, 2010), pp. 18-19.

153   '"We could have been good Germans ..."' Alan Friedman, *Agnelli and the Network of Power* (Mandarin, 1989), p. 25.

153   '"The executives of this company ..."' Caballo, *Pininfarina: Born with the Automobile*, p. 93.

153   '"Serene and systematic activity"' Giacosa, *Forty Years of Design with Fiat*, p. 70.

Chapter 29: Retribution

155   '"As a result ..."' Giacosa, *Forty Years of Design with Fiat*, p. 72.

156   '"The closer the Allies advanced ..."' Caroline Moorehead, *A House in the Mountains: The Women Who Liberated Italy from Fascism* (Chatto & Windus, 2019), p. 284.

158   '"We should hang Agnelli ..."' Friedman, *Agnelli and the Network of Power*, p. 59.

159   '"For forty years ..."' Giancarlo Galli, *Gli Agnelli. Una dinastia, un impero. 1899–1998* (Mondadori, 1995), p. 103.

Chapter 30: Wild Spirit

160   '"When I arrived in Turin ..."' Nicola Caracciolo, '*Agnelli, la Grande Storia.*' Documentary for RAI 3 TV, 30 December 1999.

161 '"Drawing hope from the very hopelessness …"' Tag Gallagher, *The Adventures of Roberto Rossellini* (De Capo Press, 1998), p. 194 .

162 '"Allow me to tell you …"' Bairati, *Vittorio Valletta*, p. 141.

162 '"Without the Americans …"' Judy Bachrach, 'La Vita Agnelli', *Vanity Fair,* April 2001.

Chapter 31: The Homecoming

162 '"He's a nutcase."' Ludvigsen, *Italian Racing Red*, p. 106 .

Chapter 32: Crossing the River Po

166 '"You send me …"' Doug Nye, 'Nothing Better than the Alfetta', *Motor Sport*, December 2019.

166 'His "long apprenticeship"' Colombo, *Origins of the Ferrari Legend*, p. 10.

167 '"The ox that pulls the cart."' Ibid., p. 14.

167 '"The sense of uselessness …"' Ibid., p. 11.

168 '"My dear Colombo …"' Ibid., p. 16.

Chapter 33: A Kind of Affliction

169 '"Too soft, too nice …"' Borgeson, *The Alfa Romeo Tradition*, p. 162.

170 '"It took more …"' Doug Nye, 'Nothing Better than the Alfetta', *Motor Sport*, December 2019.

171 '"How could we go …"' Borgeson, *The Alfa Romeo Tradition,* p. 138.

171 '"Alfa Romeo is not merely a make of automobile …"' Ibid., p. 138.

Chapter 34: Two Households in Fair Modena

173 '"I had to be ruthless …"' Lorenzo Boscarelli, *Ferrari 166* (Haynes, 1986), p. 18.

173 '"To me the number one …"' Karl Ludvigsen, 'Creating Ferrari's First Champions', *Forza*, 30 May 2019.

173 '"It gave 60 to 65 …"' Ludvigsen, *Italian Racing Red*, p. 106.

174 '"Unlimited powers …"' Ludvigsen, 'Creating Ferrari's First Champions', *Forza*, 30 May 2019.

174 '"If something doesn't work …"' Ibid.

175 '"If you were used …"' Ludvigsen, *Italian Racing Red*, p. 106.

175 '"I went and sat …"' Ferrari, *My Terrible Joys*, p. 19.

Chapter 35: Return of the Champions

176 '"I continue to race …"' Christopher Hilton, *Nuvolari* (Breedon Books, 2003), p. 200.

178 '"I did not want …"' Chris Nixon, 'Romolo Tavoni: Enzo's Right-Hand Man', *Motor Sport*, November 1998.

178 '"I'm not satisfied …"' Anthony Pritchard, *Ferrari: Men from Maranello* (Haynes, 2009), p. 332.

178 '"Mr Ferrari, I have been working …"' Ibid.

180 '"We will do it again ..."' Williams, *Enzo Ferrari*, p. 142.
180 '"Bury me in my uniform ..."' Ibid., p. 175.

Chapter 36: The Little Boat

182 '"It was like a giant compressed spring ..."' Winston Goodfellow, 'Ghia's Gilda: Siren Song for An Era', *Motor Trend Classic*, 24 January 2013.

Chapter 37: Spare Room in the Palazzo

186 'Giacosa thought it "extremely beautiful ..."' Giacosa, *Forty Years of Design with Fiat*, p. 78.
186 '"I had just finished ..."' Ibid., p. 83.
186 '"*Ngegne! Che curage ...*"' Ibid., p. 86.

Chapter 38: Merchants in the Temple

188 '"A client of Pinin's ..."' Antoine Prunet, *Pininfarina: Art and Industry, 1930–2000* (Rizzoli International, 2001), p. 56.
189 '"Pininfarina is going ..."' Caballo, *Pininfarina: Born with the Automobile*, p. 94.
189 '"Master models ..."' Ibid., p. 96.
190 '"I knew that the old ..."' Ibid., p. 97.
191 '"The Cisitalia's body ..."' Eight Automobiles, Museum of Modern Art, exhibition guide, Autumn 1951.
191 '"I felt like ..."' Caballo, *Pininfarina: Born with the Automobile*, p. 105.
191 '"I still saw myself ..."' Ibid., p. 105.

Chapter 39: *Viva Italiana*

193 '"Fashion," he explained ...' Shawn Levy, *Dolce Vita Confidential* (Weidenfeld & Nicolson, 2017), p. 45.
193 '"Italian Styles Gain Approval ..."' Ibid., p. 53.
193 '"Everyone seems interested ..."' Ibid, p. 54.
194 'Piaggio's marketing ...' Simon Martin, *Sport Italia: The Italian Love Affair with Sport* (I. B. Tauris & Co., 2011), p. 136.

Chapter 40: *El Chueco*

195 '"You had to be a bit ..."' Karl Ludvigsen, *Juan Manuel Fangio: Motor Racing's Grand Master* (Haynes, 1999), p. 12
196 '"We kept ourselves ..."' Ibid., p. 14.
196 '"The only person in church ..."' Ibid., p. 16.
197 '"He was perhaps ..."' Ferrari, *My Terrible Joys*, p. 75.
197 '"Driving as fast ..."' Karl Ludvigsen, *Juan Manuel Fangio: Motor Racing's Grand Master* (Haynes, 1999), p. 37.
197 '"First we have ..."' Ibid., p. 54.

Chapter 41: Taking on the Victors

200 ‘"He drove like a madman ..."’ Ludvigsen, *Italian Racing Red*, p. 100.

200 ‘"A man whose courage ..."’ Ibid., p. 100.

Chapter 43: Shadow of the Father

204 ‘"I only obey ..."’ ‘La morte di Ascari’, *Men on Wheels*, 27 May 2021.

205 ‘"Whereas Fangio could be ..."’ Williams, *Enzo Ferrari*, p. 163.

205 ‘"I cried for joy ..."’ Brock Yates, *Enzo Ferrari: The Man and the Machine* (Transworld, 1991), p. 241.

206 ‘"While the steel tubing ..."’ Ludvigsen, ‘Creating Ferrari's First Championships’, *Forza*, 30 May 2019.

206 ‘"The first thing ..."’ Kevin Desmond, *The Man with Two Shadows: The Story of Alberty Ascari* (Proteus Books, 1981), p. 86.

Chapter 44: New Jacket, Frayed Trousers

209 ‘"Inventive industrialisation."’ J. A. Lucas, *American Machinist*, 5 January 1928, pp. 19–23.

210 ‘"I've been told ..."’ Geoffrey Goldberg, *Lancia and De Virgili* (David Bull, 2014), p. 39.

210 ‘"A useless exercise ..."’ Johansen, *Lancia Aurelia in Detail*, p. 32.

211 ‘"It was like ..."’ Goldberg, *Lancia and De Virgilio*, p. 48.

Chapter 45: World-class Couturier

214 ‘"Engines either run well ..."’ Ludvigsen, ‘Creating Ferrari's First Championships’, *Forza*, 30 May 2019.

214 ‘"A tall young man ..."’ Caballo, *Pininfarina: Born with the Automobile*, p. 47.

214 ‘"As tightly closed ..."’ Ibid., p. 113.

215 ‘"One of us ..."’ Ferrari, *My Terrible Joys*, p. 142.

215 ‘"He was pretty gruff ..."’ Antoine Prunet, *Pininfarina*, p. 105.

Chapter 46: Chasing Ferrari

217 ‘"I cannot tell you ..."’ Francesco de Virgilio, ‘Il Motore della Lancia Aurelia’, lecture given to the AISA – Associazione Italiana per la storia dell'Automobile, Milan, 26 March 1994.

217 ‘"Someone had suggested ..."’ Goldberg, *Lancia and De Virgilio*, p. 80.

218 ‘"The B20 had a rather ..."’ Caballo, *Pininfarina: Born with the Automobile*, p. 107.

218 ‘"Then we could run ..."’ Johansen, *Lancia Aurelia in Detail*, p. 115.

219 ‘"Before I stop ..."’ Ibid., p. 121.

219 ‘"I want to win ..."’ Ibid.

220 ‘"I want to defeat Ferrari ..."’ Goldberg, *Lancia and De Virgilio*, p. 112.

Chapter 48: Contract Terminated

225 '"One Monday morning, on returning to work ..."' Ludvigsen, 'Creating Ferrari's First Championships', *Forza*, 30 May 2019.

225 '"He skilfully produced ..."' Giacosa, *Forty Years of Design with Fiat*, p. 156.

225 '"Even press agents ..."' Desmond, *The Man With Two Shadows*, p. 130.

225 '"While Alberto drove ..."' Chris Nixon, *Rivals: Lancia D50 and Mercedes-Benz-W196* (Transport Bookman, 1999), p. 79.

Chapter 49: Rockets on Wheels

228 'While the Maserati's ...' Nixon, *Rivals*, p. 115.

230 '"I never want my children ..."' Martin Williamson, 'Alberto Ascari', ESPN F1.

230 '"Alberto was secure ..."' Ferrari, *My Terrible Joys*, p. 38.

Chapter 50: Fall of the House of Lancia

234 '"Only too often ..."' Ferrari, *My Terrible Joys*, p. 38.

235 '"With the intention of promoting ..."' Nixon, *Rivals*, p. 173.

Chapter 51: British Racing Red

239 '"It is only fitting ..."' Doug Nye, *BRM* (MRP, 2003), p. 47.

241 '"It was a big jump ..."' Denis Jenkinson. *Maserati 250F* (Macmillan, 1975), p. 9.

242 '"Their continued apathy ..."' Richard Williams, *The Boy. Stirling Moss: A Life in Sixty Laps* (Simon & Schuster, 2021), p. 107.

242 '"You say my gearbox ..."' Chris Nixon, *Mon Ami Mate* (Transport Bookman, 1991), p. 103.

242 '"Mike hated the albergo ..."' Ibid., p. 103.

Chapter 52: Gentleman Driver

245 '"If you go to the movies ..."' Nixon, *Mon Ami Mate*, p. 318.

245 '"I and my old friend Jano ..."' Ferrari, *My Terrible Joys*, p. 184.

246 '"I had always deluded myself ..."' Ibid., p. 191.

246 '"The conviction has never left me ..."' Ibid., p. 191.

246 '"Eventually Peter went ..."' Ibid., p. 320.

247 '"I do not know ..."' Chris Nixon, *Mon Ami Mate*, p. 195.

Chapter 53: Ferrari's Primavera

248 '"Mr and Mrs Ferrari ..."' Ibid., p. 318.

248 '"Castellotti took Delia ..."' Ibid., p. 266.

249 '"Try to understand ..."' Ferrari, *My Terrible Joys*, p. 72.

249 '"He was going ..."' Ibid., p. 72.

249 '"A rare and perfect ..."' Ibid., p. 112.

249 '"He really was extraordinary ..."' Nixon, *Mon Ami Mate*, p. 271.

250 '"It was very strange ..."' Ibid., p. 276.
250 '"Things are getting pretty ridiculous ..."' Ibid., p. 227.
251 '"As he passed ..."' Ibid., p. 325.
251 'Musso was rushed ...' Ibid., p326.
252 '"Peter was fighting ..."' Ibid., p. 335.
252 '"There was a bruise ..."' Ibid., p. 336.
253 '"A modern Saturn ..."' Ferrari, *My Terrible Joys*, p. 154.
253 '"I'm sure he felt ..."' Nixon, *Mon Ami Mate*, p. 342.
254 '"You can write ..."' Ibid., p. 346.
254 '"Good on his good days ..."' Ferrari, *My Terrible Joys*, p. 75.
254 '"Racing was so different then ..."' Nigel Roebuck, 'Peter Collins, "This Charming Man"', *Motor Sport*, September 2008, p. 62.

Chapter 54: The Bombshell
257 '"Design the most beautiful car ..."' Peter Grist, *Virgil Exner – Visioneer* (Veloce, 2015), p. 48.
259 '"The Ghia lines ..."' David Burgess Wise, *Ghia* (Osprey, 1985), p. 50.

Chapter 56: The Ice-cream Makers
266 '"My friends swore ..."' Caballo, *Pininfarina: Born with the Automobile*, p. 118.
267 '"Have you seen ..."' Barney Sharratt, *Men and Motors of the Austin* (Haynes, 2000), p. 164.
268 '"We got it into the styling studio ..."' Jonathan Wood, 'Herald Triumph', *Thoroughbred and Classic Cars*, July 1983, p. 79.

Chapter 57: Il Boom
271 'We have to concentrate ...' Caballo, *Pininfarina: Born with the Automobile*, p. 149.
272 '"The great sacrifices ..."' Paul Ginsberg, *A History of Contemporary Italy* (Penguin, 1990) p. 192.
272 '"Supreme principle of economy ..."' Giacosa, *Forty Years of Design with Fiat*, p. 11.
274 '"The Italians wanted to become ..."' Ibid., p. 161.
274 '"The light cavalry ..."' Caballo, *Pininfarina: Born with the Automobile*, p. 124.
274 'In 1955, only 3 per cent ...' Figures from Vic George and Roger Lawson, eds, *Poverty and Inequality in Common Market Countries* (Routledge & Kegan Paul, 1980).
275 'From 100,000 units in 1950 ...' Figures from Francesca Fauri, *The Role of Fiat in the Development of the Italian Car Industry in the 1950's*, Business History Review, Summer 1996, p. 176.
276 '"Middleman for the US ..."' 'To Russia without Love', *Forbes*, 1 October 1966.

Chapter 58: L'Avvocato

278 '"The worst part ..."' 'Gianni Agnelli: The Godfather of Italian Cool', *Gentlemen's Digest*, 3 December 2024.

278 '"Marriage may have been the wisest move ..."' Friedman, *Agnelli and the Network of Italian Power*, p. 49.

278 Gianni Agnelli referenced in *Jacqueline Kennedy: Historic Conversations on Life with John F. Kennedy* (Hyperion, 2011), p. 219.

279 '"Gianni disliked self-righteous posturing ..."' 'Giovanni Agnelli by Henry Kissinger', 29 August 2007 https://www.henryakissinger.com/remembrances/foreword-for-book-on-giovanni-agnelli/

279 '"Without America ..."' Bachrach, 'La Vita Agnelli', *Vanity Fair*, April 2001.

280 '"I haven't the slightest idea ..."' *Time* magazine, 17 January 1969, p. 61.

280 '"The leading Italian industrial company ..."' 'Vittorio Valletta, il ragioniere divenuto re della Fiat', *Il Giornale*, 23 November 2023.

Chapter 59: California Dreaming

282 '"We were on a twisty stretch ..."' Doug Nye, 'Inside Track with Phil Hill', *Motor Sport*, 6 February 2019.

284 '"Everybody dies ..."' A. J. Baime, *Go Like Hell: Ford, Ferrari, and Their Battle for Speed and Glory at Le Mans* (Mariner, 2010), p. 99.

285 '"It was meeting ..."' Robert Lacey, *Ford: The Men and the Machine* (Little, Brown, 1986), p. 521.

286 '"The Pizza Queen ..."' David Halberstam, *The Reckoning* (William Morrow, 1986), p. 465.

286 '"He smok' da cigar ..."' Ibid., p. 354.

Chapter 61: Pride and Prejudices

288 '"While I doubt ..."' Baime, *Go Like Hell*, p. 102.

289 '"You do not go ..."' Ibid., p. 108.

292 '"I would like you to know ..."' John Wyer, *The Certain Sound* (Edita, 1981), p. 154.

292 '"Nothing can be done ..."' Baime, *Go Like Hell*, p. 283.

293 '"It's sad to see ..."' 'Ford v Ferrari', *RossoAutomobili* magazine https://rossoautomobili.com

Chapter 62: Palace Revolt

295 '"I fixed every mechanical thing on the farm ..."' *Twenty Three amazing quotes by Ferruccio Lamborghini* https://medium.com/@entrepreneursway0007/23-amazing-quotes-by-ferruccio-lamborghini-1f75d33fff9c

296 '"Which we entered ..."' 'Interview with Ferruccio Lamborghini', *Thoroughbred & Classic Cars*, January 1991.

296 '"All my Ferraris ..."' Ibid.

297   '"A matter of the ..."' Williams, *Enzo Ferrari*, p. 220.

297   '"She was criticising ..."' 'Romolo Tavoni: Enzo's Right-Hand Man',
      Motor Sport, November 1998.

Chapter 63: Raging Bull

299   '"Lamborghini was completely ..."' 'Giampaolo Dallara: A talent all
      made in Motor Valley' https://www.motorvalley.it/en/stories/giampaol
      o-dallara-a-talent-all-made-in-motor-valley/

300   '"I'm the one ..."' 'The real inspiration for Lamborghini's Miura'
      https://winstongoodfellow.com/blogs/blog/myth-busting-part-ii-the-rea
      l-inspiration-for-lamborghini-s-miura

301   '"Every one I build ..."' '23 Amazing Quotes by Ferruccio Lamborghini'
      https://medium.com/@entrepreneursway0007/23-amazing-quotes-by-ferr
      uccio-lamborghini-1f75d33fff9c

301   '"At 60 mph ..."' Karl Ludvigsen, 'Lamborghini Miura: The Supercar
      That Started It All', *Car and Driver*, August 1967.

Chapter 64: A Question of Attribution

303   '"I pick people ..."' Obituary, Nuccio Bertone, *Independent*,
      3 March 1997 https://www.independent.co.uk/incoming/
      obituary-nuccio-bertone-5578529.html

303   '"He wanted me to draw ..."' LIGNES/auto : interview, intimate
      Giugiaro https://lignesauto.fr/?p=16552

303   '"A bohemian lifestyle ..."' Richard Benson, 'How Giorgetto
      Giugiaro Became The Greatest Car Designer Of All Time', *Esquire*, 5
      August 2019.

304   '"Enough to buy a pair of skis ..."' Christophe Bonnaud, 'Interview,
      intimate – Giugiaro' *LIGNES/auto* https://lignesauto.fr/?p=16552

304   '"Bertone sees them ..."' Ibid.

305   '"I refused to play ..."' Jason Barlow, 'Marcello Gandini – The Miura
      annoys me a bit', *Top Gear*, 14 March 2024.

305   '"Engineering, applied to car design ..."' 'Farewell Marcello Gandini,
      Master of Design', *Auto e Design*, 13 March 2.24

305   '"Strong, stubborn and constructive ..."' Lectio Magistralis,
      Marcello Gandini, Cerimonia conferimento Laurea Honoris Causa
      in ingegneria meccanica 12 gennaio, 2024 https://www.polito.it/
      sites/default/files/2024-01/Lectio%20Magistralis%20Marcello%20
      Gandini.pdf

305   '"I must admit ..."' 'Interview, intimate Giugiaro LIGNES/auto https://
      lignesauto.fr/?p=16552

306   '"It was important for me ..."' Jason Barlow, 'Marcello Gandini – The
      Miura annoys me a bit', *Top Gear* magazine, 14 March 2024.

306   '"For the rest of my life ..."' 'Interview with Ferruccio Lamborghini',
      Thoroughbred & Classic Cars, January 1991.

Chapter 65: Marriage of Convenience

307 ' "My marriage to cars . . ." ' Video interview, Ing. Enzo Ferrari – evento 30° anniversaio Centro Dino Ferrari https://www.youtube.com/watch?v=zioYK5x5EOQ

308 ' "The demands of mass production . . ." ' The Scuderia.net, Legendary quotes from 'Il Commendatore' Enzo Ferrari https://www.thescuderia.net/forums/showthread.php/31826-

309 ' "I told him of my past . . ." ' Enzo Ferrari, *Una Vita per l'Automobile*, p. 124.

311 ' "You are not going to see . . ." ' Press release for exhibition, Italy at Work: Her Renaissance in Design Today, 30 November 1950 through 31 January 1951 at the Brooklyn Museum, New York https://www.brooklynmuseum.org/opencollection/exhibitions/859

311 ' "The automobile has become . . ." ' Jonathan Glancy, 'Benvenuto Cinquecento: Fiat's new city car', *Independent*, 21 March 1993.

312 ' "Being so young . . ." ' 'Giampaolo Dallara: A talent all made in Motor Valley' https://www.motorvalley.it/en/stories/giampaolo-dallara-a-talent-all-made-in-motor-valley/

Epilogue – 'We Are a National Army'

314 ' "Gianni had many opportunities . . ." ' Henry Kissinger, 'Remembrances', from a foreword to a book on Giovanni Agnelli https://www.henryakissinger.com/remembrances/foreword-for-book-on-giovanni-agnelli/

314 'Acting "out of a sense of duty" . . .' *Financial Times*, 22 October 1969.

314 ' "Gianni Agnelli came to Rome . . ." ' Paolo Forcellini and Maurizio Valentini, 'Fiat Appeal', *L'Espresso*, 13 October 1986.

314 ' "We were warned . . ." ' Friedman, *Agnelli and the Network of Italian Power*, p. 172.

315 ' "They brought the coffin . . ." ' 'Minijt, Gianni Agnelli, the Inimitable, *Medium*, 25 April 2022 https://medium.com/@mnijt3011/gianni-agnelli-the-inimitable-5d3a4a3cc6f3

315 Gaspare Nevola, 'The Gianni Agnelli Funeral, a national identification rite', *Berghahn Journals*, 1 September 2004 https://www.berghahnjournals.com/view/journals/italian-politics/19/1/ip190112.xml

315 ' "A man has no need for entertainment . . ." ' Robert Daley, *The Cruel sport: Grand Prix Racing 1959–1967* (Motorbooks, 2005), p. 68.

BIBLIOGRAPHY

Anderloni, Carlo Felice Bianci and Anselmi, Angelo Tito, *Touring Superleggera* (Autocritica, 1983).

Agnelli, Susanna, *We Always Wore Sailor Suits* (Viking, 1975).

Baime, A. J., *Go Like Hell: Ford, Ferrari, and Their Battle for Speed and Glory at Le Mans* (Mariner, 2010).

Bairati, Piero, *Valletta Vittorio* (UTET, 1983).

Barzini, Luigi S., *Peking to Paris* (Open Court, 1973).

Bayley, Stephen, Garner, Philippe and Sudjic, Dejan, *Twentieth-Century Style & Design* (Van Nostrand Reinhold, 1986).

Berghaus, Gunter, ed., *The Futurist Manifesto*, in *Critical Writings: Filippo Tommaso Marinetti* (Macmillan, 2007).

Borgeson, Griffith, *Bugatti by Borgeso: Dynamics of Mythology* (Osprey, 1981).

——, *The Alfa Romeo Tradition* (Automobile Quarterly, 1990).

Boscarelli, Lorenzo, *Ferrari 166* (Haynes, 1986).

Bradley, W. F., *Targa Florio* (G. T. Foulis, 1955).

——, *Motoring Racing Memories* (Motor Racing Publications, 1960).

—— and Bugatti, Ettore, *Bugatti: A Biography* (Motor Racing Publications, 1948).

Bugatti, L'Ebé, *Bugatti Story* (Vintage, 1967).

Burgess Wise, David, *Ghia* (Osprey, 1985).

Caballo, Ernesto, *Pininfarina: Born with the Automobile* (Automobilia, 1993).

Castronovo, Valerio, *Giovanni Agnelli* (UTET, 1993).

Cohen, Robin, *The Cambridge Survey of World Migration* (Cambridge University Press, 2010).

Colombo, Gioachino, *Origins of the Ferrari Legend* (G. T. Foulis, 1987).

De Seta, Cesare, *L'architettura del Novecento* (Garzanti, 1992).

Desmond, Kevin, *The Man With Two Shadows: The Story of Alberto Ascari* (Proteus Books, 1981).

Ferrari, Enzo, *My Terrible Joys* (Hamish Hamilton, 1963).

——, *Una Vita per l'Automobile* (Eredità Enzo Ferrari, 1998).

Friedman, Alan, *Agnelli and the Network of Power* (Mandarin,1989).

Frostick, Michael, *Lancia* (Dalton Watson, 1977).

Gallagher, Tad, *The Adventures of Roberto Rossellini* (De Capo Press, 1998).

Galli, Giancarlo, *Gli Agnelli. Una dinastia, un impero. 1899–1998* (Mondadori, 1995).

Giacosa, Dante, *Forty Years of Design with Fiat* (Automobilia, 1979).

Gianotti, Lorenzo, *Gli Operai della Fiat Hanno Cent'Anni* (Editori Riuniti, 1999).

Gregoire, J. A., *Best Wheel Forward* (The Sportsman's Book Club, 1966).

Grist, Peter, *Virgil Exner – Visioneer* (Veloce, 2015).

Halberstam, David, *The Reckoning* (William Morrow, 1986).

Hilton, Christopher, *Nuvolari* (Breedon Books, 2003)

Jenkinson, Denis, *Maserati 250F* (Macmillan, 1975).

Johansen, Niels, *Lancia Aurelia in Detail* (Herridge and Sons, 2006).

Kennedy, Jacqueline: *Historic Conversations on Life with John F. Kennedy* (Hyperion, 2011).

Lacey, Robert, *Ford: The Men and the Machine* (Little, Brown, 1986).

Laux, James, *In First Gear* (McGill-Queen's University Press, 1976).

Levy, Shawn, *Dolce Vita Confidential* (Weidenfeld & Nicolson, 2017).

Ludvigsen, Karl, *Juan Manuel Fangio: Motor Racing's Grand Master* (Haynes, 1999).

——, *Italian Racing Red* (Crecy, 2008).

Martin, Simon, *Sport Italia: The Italian Love Affair with Sport* (I. B. Tauris & Co., 2011).

Miller, Peter, *Conte Maggi's Mille Miglia* (The History Press, 1988)

Mondadori, Arnoldo, ed., 'Fiat': *A Fifty Years' Record* (Mondadori, 1951).

Moorehead, Caroline, *A House in the Mountains: The Women Who Liberated Italy from Fascism* (Chatto & Windus, 2019).

Nixon, Chris, *Racing the Silver Arrows* (Bloomsbury, 1986).

——, *Mon Ami Mate* (Transport Bookman, 1991).

——, *Rivals: Lancia D50 and Mercedes-Benz W196* (Transport Bookman, 1999).

Nye, Doug, *B.R.M.* (MRP, 2003).

Porter, Philip, *Stirling Moss: The Definitive Biography* (Porter Press International, 2016).

Pritchard, Anthony, *The Motor Racing Merchants* (Leslie Frewin, 1976).

——, *Ferrari: Men from Maranello* (Haynes, 2009).

Prunet, Antoine, *Pininfarina: Art and Industry* (Rizzoli International, 2001).

Schmidt, Giulio, *The Roaring Races* (Libreria dell'Automobile, 1988).

Sedgwick, Michael, *Fiat* (Batsford, 1974).

Sharratt, Barney, *Men and Motors of the Austin* (Haynes, 2000).

Sloniger, J. and von Fersen, H. H., *Performance Cars from Germany* (Robert Bentley, 1966).

Trow, Nigel, *Lancia: The Shield and the Flag* (David & Charles, 1980).

Williams, Richard, *Enzo Ferrari* (Yellow Jersey, 2001).

——, *The Boy. Stirling Moss: A Life in Sixty Laps* (Simon & Schuster, 2021).

Wyer, John, *The Certain Sound: Thirty Years of Motor Racing* (Edita, 1981).

ARTICLES, ESSAYS AND ONLINE PUBLICATIONS

Anfia. Industria Automobilistica Mondiale Nel 1982 (Turin, 1983)

'Ascari', *Il Popolo d'Italia* (Milan, 28 July 1925).

Bachrach, Judy, 'La Vita Agnelli', *Vanity Fair* (New York, April 2001).

Barlow, Jason, 'Marcello Gandini – The Miura annoys me a bit', *Top Gear* magazine (14 March 2024).

Benson, Richard, 'How Giorgetto Giugiaro Became The Greatest Car Designer Of All Time', *Esquire* (5 August 2019).

Obituary, Nuccio Bertone, *Independent* (3 March 1997.

Bonnaud, Christophe, 'Enough for a pair of skis . . .' 'Interview, intimate – Giugiaro' *LIGNES/auto* https://lignesauto.fr/?p=16552

Eight Automobiles, Museum of Modern Art, exhibition guide,
Autumn 1951.

'Engineering, applied to car design . . . Farewell Marcello Gandini,
Master of Design', *Auto e Design* (13 March 2024).

Fauri, Francesca, 'The Role of Fiat in the Development of the Italian
Car Industry in the 1950's', *Business History Review* (Summer
1996).

Forcellini, Paolo and Valentini, Maurizio, 'Fiat Appeal', *L'Espresso*
(13 October 1986).

'My marriage to cars . . .' Video interview, Ing. Enzo Ferrari – evento
30° anniversaio Centro Dino Ferrari https://www.youtube.com/
watch?v=zioYK5x5EOQ

'The demands of mass production . . .' The Scuderia.net, Legendary
quotes from 'Il Commendatore' Enzo Ferrari. https://www.
thescuderia.net/forums/showthread.php/31826-

'Ford v Ferrari', *RossoAutomobili magazine* https://rossoautomo-
bili.com

'The German Grand Prix', *Motor Sport* (September 1935).

https://www.brooklynmuseum.org/opencollection/exhibitions/859

'Giampaolo Dallara: A talent all made in Motor Valley' https://
www.motorvalley.it/en/stories/giampaolo-dallara-a-talent-al
l-made-in-motor-valley/

'Gianni Agnelli: The Godfather of Italian Cool', *Gentlemen's Digest*
(3 December 2024).

Glancy, Jonathan, 'Benvenuto Cinquecento: Fiat's new city car',
Independent (21 March 1993).

Goodfellow, Winston, 'Ghia's Gilda: Siren Song for An Era', *Motor
Trend Classic* (24 January 2013).

Goodfellow, Winston, 'I am the one . . . The real inspiration for
Lamborghini's Miura' https://winstongoodfellow.com/blogs/
blog/myth-busting-part-ii-the-real-inspiration-for-lamborghini-
s-miura

Gramsci, Antonio, 'Men of Flesh and Blood', *L'Ordine Nuovo*
(Turin, 8 May 1921).

Kissinger, Henry, 'Giovanni Agnelli by Henry Kissinger' (29 August 2007) https://www.henryakissinger.com/remembrances/forewor d-for-book-on-giovanni-agnelli/

'Interview with Ferruccio Lamborghini', *Thoroughbred & Classic Cars* (January 1991).

Italy at Work: Her Renaissance in Design Today, publicity for exhibition at the Brooklin Museum, New York, November 1950 to January 1951).

Ludvigsen, Karl, 'Lamborghini Miura: The Supercar That Started It All', *Car and Driver* (August 1967).

Ludvigsen, Karl, 'Creating Ferrari's First Champions', *Forza* (30 May 2019).

Magistralis, Lectio, 'Marcello Gandini, Cerimonia conferimento Laurea Honoris Causa in ingegneria meccanica' (12 January, 2024) https://www.polito.it/sites/default/files/2024-01/ Lectio%20Magistralis%20Marcello%20Gandini.pdf

Nixon, Chris, 'Romolo Tavoni: Enzo's Right-Hand Man', *Motor Sport* (November 1998).

Nye, Doug, 'Inside Track with Phil Hill', *Motor Sport* (8 February 2019).

Nye, Doug, 'Nothing Better than the Alfetta', *Motor Sport* (December 2019).

Owen, David, *Lancia*, Part 1, *The Vincenzo Years*, *The Automobile Quarterly*, vol. XII, no. 49 (New Albany, Indiana, 1974).

Roebuck, Nigel, 'Peter Collins: "This Charming Man"', *Motor Sport* (September 2008).

'The Royal Silverstone Meeting', *Motor Sport* (June 1950)

Schmidt, Edmondo, *Il Caso Schmidt, Da Berlino a regina Coeli* (Centro Studi PIedmontesi Turin, 2010)

'To Russia without Love', *Forbes* (1 October 1966).

'Twenty Three amazing quotes by Ferruccio Lamborghini' https:// medium.com/@entrepreneursway0007/23-amazing-quotes-by-f erruccio-lamborghini-1f75d33fff9c

'Vittorio Valletta, il ragioniere divenuto re della Fiat', *Il Giornale* (Milan, 23 November 2023).

Wood, Jonathan, 'Herald Triumph', *Thoroughbred and Classic Cars* (July 1983).

ACKNOWLEDGEMENTS

My thanks go first to Bobby Gaspar M.D., whose pioneering work in paediatric gene therapy did not preclude him from pointing out a gap in the automotive book market for a '*High Performance* of Italy'.

For over four decades, Beppe Severgnini, author and *Corriere della Sera* columnist, has been my tutor on all matters Italian. He also dismissed any misgivings I had about a foreigner venturing into such a sacred area of Italian heritage.

Many hands helped propel this daunting enterprise with words of wisdom, superior knowledge and gentle encouragement, in particular Andrew Nahum, for his enthusiasm right from the start, for sharing his own work on the subject and for reviewing the manuscript.

I am also indebted to Ronald Stern for giving me access to his exceptional Ferrari archive and for allowing me to quiz him remorselessly on the finer points of Maranello folklore.

Any lingering concerns about the madness of this undertaking were dissipated by encouraging noises – as well as wisdom – from Richard Bremner, Steve Cropley, Jason Hartcup, Patrick Uden and Richard Williams.

Nothing would have got written without my wife, Stephanie Calman, who helped me mine the mountains of research material and knock my first drafts into readable shape.

Thanks also go to Mark Aaron Byrne for donating me his entire car magazine library, Giles Chapman for some invaluable pointers, Steve Barnett, Australia's most gifted *carrozziere,* for sharing the secrets of *superleggera* and Tom Del Mar for insights into the Milanese armourers. Also, Hamish Barbour, Michael Barton, Roger

Beattie, Simon Berthon, Vivian Bush, Steve Clarke, the late Gordon Cruickshank of *Motor Sport,* Chiara Gatti, Russell Hayes, Deborah Iovine, Alan Judd, Iain MacGregor, Beth McHattie, Jay Nagley, Simon Pearson, Nigel Smith and Tim White.

Ian Marshall, late of Simon & Schuster, enthusiastically backed the project and my agent Mark Lucas has been a dedicated cheerleader along the way, as have the rest of my household, Lawrence and Lydia Calman-Grimsdale and Laura Ali.

Lastly, heartfelt thanks and respect to my exceptional editor Fran Jessop for her inspirational navigation of the text round many dangerous corners, and seeing it through to the finish line.

INDEX